Questions & Answers

Employment Law

Questions & Answers

Employment Law

THIRD EDITION

Richard Benny
Senior Lecturer in Law,
University of Surrey

Malcolm Sargeant
Professor of Labour Law,
Middlesex University Business School

Michael Jefferson
Senior Lecturer in Law,
University of Sheffield

2008 and 2009

OXFORD
UNIVERSITY PRESS

OXFORD

UNIVERSITY PRESS

Great Clarendon Street, Oxford OX2 6DP

Oxford University Press is a department of the University of Oxford.
It furthers the University's objective of excellence in research, scholarship,
and education by publishing worldwide in

Oxford New York

Auckland Cape Town Dar es Salaam Hong Kong Karachi
Kuala Lumpur Madrid Melbourne Mexico City Nairobi
New Delhi Shanghani Taipei Toronto

With offices in

Argentina Austria Brazil Chile Czech Republic France Greece
Guatemala Hungary Italy Japan Poland Portugal Singapore
South Korea Switzerland Thailand Turkey Ukraine Vietnam

Oxford is a registered trade mark of Oxford University Press
in the UK and in certain other countries

Published in the United States
by Oxford University Press Inc., New York

© Richard Benny, Malcolm Sargeant, and Michael Jefferson 2008

The moral rights of the authors have been asserted

Database right Oxford University Press (maker)

Crown copyright material is reproduced under Class Licence
Number C01P0000148 with the permission of OPSI
and the Queen's Printer for Scotland.

First published 2004

British Library Cataloguing in Publication Data
Data available

Library of Congress Cataloging in Publication Data
Data available

Typeset by Laserwords Private Limited, Chennai, India
Printed in Great Britain
on acid-free paper by
Ashford Colour Press Limited, Gosport, Hampshire

ISBN 978-0-19-923724-1

10 9 8 7 6 5 4 3 2 1

Contents

The Q&A series

Key features

The Q&A series provides full coverage of key subjects in a clear and logical way.

This book contains the following features:

- Questions
- Commentary
- Bullet-pointed answer plans
- Suggested answers
- Further reading
- Diagrams
- Glossary

 online resource centre

www.oxfordtextbooks.co.uk/orc/qanda/

Every book in the Q&A series is accompanied by an Online Resource Centre, hosted at the URL above, which is open-access and free to use.

The online resources are tailored to each different subject area and for this title include a glossary of key terms, and links to useful websites.

Preface to the Third Edition

This edition of *Questions and Answers on Employment Law*, like the previous one, has the aim of assisting law students in preparing for their assessed work in the subject, which usually takes the form of examinations and coursework. The book is no substitute for the hard work necessary to make the subject one's own, i.e. reading and critically discussing cases, legislation, articles and other materials to which students should be exposed during the course of their studies. However, it should provide useful guidance on what examiners are looking for.

Our thanks go to our editor, Helen Swann, for all her help and patience in bringing this edition to press.

As usual, there have been numerous developments in employment law during the period since the previous edition: the pace of change shows no sign of slowing down. We have attempted to state the law as we believe it to have been on 1 June 2007, although it has been possible to take some developments into account after that date.

Richard Benny
Malcolm Sargeant
Michael Jefferson

Table of Cases

Table of Statutes

Table of Statutory Instruments

Table of European Legislation

Introduction

This book is designed to be used primarily by students who are preparing for an examination in employment law. The chapters cover the main areas likely to be included in syllabuses, i.e. both individual and collective employment law, and discrimination law. The introductory sections to each chapter are intended to open out the relevant topics featured in the chapter, and to indicate the key aspects to be noted, explored, and revised.

Examination papers in employment law, as in other areas of law, usually consist of a mixture of problem-type questions and essay-type questions, usually with the preponderance of questions being of the former type. This split is reflected in the format of questions set in the text as a whole. However, it is recognized that, alongside examinations, courses often have a coursework element, so you will find a section in this book on how to approach and answer coursework questions, together with a suggested answer provided for the piece of coursework set.

Students often find examinations very difficult, and some even fear them. Much of their concern is a fear of the unknown—they have no idea exactly what questions they will encounter, and they are worried that they will not be adequately prepared for the task facing them. Such fears may be neutralized to some extent by ensuring you have a thorough grasp of the important case law and legislation in the field, which means reading, revising, and re-revising until you have made the topic your own. Engagement with the scholarly literature to be found in the law journals will deepen and extend your knowledge, as well as providing a critical insight in to various aspects of the subject.

While there is no substitute for this process of acquiring the relevant knowledge, a book like this can assist you in the later stages of revision when you are preparing for an examination, and attempting to hone your examination technique. The answers provided are suggestions, although it is intended that they offer sound guidance on the approach to be taken. To gain the most from this book, you should use it as a revision aid, and, after reading the answers a few times, as a way of improving your examination technique. The latter is best done by attempting the questions in near-examination conditions, i.e. by allowing, say, 45 minutes to write the answer, without the assistance of any textbooks or other materials.

Examiners in law (and, no doubt, in other subjects) commonly identify similar faults in examinations scripts: a failure to answer the question; a failure to use sufficient case law and or legislation to support the answer; and a failure to write in clear prose, making it difficult for the examiner to understand what the examinee is attempting to say. This book should assist you in finding out how to answer the question, but you should always read the examination and question rubrics very carefully: make sure that you know what the examiner wants you to do, and then do it. Examinees should take personal responsibility for ensuring that they enter the examination room with the requisite knowledge of case law and legislation. As with all written examinations, it is vital to write legibly in clear, intelligible prose.

Another common fault is badly mistiming the exam paper, so that, for example, examinees spend 90 minutes on one question in a three-hour exam requiring four questions to be answered. If you use this book in the way suggested in the previous paragraph, many of these faults should be alleviated, if not avoided altogether. It is also advisable to write a brief plan so that your answer has some structure to it, and it can prove useful to set down key thoughts initially, in case you forget these while in the throes of answering the question!

If you approach this book in the way indicated above, and put in the work needed to grasp the subject, you should find that the examination is not an insurmountable barrier but rather an opportunity to display your knowledge.

Employment status

Introduction

Issues concerning employment status are popular with examiners, and students may encounter whole questions or parts of questions on this topic. It is essentially a preliminary issue, and employment tribunals will consider it as such, if it is in issue. It is often crucial to determine the employment status of a person, i.e. whether they are employees or self-employed (persons in this latter category are sometimes described as 'independent contractors') because certain important employment rights flow from a finding that someone is an employee. For example, only employees (with, in most cases, the relevant period of continuous employment) may bring claims for unfair dismissal, or be made redundant and claim statutory redundancy payments. Under the common law principle of vicarious liability, principals (i.e. employers in this context) may be held liable for the tortious acts of their employees but may not be held liable for the acts of independent contractors. Further, employees are taxed under a different tax regime, with tax deducted at source under the PAYE system, whereas the self-employed pay tax at the end of the relevant tax year. Employees are said to be working under a contract *of* service, and the self-employed to be working under a contract *for* services.

Some statutes extend employment protection to another, wider category known as a 'worker', which includes an employee and which is defined in s. 230(3) of the Employment Rights Act 1996 (ERA) as:

> an individual who has entered into or works under . . . a contract of employment; or . . . any other contract, whether express or implied and (if it is express) whether oral or in writing, whereby the individual undertakes to do or perform personally any work or services for another party to the contract whose status is not by virtue of the contract that of a client or customer of any profession or business undertaking carried on by that individual.

A similar definition of a worker as someone performing any work or services personally is also contained in the discrimination statutes (the Sex Discrimination Act 1975, the Race Relations Act 1976, and the Disability Discrimination Act 1995) which extend protection against discrimination on the ground of sex, race, and disability to workers. Similarly, for example, the following employment protection rights also apply to workers as well as employees: the limits on working time and the right to annual leave under the Working Time Regulations 1998 (SI 1998/1833) (reg. 2); protection from unlawful deduction from wages (ERA, s. 230(3)); the right to be accompanied (Employment Relations Act 1999 (ERelsA), s. 13); the right to the national minimum wage (National Minimum Wage Act 1998, s. 54(3)); and the various provisions relating to the protection of part-time workers under the Part-time Workers (Prevention of Less Favourable Treatment) Regulations 2000 (SI 2000/1551) (reg. 1). Useful guidance on the determination of the question of whether an individual is a worker is given by Elias J., in *James* v *Redcats (Brands) Ltd* [2007] IRLR 296, EAT, where the obligation to provide personal service on the part of the putative worker must be the dominant feature of the relationship.

Occasionally, courts and tribunals cannot categorize a person either as an employee or as self-employed because they are found to be working under contracts which are neither employment contracts nor contracts for services but rather contracts *sui generis* (see, for example, *Ironmonger* v *Movefield Ltd* [1988] IRLR 461).

Employment status is largely a question of fact for the tribunal to decide, and its decision can be overturned only where it has erred in law or its decision is perverse (*O'Kelly* v *Trusthouse Forte Plc* [1983] ICR 728, CA). The question will only become one of law if the construction of a written document is in issue (see *Davies* v *Presbyterian Church of Wales* [1984] ICR 280, HL). In cases involving issues of employment status where personal injuries have been sustained by the claimant in the workplace, policy considerations often seem to out-weigh legal principle, leading to a finding of a contract of service, perhaps in order to bring the claimant under the employer's compulsory liability insurance (*Lane* v *Shire Roofing Co (Oxford) Ltd* [1995] IRLR 493, CA, *Ferguson* v *Dawson* [1976] IRLR 346, CA, *Lee* v *Chung* [1990] IRLR 236, PC).

Three tests have been used to determine employment status: the control test; the integration test; and the multiple test (or economic reality test). The first focused entirely upon the degree of control the 'employer' had over the worker: a large measure of control, i.e. where it could be said that the employer could stipulate not only what was to be done but how it was to be done, indicated a contract of employment, whereas a smaller degree of control would point towards self-employment.

The classic modern test for deciding employment status is embodied in MacKenna, J's decision in *Ready Mixed Concrete (South East) Ltd* v *Minister of Pensions and National Insurance* [1968] 2 QB 497. He stated that a contract of service exists if three conditions are fulfilled:

(i) The servant agrees that, in consideration of a wage or other remuneration, he will provide his own work and skill in the performance of some service for his master; (ii) He agrees, expressly or impliedly, that in the performance of that service he will be subject to the other's control in a sufficient degree to make that other master; (iii) The other provisions of the contract are consistent with its being a contract of service.

The first condition has been summarized by the courts as 'the irreducible minimum of obligation' without which a contract of employment cannot be said to exist (*Nethermere (St Neots) Ltd* v *Taverna & Gardiner* [1984] ICR 612, CA, *Carmichael and Leese* v *National Power plc* [2000] IRLR 43, HL). The second condition is known as the control test (originally, the sole test used in the nineteenth and early twentieth centuries to determine employment status), while the third allows the courts to exclude contracts with provisions that are flatly contrary to a contract of employment, such as an untrammelled power of substitution on the part of the worker (see below).

The multiple test now employed by the courts to determine employment status allows all the factors to be taken into consideration. Some may point in the direction of self-employment, such as a worker providing his own equipment or hiring his own helpers, whereas others may point towards a contract of employment, such as submitting to the complete control of another and paid holidays. It is clear that the parties' designation of the relationship as one of self-employment or employment is not determinative but rather one factor to be taken into consideration. The courts will look at the substance and not the form, and the label the parties apply may be misleading (*Ferguson* v *Dawson* [1976] IRLR, CA; *Young* & *Woods Ltd* v *West* [1980] IRLR 201, CA). However, a genuine agreement which accords with the correct legal interpretation will be upheld (*Massey* v *Crown Life Insurance Co* [1978] 2 All ER 576, CA).

Recent cases have involved contracts containing a power of substitution or delegation, i.e. a contractual provision allowing the worker to substitute another person to carry out their work. The Court of Appeal has held that a wide power of substitution is inherently inconsistent with the irreducible minimum of obligation (see *Express and Echo Publications Ltd* v *Tanton* [1999] IRLR 367, CA) but a more limited power to delegate/substitute is not necessarily inconsistent with a contract of employment (see *MacFarlane* v *Glasgow City Council* [2001] IRLR 7, EAT).

The irreducible minimum of obligation may be excluded from the contract by a clear express term. In such a case, no term may be implied to find a contract of employment (*Stevedoring & Haulage Services Ltd* v *Fuller* [2001] IRLR 627, CA).

A number of cases involving company directors holding controlling shareholdings in the companies for which they work have posed some problems for the courts. Can such persons be regarded as employees when they in fact effectively control their 'employer'? This is a question of fact, to be decided after looking at all the factors, so, in *Fleming* v *Secretary of State for Trade and Industry* [1997] IRLR 682, Ct Sess, the court held that the director of a company holding 65 per cent of the company's shares was not an employee. However, in *Secretary of State for Trade and Industry* v *Bottrill* [1999] IRLR 326, CA, the Court of Appeal held that a director who temporarily held only one share in an off-the-shelf company was an employee (see also *Sellars Arenascene* v *Connolly* [2001] IRLR 222, CA).

Particular problems arise where a person is assigned by an employment agency to a particular client. There will be a contract between the employment agency and the worker, and another between the agency and its client, but is the worker engaged under an employment contract with either the agency or its client? In *Motorola Ltd* v *Davidson and Melville Craig Group Ltd* [2001] IRLR 4, the EAT held that the indirect control of the client was sufficient to establish an employment relationship between Mr Davidson and the client. However, in *McMeechan* v *Secretary of State for Employment* [1997] ICR 549, CA, Mr McMeechan was held to be an employee of the agency for the purposes of a particular four-day temporary arrangement under which he was supplied to the client of the agency ('the end-user'), although the Court left open the question of whether he was an employee of the agency for general employment law purposes. However, the Court of Appeal in *Montgomery v Johnson Underwood Ltd* [2001] IRLR 269 held that a worker was not the employee of an employment agency (on the grounds of an absence of mutuality of obligation, and the lack of a sufficient degree of control) and, as Mrs Montgomery had not appealed the EAT's decision that she was not employed by the end-user, she could not argue in the Court of Appeal that she was the employee of the end-user. In *Dacas v Brook Street Bureau* [2004] IRLR 358, the Court of Appeal held that Mrs Dacas, who was a temporary cleaner assigned to Wandsworth Council, was not an employee of the agency on the grounds that (i) there was no obligation on the agency to supply work and no corresponding obligation to accept any work it offered and (ii) the agency had no control over her work. However, the Court of Appeal indicated, *obiter*, (by a majority) that a temp in Mrs Dacas's position is likely to be an employee of the end-user. However, with respect, this rather controversial obiter indication is open to question. The Court also stated, *obiter*, that a contract of employment may be implied between the parties. In *James v Greenwich LBC* [2007] IRLR 168, the EAT (Elias J, presiding) considered this possibility but held that (i) such a contract would be implied between the agency worker and the end-user only where a *necessary* inference could be drawn to this effect and (ii) the way in which the contract is performed is consistent *only* with such an implied contract and where it would be inconsistent with there being no such contract. This would seem to severely limit the scope of courts and tribunals to imply such a contract.

Subsequent case law on the status of agency workers who are supplied to an end-user indicates that clarification is needed in this area. To find that the worker is an employee of the agency, mutuality of obligation and a sufficient degree of control must be found to exist between the agency and the worker. In *Bunce v Potsworth t/a Skyblue* [2005] IRLR 557, CA, this was lacking, although it may be found in the relationship between the worker and the end-user (client), as was the case in *Cable & Wireless v Muscat* [2006] IRLR 254, CA. In situations where the agency exercises a high degree of control over the worker and where sufficient mutuality is established, the worker may be held to be an employee of the agency (see the rather unusual arrangements between worker and agency in *Consistent Group v Kalwak* [2007] IRLR 560, EAT).

Finally, it should be noted that questions concerning employment status often arise by way of a worker's request to his alleged employer for a 'section 1 statement' giving certain particulars of employment, pursuant to s. 1, ERA which may be issued only to employees. Students should be alert to such requests arising in problem questions as they may in fact represent a request for confirmation of the existence of a contract of employment, and thus essentially a challenge by the worker concerning employment status.

Question 1

The courts have resolved questions of employment status over the years by the application of various tests. Explain, by reference to case law, the tests used and briefly indicate the advantages and disadvantages of each test.

Commentary

Questions concerning employment status, i.e. whether a particular individual is an employee, often appear in examination papers. The type of question usually set is an essay-type question. Although essay-type questions of this kind give the student more freedom than a problem-type question, key points and principles must be covered. A logical structured approach should be adopted, with the points made supported by case law.

This question requires the student to discuss the three tests established by case law to determine employment status, but it also requires a consideration of the advantages and disadvantages of each test, i.e. students should attempt a (brief) critical evaluation of the tests, rather than simply regurgitating standard information.

There are a number of key cases to be discussed, and there have been several important developments recently in the case law concerning employment status. Students should include some discussion of these developments.

The key tests are: the control test; the integration test; and the multiple test, with the majority of the discussion focusing on the multiple test. Other important points concern: the influence of policy matters, particularly where health and safety matters arise; the problems encountered as regards liability for tortious acts by workers when they are hired by another person; and difficulties establishing who is the employer when a worker is engaged by an employment agency and assigned to a client. Another problem area concerns company directors: it may be difficult to categorize directors, particularly where they own the majority shareholding and therefore effectively own the company.

Finally, it should be remembered that some legislation is widely drafted to include not just employees but 'workers'. The definition of workers is wider than that of an employee and includes independent contractors personally carrying out work.

The following suggested answer would be appropriate where a long essay has been set as part of coursework assessment: it is too long to constitute an examination answer, although the key points covered could form the basis of any examination answer in this area.

Answer plan

- Identify the various tests developed to determine employment status (control test; integration test; multiple test), using case law to support your answer. Ensure that your answer considers the advantages and disadvantages of each test, i.e. you must engage in a critical discussion.

- Discuss the importance of policy considerations, particularly when health and safety issues arise.

- Discuss difficult areas such as workers engaged on employment agency assignments, and directors who are controlling shareholders.

- Consider and contrast the definitions of 'employee' and 'worker' in the employment legislation.

Suggested answer

The question of who is an employee is central in employment law. Employees have certain important rights, such as the right to claim wrongful or unfair dismissal, redundancy payments; they are accorded protection under the health and safety legislation and the insolvency legislation, and upon the transfer of an undertaking. The distinction is made between an employee working under a 'contract *of* service' and an independent contractor (or self-employed person) working under a 'contract *for* services'. The determination of the question of employment status has sometimes proved difficult, and the courts have therefore devised a number of tests to resolve the question. Questions of employment status are generally a question of fact rather than law (see the comments of Lord Griffiths in *Lee* v *Chung* [1990] ICR 409, PC). This means that the appellate tribunal cannot overturn the lower court's decision unless it misdirected itself in law or where the tribunal, having properly directed itself on the law, could not have reached the conclusion it did.

Definitions contained in the Employment Rights Act 1996 (the ERA) provide limited assistance. Section 230(1) of the ERA defines an employee as 'an individual who has entered or works under (or, where the employment has ceased, worked under) a contract of employment' and s. 230(2), ERA defines a 'contract of employment' as 'a contract of service or apprenticeship, whether express or implied, and (if it is express) whether oral or in writing'.

Some legislation in the employment field extends beyond employees, also covering workers: see, for example, s. 82(1) of the Sex Discrimination Act 1975 (SDA) which extends protection under the statute to those working under 'a contract personally to execute any work or labour'. This definition is sufficiently broad to cover self-employed persons who do the work themselves. Other legislation, such as the Working Time Regulations 1998 and the National Minimum Wage Act 1998 also extend to 'workers' rather than just employees. It should be noted that s. 23, Employment Relations Act 1999 gives power to the Secretary of State by order to enlarge the scope of employment protection rights by conferring such rights on individuals of a specified description, although no such order has been made yet.

The parties cannot themselves declare the nature of the relationship: it is for the courts and tribunals to determine the nature of the relationship by looking at the substance and not the form (see *Ferguson* v *Dawson* [1976] IRLR, CA; *Young & Woods Ltd* v *West* [1980] IRLR 201, CA). However, where there has been a genuine agreement, and the legal relationship accords with the parties' intentions, the court may find self-employment: see *Massey* v *Crown Life Insurance* Co [1978] 2 All ER 576, CA.

The classic statement concerning the test for whether an employment contract exists was given by MacKenna J in *Ready Mixed Concrete (South East) Ltd* v *Minister of Pensions and National Insurance* [1968] 2 QB 497, where he said:

A contract of service exists if these three conditions are fulfilled:

(i) The servant agrees that, in consideration of a wage or other remuneration, he will provide his own work and skill in the performance of some service for his master.

(ii) He agrees, expressly or impliedly, that in the performance of that service he will be subject to the other's control in a sufficient degree to make that other master.

(iii) The other provisions of the contract are consistent with its being a contract of service.

Subsequent cases have taken this statement as a guide when determining employment status.

In the *Ready Mixed Concrete* case itself, a driver who delivered concrete in his own lorry was held to be self-employed. Important factors supporting this view were the fact that he had to purchase the lorry in which he carried out his job, and he could engage a replacement driver if he was not able to perform his tasks.

In order to find an employment relationship, the court will require, at the very least, an irreducible minimum of obligation for the contract to be one of service, i.e. an obligation on the employer to offer work and on the worker to accept it: see *Nethermere (St Neots) Ltd* v *Taverna & Gardiner* [1984] ICR 612, CA.

The first test to be used by the courts in the nineteenth century was the 'control test'. This test asked what was the degree of control the alleged employer (called 'the master' in the old cases) exercised over the alleged employee ('the servant'). The courts asked whether the master could control not only what was done but also the manner in which it was done. In *Yewens* v *Noakes* (1880) 6 QBD 530, Bramwell LJ stated that, 'A servant is a person subject to the command of his master as to the manner in which he shall do his work.'

In the last century, as work became more complicated and technology increased, the simple control test proved to be inadequate as the sole determinant: certain highly skilled employees could not be said to be under the control of the employer. For example, an airline pilot cannot be said to be 'controlled' by the airline in any real sense while he or she is carrying out their work. Therefore, the control test became outmoded as the sole criterion. Although it remains important, it is no longer seen as necessarily conclusive. It is, however, often a central consideration when determining questions of employment status.

The control test was applied in cases concerning the assignment of employees by their employer to a temporary employer. Is the temporary employer or the original employer liable for the tortious acts of the employees? The control test was used to determine which of two potential employers would be vicariously liable for the torts of employees: see *Mersey Docks and Harbour Board* v *Coggins & Griffith (Liverpool) Ltd* [1947] AC 1 and *Denham* v *Midland Employers Mutual Assurance Ltd* [1955] 2 QB 437. In such temporary deemed employment, the paramount test is that of control: see *Interlink Express Parcels Ltd* v *Night Trunkers Ltd, The Times,* 22 March 2001.

Recently, the control test was considered in a number of cases involving an employment agency. Questions sometimes arise as to whether the agency or the agency's client is the employer. Employment agencies usually have direct control over the worker, but this does not necessarily mean that the agency is the employer. Direct control is not always necessary to establish the requisite degree of control to find an employment contract: indirect control may be sufficient (see *Motorola Ltd* v *Davidson and Melville Craig Group Ltd* [2001] IRLR 4, EAT, where Motorola, the client company, which had *indirect* control of a worker, was held to be the employer of Mr Davidson). Employment agencies may themselves be the employer: see *McMeechan* v *Secretary of State for Employment* [1997] ICR 549, CA, where Mr McMeechan was held to be an employee of the agency, despite a term in his contract stating that he was self-employed (see also *Montgomery* v *Johnson Underwood Ltd* [2001] IRLR 269, and *Dacas* v *Brook Street Bureau* [2004] IRLR 358, in both of which the Court of Appeal held that a worker was not the employee of the employment agency, on the grounds of an absence of mutuality of obligation, and the lack of a sufficient degree of control).

In *Cable & Wireless* v *Muscat* [2006] IRLR 254, CA, another triangular relationship case involving an agency, an agency worker and an end-user, the Court found a contract of employment between the end-user and the client, on the basis that there was sufficient mutuality and control between these parties (and the superimposition of agency-style arrangements on what had been a pre-existing employment relationship). However, where the agency has a high degree of control over the worker and where sufficient mutuality is established, the worker may be held to be an employee of the agency (see *Consistent Group* v *Kalwak* [2007] IRLR 560, EAT).

In *Dacas,* the Court of Appeal stated, *obiter,* that it might be possible to imply a contract of employment, either between the end-user and the worker or the agency and the worker. This *obiter* remark was subject to a rather restrictive interpretation in *James* v *Greenwich LBC* [2007] IRLR 168, EAT (Elias J, presiding), in which the EAT held that (i) such a contract would be implied between the agency worker and the end-user only where a *necessary* inference could be drawn to this effect and (ii) the way in the which the contract is performed is consistent *only* with such an implied contract and where it would be inconsistent with there being no such contract. This would seem to severely limit the scope of courts and tribunals to imply such a contract.

The second test that developed was the integration test. It was first identified by Somervell and Denning LJJ in *Cassidy* v *Ministry of Health* [1951] 2 KB 343, CA, where it was applied to establish that a doctor working within the NHS was an employee of the Health Authority, and Denning LJ referred again to this test in *Stevenson, Jordan and Harrison Ltd* v *MacDonald and Evans* [1952] 1 TLR 101. It asks whether a person is employed as part of the business, whether his or her work is done as 'an integral part of the business' or whether it is merely accessory to it. The test has the advantage of seeming a fairly straightforward one, although it proved to be of limited use since, in asking if a person is an integral part of the organization, it was unclear precisely what constituted 'integration' into an 'organization'.

The courts gradually moved away from seeing one factor as determinative of the issue of employment status. A more flexible approach was taken by adopting what is known as the multiple test, i.e. no single factor will be conclusive, all factors are considered and weighed to decide the question (this is sometimes called 'the multi-factorial approach'). The question asked is, looking at all the factors, some of which may point to self-employment status and others to a finding of employment, does the evidence overall point to the person being an employee? This multi-factorial test was applied by Cooke J in *Market Investigations* v *Minister of Social Security* [1969] 2 QB 173. Cooke J stated that the fundamental question was: 'Is the person who has engaged himself to perform these services performing them as a person in business on his own account?' Consideration would always have to be given to control, but it could not be regarded as the sole determining factor. Other indicia could be important, such as: whether the worker hired his own helpers; what degree of financial risk he takes; what degree of financial responsibility he has for investment; and any management responsibility undertaken.

One distinct advantage of the multiple test is that it allows the court or tribunal great flexibility: all relevant factors are considered, with no single factor being decisive. This approach is particularly useful when some factors may go toward self-employment, such as the contractual right given to the worker to substitute another worker for themselves, while other factors may point toward employment status, such as the unrestrained power to control the time and manner in which the work is performed. By looking at all the circumstances of the case, and giving appropriate weight to these (possibly opposing) factors, the court may reach a sound conclusion, without placing undue reliance on one factor as determinative. The disadvantage is that, in cases involving complex factors, it may be difficult for the parties to know whether the relationship is one of employment or not. Therefore, it may be virtually impossible to ascertain, before a court or tribunal has ruled on the matter, whether, on the one hand, a party is exposed to the obligations of an employer, such as that relating to the employer's vicarious liability for the torts of employees while in the ordinary course of their employment and, on the other hand, whether a worker has the right to claim unfair dismissal.

The flexibility inherent in the multiple test has proved useful where directors are concerned. Company directors are officers of the company and are usually employees, i.e. they work under a contract of service, but problems may arise where the director is also a controlling shareholder: see *Fleming* v *Secretary of State for Trade and Industry* [1997] IRLR 682, Ct Sess, where the court held that the managing director of a company who owned 65 per cent of the company's shares was not an employee. This conclusion was based on a number of factors: he had not drawn his salary for the last month of the company's existence; he had personally guaranteed the company's debts; he had no written contract of employment; and he held the majority of shares in the company. However, this is not to say that a director with a majority shareholding will never be held to be an employee: see *Secretary of State for Trade and Industry v Bottrill* [1997] IRLR 120, EAT, [1999] IRLR 326, CA, where the Court of Appeal held that a director who temporarily held the only share in an off-the-shelf company, pending purchase of the share by another company, was an employee. Although he was the sole shareholder, he was paid by PAYE, had a written contract of employment, and worked in the same manner as other employees. The Court of Appeal in *Bottrill* stated that questions of employment status were questions of fact and there was no hard and fast rule that a director who was a majority shareholder could never be an employee.

In cases involving health and safety at work, the courts more readily find that a worker who, for example, has been injured at work, is an employee. This finding allows the employee to claim for a breach of the employer's common law duty of care owed to employees and for compensation under the employer's insurance policy covering employees. Having such a policy on foot is a legal requirement for most employers under the Employers' Liability (Compulsory Insurance) Act 1969, as amended by the Employers' Liability (Compulsory Insurance Regulations 1998 (SI 1998/2573). The parties themselves will sometimes categorize the worker as self-employed, often because of the tax advantages flowing from this status: see *Ferguson* v *Dawson* [1976] IRLR 346, CA, where a building labourer, who was taken on as self-employed and was injured when he fell from scaffolding, was held to be an employee. The description of the relationship by the parties as one of self-employment did not preclude a finding of employment in *Ferguson*. In *Lee* v *Chung* [1990] IRLR 236, PC, the Privy Council held that a stonemason, who was injured by falling from a stool during the course of his work, was an employee. Similarly, in *Lane* v *Shire Roofing Co (Oxford) Ltd* [1995] IRLR 493, CA, the Court of Appeal held that a porch repairer/tiler who fell from a ladder and was seriously injured was an employee.

Where the contract contains a term that the worker may substitute another person to carry out their work, it would seem that this factor may weigh against finding an employment relationship. In *Express and Echo Publications Ltd* v *Tanton* [1999] IRLR 367, the contract between the parties contained a term that Mr Tanton could substitute another worker to carry out his duties if he was unable or unwilling to perform them, and he had done so on occasion. The Court of Appeal held that the right of the worker to provide a substitute is inherently inconsistent with the existence of a contract of employment. The irreducible minimum of obligation in a contract of employment involved the obligation on the part of the employee to provide his services personally. Without it, there could not be such a contract. It was, said the court, a recognition that such a contract involves mutual trust and confidence and that personal service was a requirement.

According to the EAT in *MacFarlane* v *Glasgow City Council* [2001] IRLR 7, the principle enunciated in *Tanton* does not necessarily preclude a finding of employment where there is a contractual provision allowing a limited power of substitution. The case involved gym instructors working for the council under contracts that allowed them, when they were unable to work, to find a replacement worker from a register kept by the council. The council paid such replacements directly. It regarded the instructors as self-employed, a view with which they disagreed and left their jobs, claiming constructive, unfair dismissal. The EAT stated that such a *limited* power of substitution or delegation was held not to be inconsistent with a contract of employment. The clause in *Tanton* allowed substitution by the worker at any time and for any reason, whereas that in *MacFarlane* was a limited or occasional power invoked when the workers were unable to work. (The case was remitted to the employment tribunal to decide whether the workers were employees or not.)

Questions concerning the status of casual or temporary workers can be particularly difficult to resolve. In such cases, whether there is mutuality of obligations is an important factor. In *Clark* v *Oxfordshire Health Authority* [1998] IRLR 125, CA, a 'bank nurse', i.e. one retained by the health authority on a casual basis to fill temporary vacancies as and when they arose, was held to be not an employee. There was no mutuality of obligations during the periods when she was not engaged on a contract: the health authority was not under any obligation to offer her work, nor was she under any obligation to accept it, if offered. Similarly, a finding of self-employment was made in a case concerning wine butlers, described as 'regular casuals', where there was no mutuality of obligations: see *O'Kelly* v *Trusthouse Forte Plc* [1983] ICR 728, CA.

In the House of Lords' decision in *Carmichael and Leese* v *National Power plc* [2000] IRLR 43, two 'casual as required' guides at a nuclear power station were held not to be employees. Their Lordships approved the tribunal's finding that the applicants' case 'founders upon the rock of absence of mutuality'. The guides were not obliged to take work, if offered, and the company was under no obligation to offer it.

In conclusion, it is clear that the cases provide only guidance and do not identify rigid rules. When questions of employment status arise, the legal principles must be applied to the facts of the case, and all factors must be taken into consideration. Of the three tests, the control test is now subsumed as part of the multiple test, although the degree of control over a worker is often a very important consideration. The integration test has also been absorbed into the multiple test. The multiple test allows the courts the greatest flexibility when considering all relevant factors when deciding whether a person is an employee. However, it would appear that the law in this area is in need of greater clarification, particularly in the agency cases, where application of the relevant principles and the possibility of an implied contract arising has led to some surprising results. Finally, it should be noted that personal service and mutuality of obligations are essential requirements in a contract of employment: it would seem that without these there will be no finding of a contract of service.

Question 2

Ruth has worked for Fit & Free Health Centre Ltd as a physiotherapist for the past six years. She has a contract stating that her normal working period is Monday to Friday, from 9 a.m. to 5 p.m. and her wages are paid net of tax and national insurance, which is deducted by Fit & Free. Her contract states that, with the agreement of the company, she may engage substitutes to work in her place when she is unavailable for work. This provision also states that only individuals whose names appear on a list kept by the company, who are approved by the company, may be nominated as substitutes, and Ruth may substitute in this way for no more than a total of 14 days per annum. Ruth has used this provision on two occasions in the past year, when she has been abroad with her husband, for periods of three days and six days. Advise Ruth whether she may claim unfair dismissal against Fit & Free.

Commentary

This question concerns the employment status of Ruth, who may claim unfair dismissal only if she is an employee. Ruth is a worker with a power of substitution in her contract. This problem-question requires a discussion of the relevant case law covering these points, followed by an attempt to assess the employment status of Ruth. Mention should be made of the fact that a power of substitution seems to weigh against finding employment status, in which the element of *personal* service is central (although this is subject to some qualifications).

Answer plan

- Consider the importance of determining employment status as only employees may claim unfair dismissal.
- Consider the central issue of a power of substitution and its effect on finding that Ruth is an employee, using relevant case law on substitution; discuss the element of *personal* service, which is seen as central in employment relationships.
- Consider factors in Ruth's relationship with Fit & Free pointing towards employment status and those pointing towards self-employed status.

Suggested answer

The fact that Ruth's wages are paid net of tax and national insurance contributions points toward employment status, as usually employees are paid the net amount after such deductions have been made, whereas self-employed workers are usually paid gross.

However, Ruth's contract contains a power of substitution, i.e. she is able to replace herself with another worker whose name appears on the list approved by the company.

In *Express and Echo Publications Ltd* v *Tanton* [1999] IRLR 367, Mr Tanton had worked for Express and Echo as an employee but he was made redundant in 1995. Later that year, he was re-engaged as a driver on what the company intended to be a self-employed basis (a basis which Mr Tanton accepted, at least initially). In 1996, he was sent a document for signature containing the following clause: 'In the event that the contractor is unable or unwilling to perform the services personally, he shall arrange at his own expense entirely for another suitable person to perform the services.' Although he refused to sign this document, he continued working in accordance with its terms and, occasionally, used the substitution power to provide a substitute driver. Mr Tanton was paid net of tax and national insurance because the Inland Revenue considered him to be an employee. He later applied for a statement of written particulars (a 'section 1 statement'), confirming his employment status.

The Court of Appeal held that the right of substitution was inherently inconsistent with a contract of employment, which must necessarily contain an obligation of personal service by the worker (this obligation is part of the 'irreducible minimum of obligation'). Peter Gibson LJ called such a provision 'a remarkable clause to find in a contract of service'. Further, the Court of Appeal held that the implied term of mutual trust and confidence was consistent with a requirement of personal service. The court also referred to MacKenna J's comments in *Ready Mixed Concrete (South East) Ltd* v *Minister of Pensions and National Insurance* [1968] 2 QB 497 (itself a case involving substitution by the owner/driver of a vehicle, which strongly pointed toward a finding of self-employment), where he said that one condition for a contract of service was that:

[T]he servant agrees that, in consideration of a wage or other remuneration, he will provide his own work and skill in the performance of some service for his master . . . The servant must be obliged to provide his own work and skill. Freedom to do a job either by one's own hands or by another's is inconsistent with a contract of service, though a limited or occasional power of delegation may not be.

The idea of a limited power of delegation or substitution not necessarily contradicting employment status was considered by the EAT in *MacFarlane* v *Glasgow City Council* [2001] IRLR 7. In this case, a number of gym instructors worked for the council under a contract that allowed them to provide a replacement worker from a register kept by the council when they were unable to work. The replacements were paid directly by the council. The council regarded the gym instructors as self-employed, a belief reflected in the contractual documentation sent to the workers, but they resigned and claimed constructive dismissal. Lindsay P, giving the EAT's judgment, stated that the Court of Appeal's decision in *Tanton* 'does not oblige the tribunal to conclude that under a contract of service the individual has, always and in every event, however exceptional, personally to provide his services'. He said that the clause in *Tanton* was 'extreme' in that it permitted the worker to use any substitute *at any time*, whether the worker was unable or unwilling to work, and at his own expense, whereas in the instant case there were a number of 'cumulative reasons' to distinguish the case from *Tanton*: first, the workers in *McFarlane* could only invoke the substitution clause if they were unable to work; second, the right was limited to selection of a replacement from the council's register, and the council could veto a replacement; third, the council itself sometimes arranged a replacement, without objection from the workers; and, fourth, the council paid the substitute direct. Therefore, the substitution power did not overwhelm the factors pointing toward employment, and the case was remitted to the employment tribunal.

However, the provision that Ruth may invoke the substitution clause when she is 'unavailable' for work would seem to include circumstances in which she is unwilling to work, as well as when she is unable to do so (see *James* v *Redcats (Brands) Ltd* [2007] IRLR, EAT). This provision is nearer the wide power of substitution present in *Tanton*, and might go toward a finding that personal service was not required in such circumstances.

On balance, the stronger argument seems to be that Ruth's case is closer to the *McFarlane* decision, in that she has a limited power of substitution. It is limited because, first, it applies only when she is unavailable for work; second, she must secure the agreement of the company; third, the replacements must be selected from those on the register approved by the company; and, fourth, she may only use this substitution power for a maximum of 14 days per annum. In conclusion, it is submitted that these constraints do not prevent a finding of employment status in Ruth's case.

Further reading

Busby, N., 'IR35: resolution of a taxing problem?' (2002) 31(2) ILJ 172–82.

Christensen, C., and Amarshi, R., 'A typical worker or atypical workers?' (2002) 152(7059) NLJ 1851–2.

Collins, H., Ewing, K. D., and McColgan, A., *Labour Law: Text and Materials* (Oxford: Hart Publishing, 2002), ch. 2, pp. 147–83.

'Employment law review 2002: contract of employment' (2003) 724 *IDS Brief* 17–19.

Honeyball, S., and Bowers, J., *Textbook on Labour Law*, 8th edn (Oxford: Oxford University Press, 2006), ch. 2.

Leighton, P., 'Problems continue for zero-hours workers' (2002) 31(1) ILJ 71–8.

Reynolds, F., QC, 'The status of agency workers: a question of legal principle', 35(3) ILJ 320–323.

Sargeant, M., *Employment Law*, 2nd edn (Harlow: Pearson, 2003), ch. 3, pp. 46–59.

Smith, I. T., 'Employment law brief: the "worker" definition' (2002) 152(7027) NLJ 548–9.

Smith, I. T., and Thomas, G., *Industrial Law,* 8th edn (London: LexisNexis, 2003), ch. 1, pp. 9–34.

Wigan, Z., and Cole, Kelly, 'Employee status—out of the ordinary?' (2002) 27 Empl. LJ 22–4.

'Working time: labour-only subcontractors were "workers" under the Working Time Regulations' (2002) 683 IRLB 15–16.

Wynn, M. and Leighton, P., 'Will the real employer please stand up? Agencies, Client Companies and the Employment Status of the Temporary Agency Worker', 35(3) ILJ 301–320.

Younson, F., 'Employment relationship—contracts and contractual terms—practice and procedure' (2002) 81 Empl. Lawyer 11.

2

Express and implied terms

Introduction

This chapter is devoted to express and implied contractual terms including covenants in restraint of trade. It shows in relation to covenants how a problem question may be dealt with; the student can use the same headings to write an essay on this topic. The sequence for answering questions appears in the commentary to the question but in summary it must be asked whether the clause falls within the restraint of trade doctrine; if so, does it protect a legitimate proprietary interest? If so, is the clause reasonable in the interests of the parties (and of the public)? If not, can it be 'rescued' by the doctrines of construction and severance? If not, has there been a wrongful dismissal, which will invalidate the clause? Finally, if the covenant is enforceable, which remedy or remedies will be given? This is a matter of grave importance, for a covenant which no longer applies is useless.

Question 1

Tina is a car salesperson at Karsales plc, a countrywide car dealership trading in high-powered vehicles. She knows the cost price (i.e. the cost of the cars to the dealership) as well as the selling price to customers (before any discount, which is limited to 7 per cent). Over the years she has assiduously cultivated customers, actual and potential, by playing golf, joining societies, and the like. Currently she earns some £35,000 per annum, which consists of a basic salary plus commission depending on the value of the cars she has sold. In a good year commission can be half of her pay.

Rick Shaw, the owner of Motors Ltd, has met Tina at several functions and now wishes to invite her to join his firm. He offers her £45,000 per annum. Both Motors and Karsales trade in the same market.

Tina's contract contains the following clauses.

1. 'You will not for six months after termination solicit any clients of Karsales.'

2. 'You will not at any time after termination use or disclose any confidential information belonging to Karsales.'

Advise the parties as to the validity of these clauses. Would it make any difference if, having heard of Rick Shaw's approach, Karsales dismiss Tina with immediate effect?

 ## Commentary

As always be alert to the rubric. If it states that advice as to the enforceability of covenants potentially in restraint of trade is to be provided, stick to that topic and do not deal with the law of implied terms as to confidentiality found in *Faccenda Chicken Ltd* v *Fowler* [1987] Ch 117, CA.

The following sequence is suggested:

1. Is the clause potentially in restraint of trade?

2. If so, does the clause protect a legitimate proprietary interest?

3. If so, is the clause reasonably necessary to protect that interest?

4. If so, is the clause in the interests of the public? (This question in employment law is normally subsumed under points 2 and 3 above.)

5. Does the doctrine of construction apply?

6. Does the doctrine of severance apply?

7. Has there been a wrongful dismissal?

8. Which remedy are the employers seeking? Normally they will want an interim injunction pending trial. Remedies are important throughout employment law, but particularly when considering convenants.

Not all of these problems are relevant to every restraint of trade question but simply writing something about each of these issues both means that issues are not omitted and provides a structure to the answer. Writing a paragraph or more on each, and applying the law to the facts, looks impressive to examiners. As a corollary examiners deduct marks for poor organization. Unless instructed differently, you are free to use subheadings, leaving a line between topics.

 ## Answer plan

- Legitimate proprietary interest
- Reasonable between the parties including duration and territorial extent
- Wrongful dismissal
- Remedies, especially interim injunction

Suggested answer

Proprietary interest

Covenants are enforceable only if they protect a legitimate proprietary interest: *Herbert Morris Ltd* v *Saxelby* [1916] AC 688, HL. On the facts the first clause could safeguard the employers' client base, which is an interest protectable by a restrictive covenant. Clause 1 is known as a non-solicitation clause, which is aimed at protecting customer connection. Lord Parker in *Herbert Morris* spoke of 'personal knowledge of and influence over' clients. It may be doubted whether customers will be so influenced by salespersons that they will keep coming back but the judges have treated milk roundspersons, hairdressers, and estate agents as having such influence; so it is not beyond the bounds of possibility that they may hold that car salespeople have such a customer connection. They may have personal knowledge of the clients' tastes in cars, financial position, and other matters. Such clauses are valid if they are no wider than is reasonably necessary in terms of area and duration. The area is not stated but the clause is restricted in another way, the link with the clientele. It is also restricted to a certain period of time, six months, which may be reasonable. The issue of reasonableness is one for the courts and previous cases cannot be treated as authoritative: *Dairy Crest Ltd* v *Pigott* [1989] ICR 90, CA. In the principal authority, *GW Plowman & Son Ltd* v *Ash* [1964] 1 WLR 568, CA it was held that a covenant is not unenforceable merely on the ground that the employee did not work for all the clients. Russell LJ said that since the validity of covenants is assessed at the time when the contract is entered into, it does not matter that the employee did not deal with all the customers if at the time when the contract was agreed the employee could have dealt with any or all of them. The second clause protects confidential information. Trade secrets are protectable by covenants. The law is that post-termination covenants cannot prevent the employee's skill and knowledge from being used in the service of Tina's new employers (such as the fact that she is pleasant towards clients), or protect knowledge of the general methods of running a business (e.g. the fact that a company keeps its client database on computer) and information which is publicly available, such as the selling price of cars. *Herbert Morris* is authority for these propositions. The maximum discount and the cost price may on the facts be trade secrets. If Motors knew such information, they could gain a competitive advantage over Karsales: they could attract Karsales' clients to them by undercutting their rival in the market (for a case involving discounts but not a restraint of trade one see *Faccenda Chicken Ltd* v *Fowler* [1987] Ch 117, CA, the major authority on implied terms of confidentiality).

Reasonable between the parties

Assuming that both clauses protect proprietary interests, we must tackle the next issue, whether the clause is reasonable between the parties. In respect of area covenants judges normally concentrate on the duration of the covenant and the territory covered. However, such issues may not be relevant in respect of non-solicitation and trade secrets clauses. Both have 'internal' restrictions. The first clause is restricted to clients. The firm deals with a certain type of vehicle. It is possible that the market is the whole of the UK (or less likely, the whole world), depending on the type of car. However, there is no territorial restriction and if the customers do not come from throughout the UK or perhaps from the whole world potentially the clause could fall. However, it is suggested that the restriction to 'clients of Karsales' means that the clause, so internally limited, will on these grounds be enforceable: see Harman LJ in *Plowman* v *Ash*. In the jargon there is 'functional correspondence' between the interest to be protected and the clause as drafted. In terms of length six months does not seem excessive, though each case stands on its own facts. There is time for Tina's influence over her clients to wane.

The second clause is also internally limited: to confidential information. Therefore, it does not extend to non-confidential material, and once the employers publish that information, the clause lapses. Such a restrictive covenant may apply to the whole world and the lack of a restriction as to territory is immaterial. Compare *Littlewoods Organisation Ltd* v *Harris* [1977] 1 WLR 1472, CA, where a clause would not have been upheld, had it been for longer than 12 months, because women's fashions change so quickly: protection was given to a home sales catalogue prepublication; on publication the prices, etc. entered into the public domain and the covenant, previously enforceable, became unenforceable because there no longer was an interest to protect.

Other matters

If the clauses are valid so far, they will not be invalidated by the public interest. That interest except in pension cases and other rare cases has been subsumed into the 'interests of the parties' test. If the clause is reasonably necessary in the interests of the parties, it will also be reasonable in the public interest. There are no difficulties of construction and severance is not at issue. The question which arises is whether the clauses apply to what Tina is doing (and we do not know what she proposes to do).

Assuming that the clauses do cover what she will be doing for Motors, we must investigate whether or not she has been wrongfully dismissed by Karsales. If she has, both covenants fall: *General Billposting Co Ltd* v *Atkinson* [1909] AC 118, HL. The Court of Appeal in *Rock Refrigeration Ltd* v *Jones* [1996] IRLR 675 had some doubts whether *General Billposting* survived *Photo Production Ltd* v *Securicor Transport Ltd* [1980] AC 827, HL, when the employers had drafted the contract in a way to try and avoid the rule that covenants fall on wrongful dismissal, but it is suggested that the earlier Lords' case applies with full vigour, *Securicor* not being concerned with this issue. In that event the question is whether there is a wrongful dismissal. Karsales have dismissed Tina and have done so immediately i.e. without giving the correct length of notice; do they have a cause, a justification, for dismissing her without notice? Tina is expecting to join Motors. No firm can be expected to wait until she does before seeking to enforce the covenants; otherwise the firm may lose its client base or trade secrets or both. Therefore, the claimants have the right to dismiss without notice. Therefore, there is no wrongful dismissal.

Karsales will seek an interim injunction, which is granted under the principles in *American Cyanamid Ltd* v *Ethicon Ltd* [1975] AC 396, HL. This remedy will stop Tina from acting in breach of the covenants. It cannot prevent Tina from working for Motors after the six-month period has elapsed or from using non-confidential material. The basic rule is that the claimants must have an arguable case, which apparently Karsales do. The merits (such as the reasonableness of the covenant) are not considered. However, merits are investigated if the clause will become inapplicable through lapse of time: *Lansing Linde Ltd v Kerr* [1991] 1 WLR 251, CA. Clause 1 will be rendered otiose after six months have elapsed since termination. Full trial can rarely come on in such a short period, though there is the possibility of an order for speedy trial. In that case the court can consider the merits of Karsales' contentions at the interlocutory stage. The usual equitable rules governing injunctions of all varieties apply and an interim injunction will not be granted if damages are adequate. Here the employers seem to have complied with the maxims of equity and damages will not prevent Tina from 'stealing' their clients and confidential information. Should the case proceed to full trial, Karsales will seek a final injunction (to prevent future loss) and damages (to compensate for any past breach). Damages are assessed in the normal contractual manner.

Question 2

Is it true to say that implied terms protect employees more than employers?

Commentary

This question deals with implied terms in the context of employment law and requires an in-depth treatment of how the courts and tribunals have used such terms either to promote the interests of employees at the expense of employers or vice versa. It is not simply a question of counting implied terms but of weighing them up and coming to a conclusion that is a response to the question set.

Answer plan

- The definition of implied terms including their current status and importance
- The standard employment law terminology ('implied in law' and 'implied in fact')
- The comparison: pro-employee or pro-employers?

Suggested answer

Introduction

Contracts of employment have become much more formal over the past half century or so. This development is no doubt linked to the bureaucratization of modern life but it is also connected with the switch from collective bargaining to individual contracts and with the written statement of the particulars of employment, first laid down in the Contracts of Employment Act 1963 and now consolidated in the Employment Rights Act 1996 (ERA). These changes have led to the diminution in significance of, for example, custom and practice as a source of implied obligations. Nevertheless, there is still room for implied terms, as can most easily be seen by reference to the rise of the duty of mutual trust and confidence in recent years; there is still no requirement for employment law terms to be in writing (except for merchant seamen) and provided the conditions of contract law (e.g. offer, acceptance, consideration, intent to create legal relations and legality) are satisfied, the exchange of promises is a contract of employment as in: 'Do you want this job?' 'Yes, please. How much per hour?' 'Eight quid.' 'O.K.' There is nothing in writing but there is a contract of employment. The express terms such as '£8 per hour' will be supplemented by implied terms such as the duty to serve faithfully and obligations derived from any applicable collective agreements.

The contract of employment is a contract. Therefore, not only do the conditions for being a contract apply, but so do the contractual doctrine of conditions, warranties and (no doubt) innominate terms, though employment law tends to adopt an autonomous phraseology. A complete non-payment of wages will break the contract, giving rise to an option in the employee to leave or to stay and she must make up her mind within a reasonable time (this type of term is a condition in contract terminology); however, a failure to pay every single penny because of an error in calculating pay may well not lead to such an option but relegate the employee to bringing a claim for breach of contract (this type of term is a warranty). Where there is a breach of condition and the employee accepts the breach, there is (in contract terminology) a repudiation and (in employment terminology) a constructive dismissal. Where there is a repudiation or constructive dismissal, there is a dismissal for the purposes of wrongful dismissal, redundancy payments and unfair dismissal. This point is of particular importance in respect of implied terms as fundamental terms, breach of which constitutes dismissal. Breach of the implied term of mutual trust and confidence always is a breach of a fundamental term, a breach of condition in contract parlance, and therefore such a breach gives rise to a claim, whether at common law (wrongful dismissal) or under statute (redundancy payments, unfair dismissal). When one adds that 'last straws' are a breach of this fundamental implied term *and* that the last straw need not in itself be a breach of contract (see *Omilaju* v *Waltham Forest LBC* [2005] ICR 481 (CA)), one can see how wide the term is and how much this term favours employees.

Though contracts of employment are contracts, unlike many other contracts employment ones are often intended to be of indefinite duration. If only for this reason it is impossible to foresee every eventuality and for that reason it is not possible to bargain about every item at the start of the contract: indeed, it is expected that this type of contract will be varied from time to time. If, for instance, one bargained in 1970 for a wage of £1,000 per year, one would not expect that to be paid the same in 2010. Linked with this point is the growth of implied terms after *Western Excavating (ECC) Ltd* v *Sharp* [1978] QB 761 (CA). In *Sharp* the court held that according to what is now s. 95(1)(c) of the ERA, the definition of constructive dismissal is satisfied only when the employers had acted in breach of a fundamental term in the contract; it was insufficient that they had acted unreasonably. The effect, it was thought, was that fewer employees would succeed in claiming unfair dismissal (and redundancy payments) than before because they would have to prove a breach of a fundamental term, not merely that the employers had acted unreasonably. However, the law has developed over the last 30 years in such a manner that a raft of implied terms has been formulated (or found or discovered or invented), the main one being that of mutual trust and confidence, that it can usually be said that when the employers act unreasonably, they act in breach of an implied term: see e.g. *United Bank* v *Akhtar* [1989] IRLR 507 (EAT), where the express mobility clause was qualified by an implied term that the employers would not move the employee without giving him reasonable notice. A more modern authority is *Horkulak* v *Cantor Fitzgerald International* [2005] ICR 402 (CA) where the express term that the employers could bestow or withhold a bonus at their discretion was construed as being subject to the implied term of trust and confidence that the employers would exercise their discretion in good faith and not irrationally. This application of the implied term is not far from a duty on the employers to act reasonably. Lord Steyn said in *Malik* v *BCCI SA* [1998] AC 20 (HL) that the duty of trust and confidence was defined thus: 'the employer shall not, without reasonable and proper cause, conduct itself in a manner calculated or likely to damage the relationship of trust and confidence between employer and employee'. This implied term has the potential to swallow up much of the law of terms implied in law (such as the duty of fidelity) and this is why Lord Nicholls in *BCCI* described the term as a 'portmanteau' one, like a capacious bag big enough to swallow the other implied terms.

Terms implied in law

It is usual in employment law (the phraseology derives from *Treitel on Contract*) to divide implied terms into those implied by law and those implied in fact. The latter comprise terms that arise on the facts of a particular employee's contract: for example, do these employers have a duty to provide this employee with a car? To answer that question, one has to go through the standard ways of implying terms such as business efficacy and the reasonable bystander test. However, what this question is asking about is the former set of terms, terms implied in law; that is, terms that every contract of employment has unless the express terms exclude them. In this sense, terms implied in law are 'default' terms: they apply unless expressly negated. For example, it would be a strange employment contract where there was no express and no implied provision as to pay. Such terms are also sometimes known as the 'incidents' of employment, because all employment contracts contain them unless specifically excluded.

Discussion

The list of such terms is not agreed by either courts or commentators. For example, while there is a duty to serve faithfully (or with good faith), it may be difficult to see how that term fits in with other terms: is the duty to reveal misdeeds of colleagues part of this term or a separate free-standing term? There are also difficulties with the width of some implied terms. For example, a subset of the duty of fidelity seems to be an implied term not to make illegitimate preparations during employment; however, the line between legitimate and illegitimate preparations is not clearly drawn. Nevertheless, it may be stated that the following implied terms arise in law:

- on the employee—mutual trust and confidence, duty of care, cooperation, fidelity, obedience;
- on the employers—mutual trust and confidence, duty of care, pay.

[The duties of care will not be considered here because they involve health and safety law, which is not part of this book.]

Where the duty is 'on' the employee, the employers' interests are advanced, but where it is on the employers, the reverse situation applies.

There is no implied term to provide references and there is no automatic implied term as to sick pay (in other words, there may be an implied term on sick pay, but whether there is or not depends on all the other terms of the contract). There is also no general duty on the employers to provide work (see the famous quote from Asquith J in *Collier* v *Sunday Referee Publishing Co Ltd* [1940] 2 KB 647: 'provided I pay my cook her wages regularly, she cannot complain if I choose to take any or all of my meals out') but there are exceptions, as is illustrated by *Herbert Clayton & Jack Waller Ltd* v *Oliver* [1930] AC 209 (HL) (actor; paid in part by publicity), *Turner* v *Goldsmith* [1891] 1 QB 544 (CA) (salesperson paid on commission), and *Devonald* v *Rosser & Sons* [1906] 2 KB 728 (CA) (worker paid by the piece). A recent revival of this term has occurred in defining the limits of garden leave clauses: see especially *William Hill Organisation Ltd* v *Tucker* [1999] ICR 291 (CA).

With respect to some implied terms, it must be said that it is almost impossible to visualize a contract of employment without such terms. For example, almost by definition there is a duty to obey lawful and reasonable orders. The position of employee and employers is normally one of subordination and superordination. The former is subordinate to the latter and therefore she is under a duty to obey orders. If the employee disobeys, 'the relationship is ... struck at fundamentally': per Lord Evershed MR in *Laws* v *London Chronicle (Indicator Newspapers)* [1959] 1 WLR 698 (CA). (However, the duty extends only so far: there is no duty to obey an order to falsify documents or to work in a country where one may be killed for religious or ethnic reasons.) Similarly, employees are under an obligation to serve faithfully. This duty is to be expected in a relationship such as that which exists between employers and employees. (Again, the duty extends only so far. For example, it may run up against the policy of free competition: the duty to preserve one's employers (merely) confidential information does not survive the termination of the contract.) If one looks at an illustration of an implied term in favour of employees, in this case pay, it is obvious that most (at least!) people will not work without pay. This example shows once more the fundamental nature of implied terms. It might be thought that the employees' duty to cooperate would be to similar effect but in the principal authority, *Secretary of State for Employment* v *ASLEF (No. 2)* [1972] 2 QB 455 (CA), Lord Denning MR determined that the implied term was broken when the employees worked to rule; that is, when they followed the rule-book to the letter. He held that the employees had a duty not to obstruct their employers' business deliberately. Their sticking to the express words of their contracts was a breach of contract! In *Sim* v *Rotherham BC* [1987] Ch 216 Scott J held that there was a professional obligation on teachers to cover for absent colleagues, a duty that may be part of the implied term of cooperation. That non-binding professional obligation was transmuted into a legally binding contract clause by means of an implied term!

Conclusion

In an era where employers retain the whip-hand over express terms one might have expected that the courts and tribunals would seek to restrain managerial prerogatives by extending employment protection through the use of implied terms. There is some strong indication of this approach when one looks at how express terms have been circumscribed by implied ones. Nevertheless, there is much to be said for the proposition that the judges do not use implied terms as a bulwark against employers (cf. the discussion of the duty to cooperate, above) but instead have been adept ruling against employees. Whether most judges sympathize with their 'class' mates, the employers, is a topic for another essay!

Further reading

Levin, M., and Murray, C., 'Restrictive covenants: the 21st-century approach' (2002) 29 Empl. LJ 15–18.

Lindsay, J., 'The implied term of trust and confidence' (2001) 30 ILJ 1.

McDonald, K., 'Protecting the employer's interests—covenants' (2002) 750 *IRS Employment Law* 47–60.

McDonald, K., 'Protecting the employer's interests: Part 2' (2002) 687 IRLB 3–19.

'Restrictive covenants: non-dealing covenant justifiably extended to prospective customers of employer' (2000) 636 IRLB 6–7.

Sargeant, M., *Employment Law*, 2nd edn (Harlow: Pearson, 2003), ch. 4, esp. pp. 105–11.

Smith, I. T., and Thomas, G., *Industrial Law*, 8th edn (Oxford: Oxford University Press, 2003), ch. 3, pp. 124–34.

3

Termination of the contract of employment

Introduction

This chapter focuses on the termination of the contract of employment at common law as amended by statute. It does not consider the common law action for wrongful dismissal, which is dealt with in the next chapter, or the statutory claims to redundancy payments and for a remedy for unfair dismissal, which are dealt with elsewhere. The focus in this chapter is on the modes of termination which do or do not constitute a dismissal for common law or statutory purposes. Only if there is a dismissal can there be a claim for one or more of these rights. It should be noted that the definition of dismissal varies across these rights; in particular, the expiry of a fixed-term contract is not a dismissal at law but Parliament deems the expiry of a limited-term contract without renewal to be a dismissal for the purposes of redundancy payments and unfair dismissal. It should also be noted that in respect of all three claims the courts or tribunals cannot hear the claim unless there is a dismissal; therefore, if the forum wishes to hear the merits of the case, it must hold that there has been a dismissal; there is what may be called a 'push' towards a finding of dismissal, for without such a finding there is no jurisdiction.

As the answer to Question 1 demonstrates, there are several forms of dismissal at common law: death, dissolution, frustration, expiry of a fixed-term contract, resignation, termination by mutual agreement, and performance. Each of these concepts is discussed. Question 2 considers one of those concepts in depth, frustration, and details how to approach a question on gross misconduct in the context of an action for wrongful dismissal. Such an action consists of three elements: was the worker dismissed? If so, was the worker dismissed with no or insufficient notice? If so, was the dismissal justified, or to use the correct terminology, was it for cause? As this book stresses, if there is a successful claim, the bright student then looks at the remedy or remedies. Here the remedy is damages assessed in the contractual manner because wrongful dismissal is a contractual action, to which all the contractual rules including limitation periods apply if the claim is brought in the ordinary courts. However, if the claim is brought in an employment tribunal, the limitation period is three months. For more on the comparison between wrongful dismissal and unfair dismissal, see Question 4 in Chapter 6.

Question 1

Discuss the non-dismissal forms of termination of employment contracts at common law.

Commentary

Answers should exclude redundancy payments and unfair dismissal, which are statutory claims predicated on dismissal. Nevertheless, any links should be explored. For example, where there is no dismissal, there cannot be one of these statutory claims. Therefore, the wider the concept of termination by what might be called 'non-dismissal', the less chance an employee has of qualifying for one of these rights and therefore the less opportunity a court or tribunal has of adjudicating on the dispute. Therefore, if the forum wishes to hear the dispute, it must hold that there has been a dismissal. The term 'termination' covers both termination by dismissal and termination not by dismissal (e.g. by frustration). The question is restricted to the latter. Note that for the purposes of the common law claim of wrongful dismissal 'dismissal' covers both express/actual/direct dismissal and repudiation but not the expiry of a limited-term contract.

Answer plan

- 'Non-dismissal' and its effects
- Common law (actual and repudiation) and under statute (actual, expiry of a limited-term contract without renewal, and constructive)
- Death of either party, dissolution of a partnership, insolvency of a company
- Frustration: definition and its application to illness and imprisonment
- Expiry of a limited-term contract (at common law)
- Mutual agreement and its relationship with dismissal
- Performance

Suggested answer

The contract of employment is a contract of personal service; therefore, if an employee or the employer (being a natural person) dies, the contract is terminated without dismissal. If the employer is a company which is wound up by the court or if the court appoints a receiver, the contract is terminated without dismissal. Similarly, the dissolution of a partnership terminates the contract without dismissal. Note, however, the effect of the Transfer of Undertakings (Protection of Employment) Regulations 2006 (SI 2006/246) (the TUPE Regulations). This law is reminiscent of the phrase: 'You can't flog a dead horse!' One cannot employ a dead person or be employed by one.

The contract is terminated automatically by frustration if performance becomes illegal or would produce a result radically different from that agreed or if it becomes impossible to perform the contract, provided that neither party is at fault. This doctrine, subject to the law discussed below of imprisonment, is the same as that in general contract law, as laid down in cases such as *Davis* v *Fareham UDC* [1956] AC 696, HL. If there is frustration, the contract is terminated by operation of law and there is no dismissal (except where the frustrating event is the death of the employer or the dissolution of a company, in which case the event is deemed to be a dismissal for the purposes of redundancy payments (RP): s. 136(5) Employment Rights Act 1996 (ERA)). If wages are due, they may be recovered: Law Reform (Frustrated Contracts) Act 1943. Wages falling due after frustration are not recoverable, but the court may award a sum representing wages if it considers it just and equitable to do so.

An example of frustration is *Morgan* v *Manser* [1948] 1 KB 184. A wartime call-up frustrated the contract. Employment cases tend to involve illness or imprisonment. Illness may frustrate the contract, as in *Condor* v *Barron Knights* [1966] 1 WLR 87 where the drummer in a comedy band fell mentally ill and could not drum seven nights per week. Where the contract is for a long term or is of indefinite duration, whether frustration occurs is determined by the guidelines in *Marshall* v *Harland & Wolff Ltd* [1972] 1 WLR 899 (Donaldson P) and *Egg Stores (Stamford Hill) Ltd* v *Leibovici* [1977] 1 WLR 260, EAT: what were the terms of the contract including any provision as to sick pay? How long was the job likely to last? (It is more likely that a short-term contract will be frustrated than a long-term one.) What is the nature of employment? (The holder of a key post is more likely to have his or her contract frustrated than another.) What is the nature of the illness and what are the prospects of recovery? How long has the employee worked for the employers? (The longer the length, the less likelihood there is of frustration.) Is there a risk of a RP or a remedy for unfair dismissal (UD) or both? Have wages continued to be paid? What have the employers done or said? Was it reasonable for the employers to wait any longer? The Court of Appeal in *Notcutt* v *Universal Equipment Co (London) Ltd* [1986] 1 WLR 641, the leading authority, held that frustration could apply even when the contract was terminable by a short period of notice. The employee had a heart attack, which frustrated the contract. The date of frustration was the day when his doctor told him that he would probably not work again. The fact that the employment was terminable by one week's notice was immaterial when the parties had the expectation that it would continue indefinitely.

The principal problem arises in relation to imprisonment. It would seem axiomatic that if someone is imprisoned, then that person is at fault and therefore the doctrine of frustration does not apply. However, Lord Denning MR said in *Hare* v *Murphy Bros.*

[1974] ICR 603, CA that frustration was caused not by the accused's misconduct but by the sentence of the court. Sentencing was outwith the control of the parties and therefore the frustrating event was not self-induced. The time of frustration is the date when it is commercially necessary to replace the employee: *Chakki* v *United Yeast Co Ltd* [1982] ICR 140, EAT. The main authority is *FC Shepherd & Co Ltd* v *Jerrom* [1985] ICR 552, CA. It was held that a contract of employment may be frustrated but that principle does not apply when the parties have foreseen the alleged frustrating event. An apprentice's contract contained a clause that his employers could dismiss him for misconduct. He was imprisoned. Since the parties had foreseen the misconduct through using terms dealing with the situation in the contract, there was no frustration when the employers were seeking to rely on the misconduct. However, if it had been the apprentice (or employee) who had sought to rely on his own misconduct, there would have been frustration.

Courts and tribunals have to be astute to determine whether or not there has been frustration because if there has, there is no dismissal and therefore no claim for UD, RP, or wrongful dismissal. If the forum wishes to hear the case, it must hold that frustration has not occurred. For this reason the concept remains malleable to some extent. It is suggested that Lord Denning MR's decision as to the basis of frustration where there is imprisonment is decidedly weak and may not survive challenge in the Lords.

Another way of terminating the contract at common law without dismissal is the expiry of a fixed-term contract. A break clause does not mean that the contract is not for a fixed term: *Dixon* v *BBC* [1978] QB 438, CA. However, the non-renewal of a limited-term contract is deemed to be a dismissal for the purposes of RP and UD: s. 136(1)(b) and s. 95(1)(b), ERA (both as amended) respectively.

As can be imagined, many contracts end by the employee's resigning. This is one instance of termination by mutual consent. Again there is no dismissal. For instance, in *SW Strange Ltd* v *Mann* [1965] 1 WLR 629, CA an employee's contract to serve as manager was terminated by agreement. In that contract there was a covenant in restraint of trade. That clause was not included in a contract which the employee had when he ran one department of the employers. Therefore, the employers could not enforce the covenant when the employee left.

Courts and tribunals must be aware that where there is a termination by agreement, there is no dismissal and thus no possibility of a wrongful dismissal (WD), RP, or UD claim, as in *Birch* v *University of Liverpool* [1985] ICR 470 demonstrates. Two members of staff applied for early retirement. The scheme gave them more money than did the statutory RP system, and compensation expressly covered a statutory RP. It was held that the contracts had been terminated by mutual consent. Therefore, there was no dismissal for the purposes of RP and the employers could not get a RP. Compare *Caledonian Mining Co Ltd* v *Bassett* [1987] ICR 425, EAT. When the employers asked employees if they were interested in work for other employers, the employees were obliged to seek work elsewhere; their resignation was not by consent, and there was constructive dismissal.

The leading authority, which shows that the courts are careful not to let employers have a free rein when it comes to termination by agreement, is *Igbo* v *Johnson Matthey Chemicals Ltd* [1986] ICR 505, CA. The employee requested leave to visit her children. She was granted it subject to a condition that if she did not return to England by a certain date, her contract would be automatically terminated. She was not back by that date. The court held that the condition was a means of evading her employment rights and was for that reason void under what is now s. 203, ERA. The court opined that if employers could insert such a clause, they would do so, thereby depriving employees of their rights. The question to be asked is: 'Who really terminated the contract of employment?': *Martin* v *MBS Fastenings (Glynwed) Distribution Ltd* [1983] ICR 511, CA.

Finally, a contract of employment is terminated by performance, i.e. when all the duties under it are performed.

It is suggested that in general the courts and tribunals show that they are keen not to let employers determine the outcome of the question whether an employee has been dismissed or not, for only if there is a dismissal can they deal with the merits of the case. Their jurisdiction depends on a finding of dismissal: where there is no dismissal, there is no claim for RP, UD, or WD.

Question 2

Tina has recently been appointed Head of Catering at Twistleton College, having spent the previous five years as Deputy Head of a similar college in Australia. She has a contract which states that she is dismissable with three months' notice. The contract also provides that she is subject to a discipline procedure based on the ACAS Code of Practice. She has now found herself the subject of an investigation into her running of the department. The panel of investigators found that she had mismanaged the budget of the department by overspending on hospitality. The members of the panel said that her reckless overspending constituted gross misconduct and the College has sent her a letter notifying her that she has been dismissed without notice.

Steve, the Deputy Head, has been told to 'act up'; that is, to take on Tina's management role with some increase in his salary. He also has to continue with his normal job. He found that he could not cope with the strain of doing two jobs and has had to take time off work. His doctor has told him not to go back for at least 12 weeks. It is uncertain how long after that period Steve will be able to return to work, but it will be about eight more weeks. The College has written to him stating that the contract under which he has been employed has been frustrated.

Advise Tina and Steve.

Commentary

The question tells the candidate part of the areas of law which require discussion, in particular frustration. In relation to Tina there is a mention of dismissal. There is a tendency to launch into unfair dismissal, but the facts do not give rise to such a claim because Tina has not been an employee of the College for one year. Therefore, the question seeks a discussion of wrongful dismissal. Similarly the student should be aware that in relation to Steve, discussion of the Disability Discrimination Act 1995 is irrelevant because the illness is not expected to last for 12 months or more.

Answer plan

- Wrongful dismissal
- Notice at law (express/implied) and under statute
- 'Cause'
- Breach of contract
- Damages as the remedy
- Frustration: the application of the doctrine to sickness

Suggested answer

The question states that Tina has been dismissed. She has only recently been appointed Head; therefore, she does not have the one year's continuous employment normally demanded before she qualifies to bring a claim for unfair dismissal. There is nevertheless the possibility of her bringing a claim for wrongful dismissal. She has been dismissed and the dismissal has been one without notice. On the facts she should have been given three months' notice, as stated in her contract (the statutory period in s. 86 of the Employment Rights Act 1996 (ERA) would have been shorter and it is the longer period which applies), but she has been given none. Therefore, the dismissal is 'wrongful'; that is, she has been provided with no or insufficient notice. The issue then becomes one of enquiring whether or not the College has a 'cause', a justification, for instant dismissal. Gross misconduct is such a cause, but has Tina behaved in such a way? If there was an express term to that effect, there would be gross misconduct (see *Uzoamaka* v *Conflict and Change Ltd* [1999] IRLR 624); however, there is no mention of such a term. Accordingly, implied terms should be investigated. Among examples of gross misconduct are theft, obtaining secret profits, disobeying lawful orders, and violence. Somewhat nearer to the present case is *Taylor* v *Alidair Ltd* [1978] ICR 445, CA, where one bumpy landing amounted to gross negligence justifying dismissal. If there is such behaviour, the employers are justified in sacking Tina with no contractual notice, and the statutory period of notice also does not apply (s. 86(6), ERA). If, however, there was no cause, then the dismissal is wrongful and Tina could obtain damages for the notice period, here three months' salary subject to the usual deductions such as mitigation. Her claim would be heard in the civil courts or if the amount was less than £25,000 as it presumably will be here, in the employment tribunal: note that in the event, the courts and tribunals have concurrent jurisdiction. If the forum is the tribunal, the limitation period is only three months, even though the claim is one for breach of contract.

Tina's contract also provides for a discipline procedure. This procedure has not been invoked. Therefore, the College is in breach of contract and can be sued for damages in the normal way. The aim of contractual damages is to put the parties into the position they would have been in, had the contract been performed. Therefore, damages would be assessed on the basis of: 'how long would the procedure have taken?' *Gunton* v *Richmond Borough Council* [1990] ICR 755 illustrates the manner in which the courts reach the quantum. Again the usual contract rules on deductions apply and the claim would be heard either in the civil courts or if for under £25,000 in the employment tribunal. There is also the possibility of obtaining the equitable remedy of an injunction to prevent the dismissal taking place. The normal equitable rules apply, e.g. Tina must come with clean hands. An injunction will also not be ordered where damages are adequate. The type of injunction which Tina will be seeking immediately is an interim one to preserve the position, the status quo, until trial. Under the law laid down by the House of Lords in *American Cyanamid Co* v *Ethicon Ltd* [1975] AC 396 she has merely to show an arguable case that her employers are in breach of contract, which she surely can demonstrate on the facts.

Steve may well have been employed for more than one year continuously by the College. Therefore, there is the possibility of both a wrongful and an unfair dismissal claim. However, there is for both claims the requirement of a dismissal and there will be no dismissal if the contract has been frustrated. Frustration bears its normal contract law definition (the contract comes to an end by law and not by dismissal when performance is radically different from that envisaged, or the contract becomes illegal or the contract cannot be performed—impossibility, in all cases without either party being at fault), and illness is a potentially frustrating event, for sickness means that the contract cannot be performed as intended by the parties (cf. the *Coronation* cases—e.g. *Krell* v *Henry* [1903] KB 740, on which see McElray and Williams (1940) 4 MLR 241 and (1941) 5 MLR 1). Whether it is so depends on the tests laid down in *Marshall* v *Harland and Wolff Ltd* [1972] 1 WLR 899, NIRC and *Egg Stores (Stamford Hill) Ltd* v *Leibovici* [1977] ICR 260, EAT. We do not know the terms of the contract including any reference to sick pay but presumably for a person of his status there would be a clause to the effect that he would receive sick pay for, say, six or twelve months. The employment was intended to be indefinite. The job looks like a key one. We know that Steve will return in the not too distant future. We do not, however, know how long he has worked at the College, but perhaps in the light of his job title it may have been some time. It looks as if no replacement has been found yet, so the College is not at risk of making a redundancy payment or paying compensation for unfair dismissal or both to a replacement. Wages may well have continued to be paid. The employers do, however, want to treat the contract as frustrated and it may be that they can wait no longer before engaging a new person in Steve's post. Certainly sickness is not the fault of either party. It is suggested that the contract is not frustrated and that the letter from the employers could be seen as a breach of the duty of trust and confidence, in which case there is a constructive dismissal. There may be a fair dismissal for illness, which is part of the 'capability' reason for the purposes of unfair dismissal. All will turn on whether the reasonableness test in s. 98(4), ERA has been satisfied. There has been no consultation with Steve and the employers seem not to have used the doctor's report as a basis for deciding what to do. *Spencer* v *Paragon Wallpapers Ltd* [1977] ICR 301 suggests that employers consider: the nature of the illness, the possible length of the absence, the personal circumstances of the employee, the urgency of finding a replacement, and the size and nature of the firm. While there is not evidence as to all of these factors, as *Spencer* holds, the question is basically one of whether the employers can reasonably be expected to wait any longer or not. Certainly the lack of consultation may be decisive in the mind of the tribunal: *East Lindsey DC* v *Daubney* [1977] ICR 566. If the dismissal was unfair, the usual remedies of reinstatement, re-engagement, and compensation (in that order) are available. Note too that Steve may also have an action for negligence against his employers for overloading him. See especially *Walker* v *Northumberland CC* [1995] IRLR 35 (Colman J) (on stress, as here) and *Johnstone* v *Bloomsbury HA* [1992] QB 333 (on overwork, also as here). The former case was a tort action for negligence; the latter a contract case on possible breach of the term of trust and confidence.

In conclusion it is suggested that Tina may lawfully be dismissed without notice but that the employers should have used the contractual discipline procedure, and that Steve's contract is not frustrated but that he may well have been dismissed unfairly.

Further reading

'Contracts of employment: frustration—long-term illness' (2001) 699 *IDS Brief* 10–11.

Sargeant, M., *Employment Law,* 2nd edn (Harlow: Pearson, 2003), ch. 5, esp. pp. 117–31, 163–70.

Smith, I. T., and Thomas, G., *Industrial Law,* 8th edn (Oxford: Oxford University Press, 2003), ch. 7, pp. 446–68.

Yew, J., 'Wrongful dismissal—recent developments' (2001) 75 *Employment Lawyer* 18–19.

4

Continuity of employment

Introduction

Continuity of employment is an important concept in employment law. Some employment protection measures depend upon having a minimum period of continuous employment. To be able to make a complaint of unfair dismissal, for example, in accord with Part X of the Employment Rights Act 1996 (ERA), an individual is required to be an employee with at least one year's continuous employment, usually, but not always, with the same employer. This qualifying period has been subject to change, depending upon which political party constitutes the government. Before the Conservative Party's win in 1979 the period was six months. Successive Conservative governments progressively increased this to two years, until it was reduced to one year again after the Labour Party won the general election in 1997.

It is important to remember that not all areas of employment protection need this minimum period of service. Perhaps the most important exception is in the field of discrimination. No period of continuous employment is required if an individual wishes to bring a claim for discrimination on any of the forbidden grounds (race, religion or belief, sex, sexual orientation, disability or age). Indeed the relevant statutes provide for protection during the process of applying for a job, so protection is offered before an individual even starts work. Similarly, for example, there is no service requirement with regard to the right to be paid the national minimum wage.

Issues related to the complex area of transfers of undertakings are included in this chapter because one of the effects of the Transfer of Undertakings (Protection of Employment) Regulations 2006 (SI 2006/246) (the TUPE Regulations) is to maintain continuity of employment when there has been a change in the employer as a result of a relevant transfer.

Continuity

In order to answer any exam question relating to continuity of employment, it is necessary to be aware of a number of issues. These are related to the start date, the definition of a week that counts for continuity purposes, the effect of absences from work, and industrial disputes.

The start date

An employee's period of continuous employment begins on the day on which the employee starts work. In *General of the Salvation Army* v *Dewsbury* [1984] IRLR 222 a part-time teacher took on a new full-time contract which stated that her employment began on 1 May. As 1 May was a Saturday and the following Monday was a bank holiday, she did not actually commence work until Tuesday 4 May. She was subsequently dismissed with effect from 1 May in the following year. The issue was whether she had one year's continuous employment. The EAT held that the day on which an employee starts work is intended to refer to the beginning of the employee's employment under the relevant contract of employment and that this may be different from the actual date on which work commences.

The week that counts

Section 212(1), ERA provides that any week during the whole or part of which an employee's relations with his or her employer are governed by a contract of employment counts in calculating the employee's length of employment. A week is defined as a week ending with Saturday or, for a weekly paid employee, a week ends with the day used in calculating the week's pay; see s. 235(1), ERA. Thus if a contract of employment exists in any one week, then that week counts for continuity purposes. In *Sweeney* v *J & S Henderson* [1999] IRLR 306 an employee resigned from his employment on a Saturday and left immediately to take up another post. The individual returned to the original employer the following Friday, to recommence work. The employee was held to have continuity of employment as a result of there not being a week in which the contract of employment did not apply. This was despite the fact that the employee worked for another employer during the intervening period. The employee worked under a contract of employment with the employer during each of the two weeks in question and thus fulfilled the requirements of the Act.

Absences from work

There are a number of reasons for which a person can be absent from work without breaking the statutory definition of continuity of employment: s. 212, ERA. These include:

(a) absences through sickness and injury;

(b) absences resulting from a temporary cessation of work;

(c) custom and practice.

A change of employer

Although the continuity provisions normally apply to employment by one employer, s. 218(1), ERA, there are situations where a transfer from one employer to another can preserve continuity of employment. One such situation is when there is a relevant transfer under the TUPE Regulations. The TUPE Regulations create a situation where it is as if the original contract of employment was agreed with the new employer. Thus an employee's period of service will transfer to the new employer.

There has been an enormous amount of litigation, both in the UK courts and at the European Court of Justice, concerning the provisions of the Acquired Rights Directive, 77/187/EEC, and the TUPE Regulations. The Directive was amended in 1998, Directive 98/50/EC (now consolidated into Directive 2001/23/EC), and the Regulations in 2006.

The 2006 Regulations define much more explicitly the meaning of a transfer of an undertaking. This has been a major source of litigation. Regulation 3(1)(a) of the 2006 TUPE Regulations states that the Regulations apply, firstly, to a transfer where there is a transfer of an economic entity that retains its identity and, secondly, to a service provision change. An economic entity is defined in reg. 3(2) as 'an organised grouping of resources which has the objective of pursuing an economic activity, whether or not that activity is central or ancillary'. Regulation 3(1)(b) provides that the Regulations also apply to a service provision change. These are relevant to outsourcing situations and are meant to ensure a wide coverage of the Regulations. A service provision change takes place when a person (client) first contracts out some part of its activities to a contractor; when such a contract is taken over by another contractor (so-called second-generation transfers); and when the client takes back the activity in-house from a contractor. Whereas, however, a relevant transfer consists of an 'organised grouping of resources', a service provision change requires there to be 'an organised grouping of employees, situated in Great Britain, which has, as its principal purpose, the carrying out of activities concerned'.

Other issues dealt with include transfers out of insolvency. The government wished to encourage a rescue culture by making such transfers easier to achieve. The TUPE Regulations had been seen as an obstacle to rescuing all or part of an insolvent company, because the rescuer might have been obliged to take on all the insolvent organization's employees on their current terms and conditions.

Where a trade, business, or undertaking is transferred to a new employer, then continuity is also preserved by s. 218(2), ERA and the employee's length of service moves to the new employer, although, as pointed out in *Nokes* v *Doncaster Collieries* [1940] AC 1014, this is likely to require the knowledge and consent of the employee. There are a number of specific situations where continuity is also preserved, see s. 218(3)–(10), ERA 1996.

Section 219, ERA provides that the Secretary of State may make provisions for preserving continuity of employment. The current regulations are the Employment Protection (Continuity of Employment) Regulations 1996 (SI 1996/3147), which serve, in reg. 2, to protect continuity of employment, in relation to a dismissal, where an employee is making a complaint about dismissal or making a claim in accordance with a dismissal procedures agreement. Continuity is also protected, in relation to a dismissal, as a result of any action taken by a conciliation officer or the making of a compromise agreement.

Question 1

Critically consider the approach of statute and the courts to the concept of 'continuity of employment' in relation to employment protection.

Commentary

Continuity of employment is important because a number of statutory rights depend upon it. The question requires you to display your knowledge about what is meant by continuity of employment and when it does and does not apply.

There is a lot of material on this subject and one challenge in answering the question is to remain focused. It would be quite easy to wander off into detailed discussions of those areas which require a minimum period of continuity of employment, e.g. in making a claim for unfair dismissal. It would be wrong to end up discussing unfair dismissal rather than the concept of continuity.

Answer plan

- Why is continuity of employment important?
- When does continuous employment commence?
- What is continuous employment?
- Some absences do not break continuity.
- The rules normally apply to employment with one employer except where continuity is transferred.

Suggested answer

Continuity of employment is important as a number of statutory rights, such as the right to be protected from unfair dismissal, the right to receive written reasons for a dismissal, the right to take parental leave, and the right to extended maternity leave, depend upon the employee having one year's continuous employment with an employer.

An employee's period of continuous employment begins, as stated in s. 211, ERA, on the day on which the employee starts work. In *General of the Salvation Army* v *Dewsbury* [1984] IRLR 222 the EAT held that the day on which an employee starts work is intended to refer to the beginning of the employee's employment under the relevant contract of employment and that this may be different from the actual date on which work commences.

There is a presumption that an individual's period of employment is continuous, unless otherwise shown: s. 210(5), ERA. Thus the onus is on those that wish to challenge the presumption to show that there was not continuous service within the definition in the Act. It is likely, however, that the presumption of continuity only applies to employment with one employer.

Section 212(1), ERA states that any week during the whole or part of which an employee's relations with his or her employer are governed by a contract of employment counts in computing the employee's period of employment. A week is defined, in s. 235(1), ERA as a week ending with Saturday or, for a weekly paid employee, a week ends with the day used in calculating the week's remuneration. Thus if a contract of employment exists in any one week then that week counts for continuity purposes, see *Sweeney* v *J & S Henderson* [1999] IRLR 306, where an employee worked under a contract of employment with the employer during each of the two weeks in question and thus fulfilled the requirements of s. 212(1), ERA. This was despite the fact that the employee worked for another employer during the same period.

The employment concerned must relate to employment with one employer (s. 218(1), ERA), although this can include associated employers. The test for control amongst such employers is normally decided by looking at who has the voting control, but there might be, in exceptional circumstances, a need to look at who has de facto control: see *Payne* v *Secretary of State for Employment* [1989] IRLR 352.

The question of whether such a rule can amount to indirect sex discrimination or whether it can be objectively justified was considered in *R* v *Secretary of State for Employment ex parte Seymour-Smith and Perez* [2000] IRLR 263. This case was brought when the qualifying period was two years and the complainants were individuals who were stopped from bringing a complaint for unfair dismissal because they did not have the necessary two years' continuous service. They complained that the proportion of women who could comply with the two-year qualifying period was considerably smaller than the proportion of men. The House of Lords referred a number of questions to the European Court of Justice, who replied ([1999] IRLR 253, ECJ) that the entitlement to compensation and redress for unfair dismissal came within the scope of Art. 119 of the EC Treaty (now Art. 141) and the Equal Treatment Directive 1976. The government argued that the extension of the qualifying period should help reduce the reluctance of employers to take on more people. The court was sympathetic to the government's case and accepted objective justification and also that the qualification period did have a disparately adverse effect on women.

Absence from work means not performing in substance the contract that previously existed between the parties. Such a definition applied to a coach driver whose work was greatly reduced by the miners' strike in 1984. A substantial part of the individual's work was removed, but the employee was able to claim a temporary cessation of work: see *GW Stephens & Son* v *Fish* [1989] ICR 324.

There are a number of reasons for which a person can be absent from work without breaking their statutory continuity of employment. These are, first, if the employee is incapable of work as a result of sickness or injury: s. 212, ERA. Absences of no more than 26 weeks under this category will not be held to break continuity. Second, if there is a temporary cessation of work. According to s. 212(3)(b), ERA, absence from work on account of a temporary cessation of work will not break continuity of employment. The word 'temporary' is likely to mean a short time in comparison with the period in work. Thus seasonal workers who were out of work each year for longer than they actually worked could not be considered to have continuity of employment: see *Berwick Salmon Fisheries Co Ltd* v *Rutherford* [1991] IRLR 203. In *University of Aston in Birmingham* v *Malik* [1984] ICR 492 an individual who was employed on regular fixed-term contracts to teach was held to have continuity. During the summer the employee prepared for the coming year's teaching and the EAT decided that this amounted to a temporary cessation of work. A similar decision was reached in *Cornwall County Council* v *Prater* [2006] IRLR 362 where an individual who worked on a number of assignments as a home tutor over a period of 10 years was held to be an employee. The breaks between assignments were to be treated as temporary cessations of work. Third, absence from work in circumstances under which, by custom or arrangement, the employee is regarded as having continuity of employment, may not break the statutory concept of continuity. In *Booth* v *United States of America* [1999] IRLR 16 the employees were employed on a series of fixed-term contracts with a gap of about two weeks between contracts. On each return to work they were given the same employee number, the same tools and equipment, and the same lockers. Despite the employees arguing that this arrangement was designed to defeat the underlying purpose of the legislation, the EAT could not find an arrangement which would require, in advance of the break, some discussion and agreement that continuity could be preserved. It was clear that the employers did not want such an arrangement.

A week does not count for the purposes of calculating continuity of service if during that week, or any part of it, the employee takes part in a strike: s. 216, ERA. Periods when the employee is subject to a lockout do count for continuity purposes. However, in neither case is continuity itself broken.

Although the continuity provisions normally apply to employment by one employer, there are situations where a transfer from one employer to another can preserve continuity of employment. One such situation is when there is a relevant transfer under the TUPE Regulations. These Regulations create a situation where it is as if the original contract of employment was agreed with the new employer. Thus an employee's period of service will transfer to the new employer.

Where the trade, business, or undertaking is transferred to a new employer, then continuity is also preserved by s. 218(2), ERA and the employee's length of service moves to the new employer: see *Nokes* v *Doncaster Collieries* [1940] AC 1014.

Question 2

The XYZ Fruit Co. Ltd has decided to reduce its work force. It plans to achieve this by dismissing all those with less than one year's continuous service, so that none of the individuals concerned can make a claim for unfair dismissal. The dismissals took effect on Friday, 14 June 2002.

A number of those sacked believe that they have cause for complaint and come to you for help. You are asked to give each individual legal advice with regard to their circumstances in relation to having sufficient continuity of employment in order to make a claim:

- Julia thinks that the requirement to have one year's continuous employment before an unfair dismissal claim discriminates against women workers.

- Joshua joined the company on 13 June 2001, but has been absent from work for the last three months because of an injury sustained at work. It is not known at the present time whether this injury will permanently stop him from returning to work.

- Tom is a fruit packer who has worked for the company off and on for three years. His work tends to be seasonal and he is laid off when there is little or no fruit to pack.

- Mina is an executive who has only been with the company since September 2001. She joined because her previous employer, by whom she had been employed for six years, was taken over by the XYZ Fruit Co.

Commentary

This question concerns issues related to continuity of employment and you are asked to consider each one in turn. There are four people to advise, so you will need to be very focused in your answer in order to deal with all four in the limited time available. Julia's complaint is about the interesting subject of sex discrimination and continuity; Joshua's problem is about how time spent absent through sickness is counted for continuity purposes and there is also the suggestion that he might be permanently disabled; Tom's problem is whether it is possible for seasonal workers to establish continuity; and the issue for Mina is whether her employment transferred in order to maintain her continuity of employment.

Answer plan

- Does the requirement for one year's continuous employment amount to sex discrimination?
- Does absence due to a work-related illness break continuity of employment?
- What effect does a temporary cessation of work have upon continuity of employment?
- Is it possible to count service with a previous employer for the purposes of continuity of employment?

Suggested answer

In order to establish a claim for indirect discrimination, under s. 1(2)(b) of the Sex Discrimination Act 1975, the continuous service requirement would need to have been shown to be a provision, criterion, or practice which equally applied to male workers, but which would be to the detriment of a considerably larger proportion of women than men and could not be shown to be justifiable.

This issue of indirect sex discrimination was considered in *R v Secretary of State for Employment ex parte Seymour-Smith and Perez* [2000] IRLR 263. This case was brought when the qualifying period was two years and the complainants were individuals who were stopped from bringing a complaint for unfair dismissal because they did not have the necessary two years' continuous service. They complained that the proportion of women who could comply with the two-year qualifying period was considerably smaller than the proportion of men. The House of Lords referred a number of questions to the ECJ ([1997] IRLR 315). The ECJ held ([1999] IRLR 253) that the entitlement to compensation and redress for unfair dismissal came within the scope of Art. 141 of the EC Treaty and the Equal Treatment Directive, but that it was for the national courts to verify whether the statistics showed that the measure in question had a disparate impact on men and women. The court accepted that the qualification period could have a disparately adverse effect on women and that the onus was on the Member State to show that the alleged discriminatory rule reflected a legitimate aim of its social policy, that this aim was unrelated to any discrimination based on sex. The government argued that the extension of the qualifying period should help reduce the reluctance of employers to take on more people. The court was sympathetic to the government's case and accepted objective justification.

It would seem unlikely, therefore, that Julia's complaint would be successful, as the period of continuous service required has, since 1999, been reduced to one year. In order to arrive at a different conclusion it would need to be shown that the government's justification no longer applied.

Joshua appears to have the necessary one year's continuous employment to make a claim for unfair dismissal. The question here is whether the period of absence due to a work-related illness is to be counted as part of that service. If it is not, then he will have less than the period required. Section 212(3)(b), ERA provides that any week during the whole or part of which an employee is incapable of work in consequence of sickness or injury counts in calculating the individual's period of employment. Section 212(4) provides that absences of no more than 26 weeks under this category will not be held to break continuity. There needs to be a causal relationship between the absence and the incapacity for work in consequence of sickness or injury. The absence from work also needs to be related to the work on offer: see *Pearson v Kent County Council* [1993] IRLR 165. If Joshua had been offered different work, for which he was suitable, from that which he normally did, the tribunal would have to decide whether the employee was absent from that newly offered work as a result of the sickness or injury.

Although it is likely that Joshua will be successful in his claim that he does have sufficient continuity of service to make a claim for unfair dismissal, there also appears to be an issue related to disability. If he were able to show less favourable treatment as a result of a disability—s. 5, Disability Discrimination Act 1995—then he might have a substantial claim under that Act. The employer's knowledge of an applicant's disability is irrelevant when considering whether an individual has been treated less favourably for reasons of disability: see *London Borough of Hammersmith and Fulham* v *Farnsworth* [2000] IRLR 691.

Tom has three years' service, but as a seasonal worker. This means that there are periods when he will not be working. The issue is what effect these temporary cessations of work have on his continuity of employment. According to s. 212(3)(b), ERA, absence from work on account of a temporary cessation of work will not break continuity of employment. The word 'temporary' indicates a period of time that is of relatively short duration when compared to the periods of work. Although it was possible to look back over the whole period of an individual's employment in order to come to a judgment, temporary still was likely to mean a short time in comparison with the period in work: see *Berwick Salmon Fisheries* v *Rutherford* [1991] IRLR 203. Thus seasonal workers who were out of work each year for longer than they actually worked could not be considered to have continuity of employment: see *Flack* v *Kodak Ltd* [1986] IRLR 255, CA, where a group of seasonal employees in a photo-finishing department tried to establish their continuity of employment.

Other seasonal workers who were regularly out of work for long periods were in the same position, even though, at the beginning of the next season, it was the intention of both parties that they should resume employment: see *Sillars* v *Charrington Fuels Ltd* [1989] IRLR 152, CA. See *University of Aston in Birmingham* v *Malik* [1984] ICR 492, where breaks in July and August, during which an academic prepared future teaching, were held to be a temporary cessation, not breaking the individual's continuity of employment. In Tom's case, therefore, one would need more information about the overall period of employment and the periods of absence to come to any conclusion, although the precedents would suggest that he is unlikely to succeed in a claim.

Mina has apparently less than the necessary one year's service, but there is the possibility that her time spent with her previous employer will have transferred, so that all the previous six years' service can be added to her time spent at the XYZ Fruit Co. This may have been achieved by the operation of the Transfer of Undertakings (Protection of Employment) Regulations 2006 (the TUPE Regulations). If her work was part of an entity that retained its identity on transfer (see *Spijkers* v *Gebroeders Benedik Abattoir* [1986] ECR 1119), and the transfer was not achieved only by a share purchase (see *Berg and Busschers* v *Besselsen* [1989] IRLR 447), then her continuity of service may have transferred also. Where the trade, business, or undertaking is transferred to a new employer, then continuity is also preserved by s. 218(2), ERA and the employee's length of service moves to the new employer. There have been difficulties in defining when a business has transferred, rather than a disposal of assets taking place. *Melon* v *Hector*

Powe Ltd [1980] IRLR 447 concerned the disposal, by the employer, of one of two factories to another company. The disposal included the transfer of the work in progress and all the employees in the factory. The court held that there was a distinction between a transfer of a going concern, which amounted to a transfer of a business which remains the same business, but in different hands, and the disposal of part of the assets of a business.

Further information is therefore required, in Mina's case, with respect to whether a transfer took place, before it can be established whether there is sufficient continuity of service to make a claim for unfair dismissal.

Question 3

In June 2007 Mel had been employed by Contract Cleaners Ltd (CCL) for some three years. He had been employed on a contract for the cleaning of Middlesex Airport during the whole of this period. The cleaning contract has just been put out for re-tendering and won by New Cleaners Ltd (NCL).

The new contractor does not take over any of the assets of CCL and refuses to employ any of their employees. Instead NCL moved their own employees and equipment into the airport to carry on the cleaning work.

CCL claimed that there has been a transfer of an undertaking, in accordance with the Transfer of Undertakings (Protection of Employment) Regulations 2006 (TUPE Regulations). As a result CCL refused to make Mel and his colleagues redundant, claiming that they were now employed by NCL. This was denied by NCL.

Advise Mel and his colleagues as to whether the TUPE Regulations apply in their situation, whether they have a claim, what they have a claim for, and against whom.

Commentary

The question is about the applicability of the TUPE Regulation in relation to outsourcing. This is a subject that has been considered by the European Court of Justice (ECJ) on a number of occasions and has also resulted in many cases in employment tribunals and at the Employment Appeal Tribunal. There are also apparently contradictory decisions in the ECJ and in the Court of Appeal.

This question is inviting you to display your knowledge of these contradictions. The transferor employer claims that the Regulations do apply, while this is denied by the transferee employer. The best way of answering the question is to begin with an explanation of what protection is offered by the Regulations and what are the consequences of deciding whether they apply or not. There will then need to be an analysis of the cases leading to the current situation and why it is not certain what the outcome of any litigation will be.

Answer plan

- What is the purpose and effect of the TUPE Regulations?
- When does a relevant transfer take place?
- How did the European Court of Justice define a transfer of an undertaking?
- How did the Court of Appeal deal with the confusion resulting from the European Court of Justice decisions?
- What is meant by a service provision change?

Suggested answer

The Transfer of Undertakings (Protection of Employment) Regulations 2006 replaced the 1981 Regulations of the same name (the TUPE Regulations). These were introduced to give effect to the Acquired Rights Directive (Directive 77/187/EEC, amended in 1998, Directive 98/50/EC and consolidated into Directive 2001/23/EC). The purpose of the Directive and the TUPE Regulations is to safeguard the employment relationship and contracts of employment of employees in the event of there being a change in the natural or legal person who is their employer. In the event of there being such a change all the transferor's rights and obligations arising from the contract of employment are transferred to the transferee employer. In this case it will be as if Mel's contract of employment had been entered into with NCL Ltd. Regulation 4(1), TUPE Regulations, provides that a transfer does not operate to terminate a contract of employment. Regulation 7(1) provides that any dismissal for reasons connected to the transfer will be unfair in accordance with Part X of the Employment Rights Act 1996 (ERA).

The outcome in this case will depend upon whether a relevant transfer or a service provision change has taken place. If such a transfer or change has occurred, then Mel will have a claim against NCL. As he has the necessary minimum of one year's continuous service and was employed at the time of the transfer (see *Litster* v *Forth Dry Dock Engineering* [1989] IRLR 161), he will be able to make a claim for unfair dismissal. If no transfer has taken place then his claim will rest against CCL.

In *Berg and Busschers* v *Besselsen* [1989] IRLR 447 the European Court of Justice held that the Directive applied as soon as a change occurs of the natural or legal person operating the undertaking. The test, therefore, is whether the change in contractors has resulted in a change in the natural or legal person running the operation.

The European Court of Justice (ECJ), in *Spijkers* [1986] ECR 1119, defined a transfer of an undertaking as the transfer of an economic entity that retained its identity. The case concerned an abattoir which was sold by a company which then became insolvent. The abattoir was closed for a period and Mr Spijkers was not employed by the new owners. The ECJ looked at the purpose of the Acquired Rights Directive and concluded that it was to ensure the continuity of existing employment relationships. The Court listed a variety of factors which might indicate whether the entity had retained its identity and stated that each of these factors was only part of the assessment. One had to examine what existed before the transfer and then examine the entity after the change in order to decide whether the operation was continued.

In *Rask and Christensen* [1993] IRLR 133 the ECJ considered a situation where a company had outsourced its internal catering operation. The Court relied upon the decision in *Spijkers* and the various factors that had been listed in that case. It concluded that there was an economic entity that retained its identity, and therefore a relevant transfer had taken place.

In the case of *Dr Sophie Redmond Stichting v Bartol* [1992] IRLR 366 it was established that the transfer need not be that of a commercial organization. This case concerned a charity that provided assistance to drug-dependent people living in the Netherlands. The funding for the enterprise was provided by the local authority. When this funding was switched from one organization to another, the Court held that a transfer of an undertaking had taken place and that the entity had retained its identity.

This whole approach reached its climax in the case of *Schmidt* [1994] IRLR 302, which concerned a part-time cleaner in a bank branch office. The ECJ concluded that the Directive could be applied to a situation such as the outsourcing of work carried out by a single person. It also concluded that the absence of the transfer of tangible assets was not conclusive.

The important outcomes of this judgment were that, first, the size of the operation was not an issue; second, that the test is whether the activity continued or resumed after the transfer; and third, that there need not be a transfer of tangible assets, even in a labour-intensive activity such as the cleaning of a bank branch office. This view was confirmed in *Merckx* [1996] IRLR 467 where a company which held a Ford dealership had gone into liquidation. Ford awarded the dealership to another business and the Court held that there had been a relevant transfer, even though no tangible assets had passed to the new dealership from the old. The activity of the dealership continued in the same sector and subject to similar conditions. This approach was followed in the United Kingdom, in, for example, *Kenny v South Manchester College* [1993] IRLR 265 and *Wren v Eastbourne District Council* [1993] IRLR 245. Both of these cases concerned outsourcing.

Confusion as to the meaning of what is a transfer of an undertaking was then caused by the ECJ in *Süzen* [1997] IRLR 255. This case also concerned a cleaning activity, but of a secondary school. The Court held that an entity cannot be reduced to the activity that it carries out. The transfer of an activity only, such as cleaning, could not be a relevant transfer. This seemed to weaken the application of the Directive. It might now be possible for a transferee employer, in a labour-intensive business, to deny the applicability of the Regulations by not transferring any assets and not transferring any of the current employees working on a contract.

It has also led to two decisions of the Court of Appeal which appear to contradict each other. *Betts v Brintel Helicopters* [1997] IRLR 361 concerned the transfer of a helicopter ferrying contract to and from oil rigs in the North Sea. There was no transfer of assets or people, so the Court of Appeal followed *Süzen* and held that there had not been a relevant transfer. In contrast to *Betts* the Court of Appeal held, in *ECM* (*Vehicle Delivery Service*) *Ltd* v *Cox* [1999] IRLR 599, that a relevant transfer took place in somewhat similar circumstances. ECM won one of two contracts, during a re-tendering exercise. ECM Ltd argued that all that was transferred was an activity and not any assets or employees. The Court concluded that a relevant transfer might have taken place if the staff had transferred, so the employer's motivation in failing to take on these staff could be questioned and be a reason for a relevant transfer.

The Government tried to resolve these issues by not only clarifying the meaning of a transfer of an undertaking in the 2006 Regulations, but also by introducing the concept of a service provision change. Regulation 3(1)(b) provides that the Regulations also apply to a service provision change. These are relevant to outsourcing situations and are meant to ensure a wide coverage of the Regulations. A service provision change takes place when a person (client) first contracts out some part of its activities to a contractor; when such a contract is taken over by another contractor (so-called second generation transfers); and when the client takes back the activity in-house from a contractor. Whereas, however, a relevant transfer consists of an 'organised grouping of resources', a service provision change requires there to be 'an organised grouping of employees, situated in Great Britain, which has, as its principal purpose, the carrying out of activities concerned'.

It is probable, although it cannot be said with absolute certainty, that an employment tribunal will hold that a service provision change has taken place. It would have been much less certain prior to the 2006 Regulations, although it would have been likely to have been shown to be a relevant transfer. In this situation Mel will have a claim against the transferee, NCL. A refusal to transfer employees is automatically an unfair dismissal as in Part X of the ERA. If the employment tribunal concludes that there has not been a relevant transfer, then Mel and his colleagues continue to be employees of CCL. They may have a claim for unfair dismissal and for redundancy payments against CCL.

Question 4

The Transfer of Undertakings (Protection of Employment) Regulations 2006, have the effect of simplifying the 1981 Regulations and of expanding their scope. The result is likely to be greater certainty of application and less litigation than in the past.
   Critically discuss this statement.

 Commentary

The government replaced the Transfer of Undertakings (Protection of Employment) Regulations 1981 (the TUPE Regulations) in 2006 with new Regulations of the same name, with the aim of simplifying them and making it easier to know when to apply them. This question is really testing your knowledge of the changes and asking you to critically consider them in order to assess whether their aims will be achieved.

Answer plan

- There has been confusion as to the applicability of the original TUPE Regulations.
- The government has introduced the concept of service provision changes.
- The special problems related to outsourcing.
- Transfers of insolvent enterprises.
- Changing terms and conditions.
- Conclusions.

Suggested answer

The replacement of the Transfer of Undertakings (Protection of Employment) Regulations 1981 (the TUPE Regulations), which took place in 2006, are the result of amendments to the Acquired Rights Directive, Directive 98/59/EC amending Directive 77/187/EEC.

One of the issues that has caused a great deal of litigation, both in the domestic courts and in the European Court of Justice (ECJ), is when precisely the Regulations apply in outsourcing situations. For a long time there had not been any of the clarity of application needed by employers and their legal advisers. There have been apparently contradictory judgments in *Schmidt* [1994] IRLR 302 and *Süzen* [1997] IRLR 255 at the ECJ, subsequently reflected in *Betts* v *Brintel Helicopters* [1997] IRLR 361 CA and *ECM Ltd* v *Cox* [1999] IRLR 599 in the Court of Appeal in the UK.

The government has gone back to the starting point, defined in *Spijkers* [1986] ECR 1119, that the key question is whether there has been a transfer of economic entity that has retained its identity. If the answer was yes then there was likely to have been a relevant transfer of an undertaking for the purposes of the Acquired Rights Directive. The ECJ defined an economic entity as 'an organised grouping of resources which has the objective of pursuing an economic activity'.

The 2006 Regulations have followed this definition of an economic entity and further developed it by introducing the concept of 'service provision changes'. A service provision is where a party enters into an arrangement to contract out to another organization the ongoing provision of a service or services. This can include the initial contracting out of the service, the changes of contractors that might result from further competitive tendering, and the situation where the service provision is taken back in house. The new Regulations will result in two questions being asked to decide if there is a relevant transfer. These are, first, is there a service provision change to take place and, second, are there, prior to the change, employees assigned to an organized grouping of employees, the principal purpose of which is to perform the service activities in question specifically on behalf of the client concerned? If so, then the employees assigned to the organized grouping shall then be treated in the same way as where the Regulations do apply.

One of the problems in second-generation transfers of contracts, i.e. when a contract changes hands as a result of competitive tendering, is that the new contractor is not always aware of all the liabilities owed to employees that transfer across. There are also other liabilities, such as any actions that employees take against their employer for such matters as breaches of statutory rules on health and safety or discrimination. These have transferred with other liabilities, making the new employer, the transferee, liable for all sorts of costs which may not have previously been known: *see DJM International Ltd* v *Nicholas* [1996] IRLR 76.

The amended Directive gave Member States the option to introduce changes requiring the transferor to notify the transferee of all outstanding rights and obligations in relation to the employees who will be transferred. The government has taken advantage of this option and introduced a number of simple rules and provide that the transferor in a prospective transfer is to be required to give the transferee written notification of all the rights and obligations in relation to employees to be transferred. If any of these rights and obligations change before the transfer, then there must be written notification of the changes. If special circumstances make this not reasonably practicable, then it must be done as soon as is reasonably practicable, but no later than the completion of the transfer.

This will help enormously those contractors who have suffered as a result of inadequate information, although it still does seem to leave open potential loopholes. Will contractors, for example, be able to change their pricing if there are late notified changes to the employees' terms and conditions?

The original Directive made no mention of transfers out of insolvent enterprises, even though many transfers of undertakings result from the rescue of part or the whole of insolvent undertakings. The ECJ recognized at an early stage that this created a problem for the rescue of such businesses: see *Abels* v *Administrative Board* [1985] ECR 469, ECJ. If the new employer was required to take on all the employees of the insolvent business together with their current terms and conditions and any other liabilities in relation to them, then this might act as a significant disincentive. The 1981 TUPE Regulations tried to circumvent this by introducing the concept of 'hiving down', but this has not been an issue since the case of *Litster* [1989] IRLR 161, HL.

The purpose of the changes is to encourage a rescue culture by making transfers out of insolvency easier to achieve. The government's approach is that the government would pay any debts, owed by the insolvent transferor, to the employees up to the limits set in the ERA. This will include debts to employees who are still in work by virtue of having transferred. The government appears to be treating the employees as if they had been working for an insolvent enterprise and had not been rescued by a transfer. This is, presumably, likely to be a less expensive option for them than allowing the enterprise to go into liquidation and the work force becoming unemployed. The remaining debts are transferred to the transferee.

Under the 1981 Regulations it was not possible to change the terms and conditions of employees by reason of the transfer; see *Wilson v St Helens Borough Council* [1998] IRLR 706, HL. It was possible to change them, however, if the change is as a result of an 'economic, technical or organisational reason entailing a change in the work force' (an ETO reason). The meaning of what is an ETO reason has been less than clear. Unfortunately the 2006 Regulations do not seem to attempt any clarification of the meaning of these terms, although they do suggest that the new Regulations will make it easier to make transfer-related changes for an ETO reason. These will be subject to the normal rules regarding the ability of an employer to change the terms and conditions of employees.

In insolvency situations, however, the proposals follow the amended Directive and provide for situations when it will be possible to make such changes. When there is no ETO reason, it will still be possible to make changes if they are reached by agreement between either the transferor or the transferee and the appropriate representatives of the employees, and they are designed to safeguard employment opportunities by ensuring the survival of the undertaking or business concerned.

Two of the objectives to any reform of the TUPE Regulations must be the establishment of certainty of application and, linked to this, an end to the unfairness in the treatment of affected employees. This unfairness is especially evident in relation to those in the private sector and those who are affected by second-, and further, generation transfers.

Further reading

Barrett, G., 'Light acquired on acquired rights: examining developments in employment rights on transfers of undertakings' (2005) 42 *Common Market Law review* 1053–1105.

Sargeant, M., 'TUPE: the final round' (Sept. 2006) Journal of Business Law 549–67.

Sargeant, M., and Lewis, D., *Employment Law,* 4th edn (Harlow: Pearson, 2008).

http://www.berr.gov.uk/files/file20761.pdf for a Government guide to the Transfer Regulations 2006.

5

Statutory employment protection and related contractual issues

Introduction

This chapter concerns various statutory employment protection rights lying outside the scope of the law on unfair dismissal, redundancy, collective labour law, and discrimination (sex, race, disability, religion or belief and age), which are considered in other chapters of this book, and those rights which are dealt with in Chapters 9 and 10. It also considers related statutory provisions and contractual issues concerning disciplinary procedures for breaches of contract by the employee, including the implied terms regulating this aspect of the employment relationship. Students may encounter the areas of employment law within the scope of this chapter in examination questions, or parts of questions, although generally it is unlikely that examiners would set an entire question on such issues. However, questions on implied terms and repudiatory breaches of contract tend to occur quite frequently in examination papers.

One important right available to qualifying employees, i.e. generally, those with one year's continuous employment by the effective date of termination (EDT), is the right to request written reasons for dismissal, under s. 92 of the Employment Rights Act 1996 (ERA). Employees who have been dismissed while pregnant or while on maternity or adoption leave are entitled to such written reasons, irrespective of their period of continuous employment, and without the need to request them (see ERA, s. 92(4) and (4A)). Knowing the reason given by the employer may assist the employee who wishes to lodge an application at an employment tribunal claiming unfair dismissal, since a dismissal must be for one of six potentially fair reasons as stipulated in the ERA. Any reason lying outside the scope of these six potentially fair reasons is susceptible to attack by the applicant, who may wish to challenge the reason on this basis. The written statement of the reason for dismissal is admissible in evidence in any proceedings: ERA, s. 92(5). It is possible to extend the EDT for, inter alia, the purpose of calculating the period of continuous employment in relation to the employee's request for written reasons by adding on the statutory minimum notice period under s. 86, ERA: see ERA, s. 92(7). This only applies where the dismissal is not for gross misconduct (ERA, s. 86(6)).

The employer has 14 days in which to provide the statement: ERA, s. 92(2), after which an application to the tribunal may be made for failure to provide a written statement or for failing to provide an inadequate or untrue statement. The remedy is two weeks' pay, which is not subject to the statutory maximum: ERA, s. 93(2)(a) and (b).

Another area with which students should be familiar is the provisions relating to the statutory minimum notice periods referred to above. Under the statutory provisions, employers must give one week's notice to employees who have worked for between one month and two years, with one further week's notice for each year completed after that two-year period, up to a maximum of 12 years. Employees must give one week's notice of resignation if employed for one month or more: ERA, s. 86(2). These rights to notice may be waived, and a payment in lieu of notice may be made: ERA, s. 86(3). Either party may terminate the contract as a result of the conduct of the other party: ERA, s. 86(6). This provision relates to the right of either party to terminate the contract summarily for a repudiatory breach of contract. The statutory minimum notice period is also important when computing the 'calculation date' for redundancy payment purposes where shorter notice has been given (ERA, ss. 225 and 226), as that date is the date when the notice would have expired, after adding on the statutory minimum.

The right to be accompanied as specified in the Employment Relations Act 1999 (ERelsA), s. 10, is another important right which is sometimes brought into exam questions. This right applies to workers (rather than just employees) who are required or invited to a disciplinary or grievance hearing. Such workers may request that they be accompanied by either a fellow worker or a trade union official. The person accompanying may address the hearing and confer with the worker during the hearing. Students should also be familiar with the provisions in s. 10 relating to a worker requesting postponement of the hearing because the person accompanying them is not available at the time proposed for the hearing: ERelsA, s. 10(4). The worker may propose an alternative time which must be reasonable, and within five working days (beginning with the first working day after the day proposed by the worker): s. 10(5). Workers accompanying such employees under s. 10 must be given time off to do so: s. 10(6). Familiarity with ss. 11 (complaint to a tribunal) and 12 (detriment and dismissal) for infringements of these s. 10 rights is advisable.

When considering any disciplinary or grievance issues arising in exam questions, students should be aware of the ACAS *Code of Practice on Disciplinary and Grievance Procedures* (2000). This sets out model procedures for both disciplinary and grievance procedures, although it does not have statutory force, and a failure to follow the Code is not necessarily fatal to an employer's defence. The Code may be taken into account by employment tribunal in hearings (see the Trade Union and Labour Relations (Consolidation) Act 1992 (TULRCA), s. 207). For disciplinary matters, the Code suggests a first warning (oral for minor infringements, written for more serious matters), followed by a final written warning if there is a failure to improve (the employer may move to this immediately if the behaviour is sufficiently serious), followed by dismissal or other sanction (such as transfer, demotion, suspension without pay, etc.) if there is still no improvement in behaviour.

Students should also be familiar with the model grievance procedure given in the ACAS Code, which is split into first stage, second stage, and final stage: paras 42–5. It should also be noted that the Employment Act 2002, Sch. 2, which came into force on 1 October 2004, lays down two statutory procedures: a dismissal and disciplinary procedure (DDP) and a grievance procedure (GP). With limited exceptions (such as where the retirement dismissal procedure is applicable) employers must follow the DDP when dismissing or disciplining employees with one year's continuous service. Failure to do so makes the dismissal automatically unfair (ERA, s. 98A). The DDP involves a three-step procedure: in Step 1, the employer must set out the problem in writing; in Step 2, the employer must invite the employee to a meeting to discuss the matter; in Step 3, an appeal must be arranged, if the employee requests one. Under the GP, employees must state their grievance in writing. The employee must be invited by the employer to meet to discuss the matter, then the employer must inform the employee of his response after the meeting, and the employee's right of appeal. If there is an appeal, the employee must be invited to a further meeting. Employment Tribunals may adjust any award made (either up or down) by a minimum of 10 per cent and up to a maximum of 50 per cent where there has been a failure by either the employer or employee to follow the statutory procedures (Employment Act 2002, s. 31).

The overall operation of the statutory DDP and GP in workplace disputes was reviewed in the Gibbons Review (see Michael Gibbons, *A Review of Dispute Resolution in Great Britain* (DTI, March 2007). The Review recommended that the procedures be abolished and replaced with a set of non-prescriptive rules, with an emphasis on mediation and conciliation.

Furthermore, alongside the statutory GP, there is a common law implied term that an employer must deal promptly with grievances raised by employees. Any breach of such a term may amount to a breach of the implied term of trust and confidence: *Goold (Pearmark) Ltd* v *McConnell* [1995] IRLR 516, EAT.

Finally, disciplinary offences usually involve a breach of contractual duties, express and/or implied. Students should be aware of this when considering the common law position concerning the implied terms of obedience to lawful orders, co-operation, and trust and confidence (indeed, the first two may be seen as aspects of the implied term relating to trust and confidence). In this context, it is advisable to have a sound knowledge of the law on summary dismissals for repudiatory breaches of contract: see, for example: *Western Excavating (ECC) Ltd* v *Sharp* [1978] QB 761, CA; *Laws* v *London Chronicle (Indicator Newspapers) Ltd* [1959] 1 WLR 698; *Secretary of State for Employment* v *ASLEF (No. 2)* [1972] 2 QB 455, CA: *Ticehurst* v *British Telecommunications plc* [1992] ICR 383, CA.

Question 1

Tim has worked as an accountant for Digit & Numbacrunch, a firm of accountants, for a continuous period of 51 weeks. Although he has a three-month contractual notice period, he is dismissed without notice and without any explanation being given as to the reason for his dismissal, although he believes it is because he had an argument with David, the Managing Director, last week. Susan has worked for Digit & Numbacrunch for three months as a receptionist. Susan has recently discovered that she is pregnant and she informed the firm of this fact yesterday. She was immediately dismissed by the firm, without notice (her contractual notice period is one week), and without being given a reason.

Advise Tim and Susan as to their rights to obtain reasons for their dismissal and any remedies available to them under this right.

Commentary

This question requires a consideration of the provisions relating to the right to request written reasons for dismissal, including the qualifying period normally required in order to exercise such a right, and any exceptions to the qualifying period, together with a discussion of the remedies available to Tim and Susan.

Answer plan

- Consider the provisions on the right to request written reasons for dismissal, especially the qualifying period required, together with exceptions to this, e.g. in cases of pregnancy.
- Consider the qualifying period normally required to claim unfair dismissal.
- Consider the statutory minimum notice periods, and the exceptions to the qualifying period requirement.
- Consider the other remedies available to Tim and Susan: unfair dismissal and (in Susan's case) sex discrimination (only a brief mention is necessary, to show that you are aware of the range of potential claims—note that the wording of the question requires you to focus upon their remedies as to their rights to obtain reasons for their dismissal).
- Consider briefly the statutory disciplinary and grievance procedures available to Tim and Susan.

Suggested answer

Under s. 92 of the Employment Rights Act 1996 (ERA), employees have a right to be provided by their employer with a written statement giving particulars of the reasons for their dismissal, where termination is with or without notice, or the expiry of a fixed-term contract (the provision does not apply to a constructive dismissal: s. 92(1)). This is a valuable right for employees who wish to bring a claim of unfair dismissal, since, to resist such a claim, employers will want to bring the reason for dismissal under one of the potentially fair categories for dismissal under the ERA, and employees will be seeking to challenge the reason identified, or the procedure adopted by the employer in relation to the reason given. Further, the written statement of the reason for dismissal is admissible in evidence in any proceedings: ERA, s. 92(5). The qualifying period for this entitlement is one year's continuous employment by the effective date of termination (EDT) (ERA, s. 92(3) as amended), although this is subject to the exceptions set out in s. 92(4) and (4A) relating to pregnancy and childbirth, maternity leave and adoption leave.

Tim has accrued only 51 weeks of continuous employment, so it would seem that he does not qualify for the entitlement, as his EDT is the date of termination of the contract (ERA, s. 97(1)(b)), but, since he has been continuously employed for more than one month, he is entitled to the statutory minimum notice period of one week (ERA, s. 86(1)(a)), which is added on to his period of continuous employment, for the purposes of calculating this period, ending with the EDT: ERA, s. 92(7). This would give him the necessary 52 weeks of continuous employment, which means that he would qualify to request written reasons for dismissal. Tim may not add on the contractual notice period to his length of continuous service for the purpose of calculating the qualification period: see *Fox Maintenance Ltd* v *Jackson* [1978] ICR 110, EAT.

The only difficulty may be if the employer argues that Tim's dismissal was for gross misconduct, in which case the employment tribunal may not extend the EDT (ERA, s. 86(6)), but an employer may not categorize conduct as 'gross misconduct' simply in order to prevent the extension of the EDT under the section: see *Lanton Leisure Ltd* v *White & Gibson* [1987] IRLR 119 in which the EAT held that, before such an argument is allowed, an enquiry on the merits is necessary to determine whether there was conduct to justify termination without notice.

Therefore, Tim may request from his employer written reasons for dismissal under s. 92, which the employer must provide within 14 days of the request: ERA, s. 92(2). If the employer unreasonably fails to provide such a statement, or if he believes that the reasons given are inadequate or untrue, Tim may complain to the employment tribunal under the ERA, s. 93 within three months of the EDT. If the tribunal finds that the complaint is well founded, it 'may make a declaration as to what it finds the employer's reasons were for dismissing the employee', and it may award two weeks' pay to Tim (ERA, s. 93(2)(a) and (b)), which is not subject to the statutory maximum.

Susan clearly does not have one year's continuous employment, having worked for only three months, and adding on the one week of minimum statutory notice would not assist her. However, because she was dismissed while she was pregnant, she is entitled to a statement of written reasons for dismissal, irrespective of her length of continuous employment, *and* without having to request it: ERA, s. 92(4). As in Tim's case, if written reasons are not supplied to her, or if she believes that they are inaccurate or untrue, Susan may apply to the employment tribunal under s. 93, within three months of her EDT, for the remedies available under that section, already discussed. She may also claim sex discrimination, since it appears that the dismissal is because she is pregnant.

Finally, the employer has failed to follow the statutory DDP in the cases of both Susan and Tim, which would make the dismissals automatically unfair (Employment Act 2002, Sch. 2).

Question 2

(a) Chris and Fred

Fred has worked for Soopa Doopa Cleaners Ltd for two months. Last week, Chris, his friend and work colleague, who has worked for the company for two years, was informed that a disciplinary hearing was to be held in three days' time concerning an incident of fighting at work involving Chris. Chris has been informed of the charges against him, and he has been given all the evidence in the company's possession, including witness statements. He has requested that Fred be allowed to accompany him to the hearing, speak on his behalf, and advise him during the hearing. Chris also informs the company that Fred will not be available in three days' time, since he does not return from holiday for another four days, and asks for the hearing to be postponed until Fred's first day back at work. Soopa Doopa's Manager, Charles, tells Chris that the hearing cannot be postponed, and that Fred will not be given time off to accompany him. When Chris informs Fred of this by telephone, Fred telephones Charles and insists that he be given time off to accompany Chris, and that the hearing date be postponed until his return to work. Charles refuses these requests, and tells Fred, 'Since you're being so stroppy, you can consider yourself dismissed with immediate effect.'

Advise Chris and Fred as to any rights they may have as regards the disciplinary hearing matter, and indicate the remedies available to them.

(b) Tina

Tina has worked as a bar-person for Plinkers Wine Bar Ltd for two years. Over the last two months, she has been 30 minutes late for work on 18 occasions, with the same excuse, i.e. that she had been partying the night before and could not get up in time for work. Plinkers has a disciplinary code incorporated into all its contracts of employment which states that, for misconduct (including lateness), employees will receive an oral warning (after investigation of the matter), followed, in the case of repetition of the offences, by a first written warning, followed, in the case of further repetition of the offences, by a second written warning. If the offences are repeated, a final written warning will be given and, if no improvement occurs, dismissal will be the penalty imposed. Appeals may be made to the Managing Director within seven working days of the disciplinary decision.

After giving her excuse on each occasion, Tina has received an oral warning from Tom, Plinkers Bar Supervisor, after her first three late arrivals for work, together with a warning that, if her timekeeping did not improve over the next two weeks, she would receive her first written warning. After further late arrivals, she was given her first and second written warnings, with an indication that, if her timekeeping did not improve over the next two weeks, she would be given a final written warning. As her timekeeping did not improve, Tina was given her final written warning last week. She was told that, if her timekeeping did not improve over the next week, she may be dismissed. Over the last week, her late arrival on several occasions led Paul, the Managing Director, to suspend Tina on full pay for three weeks, to allow her to sort herself out. Paul warned Tina that any further lateness would lead to summary dismissal.

Advise Tina of her rights, if any, as regards the disciplinary action taken by Plinkers.

(c) Simon

Simon works as a computer software adviser and servicing specialist for SupaFast Internet Technology Systems Ltd. The trade union to which he belongs is in dispute with the company over terms of employment. It has instructed its members to refuse to carry out some of their duties, namely servicing computers, and Simon has informed his line manager, Terry, that he will not be servicing computers until further notice, only giving advice to customers on software enquiries. Terry informs Simon that SupaFast will not accept anything less than the carrying out by employees of all their duties, and sends Simon home, telling him that he will not be paid at all unless he agrees to work normally. Terry also points out to him that his contract contains a clause stating, 'The Company may refuse anything less than the carrying out of all your contractual duties, or your willingness to carry out all such duties where no work is available.' Advise Simon as to any rights he may have against the company.

Commentary

(a) Chris and Fred

This question concerns the right to be accompanied to a disciplinary or grievance hearing, pursuant to the Employment Relations Act 1999, s. 10 and the statutory disciplinary procedures under the Employment Act 2002, Sch. 2. Your answer should deal with the rights and remedies of both Chris, as the employee invoking the right, and Fred, as the employee who is to accompany Chris.

(b) Tina

This question requires a discussion of Tina's behaviour and Plinkers' contractual disciplinary procedure. The company's disciplinary procedure should be compared with the statutory disciplinary procedures under the Employment Act 2002, Sch. 2 and the ACAS *Code of Practice on Disciplinary and Grievance Procedures*, as the latter provides important (non-statutory) guidance on fair procedures to be followed.

(c) Simon

Simon's case requires a discussion of the situation where an employee refuses to carry out part of their contractual duties. Issues to be discussed include: express and implied terms; breach of contract; the employer's position concerning an offer by the employee to perform only part of their contractual duties; and penalties imposed for a refusal to carry out all contractual duties.

Answer plan

- Chris and Fred
  - Consider the right to be accompanied to a disciplinary or grievance hearing.
  - Consider the remedies available for infringement of both the employee's right and the accompanying colleague's right (automatically unfair dismissal of Fred).
  - Consider the statutory disciplinary and grievance procedures under the Employment Act 2002, Sch. 2.
- Tina
  - Discuss the company's contractual disciplinary procedure, and compare it with the ACAS procedure.
  - Consider Tina's remedy for suspension without pay, in breach of the company's disciplinary procedure.
- Simon
  - Consider the issue of refusal to carry out contractual duties; express and implied terms; repudiatory breach of contract; and the offer to carry out part-work only.
  - Consider the contractual remedies for refusal to carry out contractual duties.

Suggested answer

(a) Chris and Fred

Under the Employment Relations Act 1999 (ERelsA), s. 10, a worker who is invited to attend a disciplinary or grievance hearing is entitled to be accompanied by either a trade union official or a fellow worker of their choice. (The term 'worker' is wider than 'employee' which is used in unfair dismissal law, and includes employees and others such as agency workers and home workers: ERelsA, s. 13.) Although the company has not refused Chris's request, its behaviour in refusing to postpone the hearing and in allowing Fred time off to attend it is clearly an infringement of the section. Chris has the right to nominate 'any of the employer's workers' to accompany him (ERelsA, s. 10(3)(c)), and, where the chosen companion will not be available at the time proposed for the hearing, and the worker proposes an alternative time within five working days of the proposed hearing date, the employer must postpone the hearing to the time proposed: ERelsA, s. 10(4)(b), (c), (5)).

Here, we are told that the hearing is to take place in three days' time and that Fred returns from holiday in four days' time, so it seems that Chris's request to postpone the hearing until Fred's first day back will be within the five-day period (s. 10(5)(b), which requires that the alternative time must 'fall before the end of the period of five working days beginning with the first working day after the day proposed by the employer'). It will be a question of fact as to whether the time proposed by Chris satisfies this requirement. Further, under the ERelsA. s. 10(6), Fred must be given time off during working hours to accompany Chris to the hearing, and the company's refusal to allow this means that Chris may make a complaint to the employment tribunal under s. 11(1). The complaint must be brought within three months of the employer's failure to comply with s. 10, although the tribunal may extend this period where it is not reasonably practicable to present the complaint within this period: ERelsA, s. 11(2). The remedy is two weeks' pay, subject to the statutory limit: ERelsA, s. 11(3).

Fred has clearly been subjected to a detriment (the dismissal) for a reason connected with his attempt to accompany Chris to the hearing and he may claim under the Employment Relations Act, s. 12. Further, although he has only two months' continuous employment, the reason for his dismissal is an automatically unfair one, for which no qualifying period is required: ERelsA, s. 12(3), (4).

Under the Employment Act 2002, Sch. 2, the company is required to follow the statutory disciplinary procedures as regards both Fred and Chris. This requires the employer to : (i) provide written details of the problem to the employee; (ii) arrange a meeting to discuss the problem; and (iii) arrange an appeal, if requested. Clearly, both (i) and (ii) have been complied with in Chris's case, although it seems the meeting has been delayed because of the problems concerning Fred. Schedule 2, para. 12 stipulates that 'each step and action under the procedure must be taken without delay'. Depending on the delay in arranging a hearing, the company may have infringed this requirement.

(b) Tina

Tina's persistent lateness without justification is clearly a disciplinary matter, and it should be noted that Plinkers' contractual disciplinary procedure is closely based on the ACAS *Code of Practice on Disciplinary and Grievance Procedures* (2004). This Code may be particularly important in cases of disciplinary dismissal: see *West Midland Co-operative Society Ltd* v *Tipton* [1986] AC 536, HL). The Code states (para. 1), 'Disciplinary rules and procedures help to promote orderly employment relations as well as fairness and consistency in the treatment of individuals.'

Plinkers' contractual disciplinary provisions closely follow the ACAS Code recommendations of a formal procedure consisting of: an oral warning, followed by a first written warning, final written warning, and then dismissal or other sanction (paras 8–32). Plinkers' procedure differs only in that it has two written warnings before the final written warning. Further, the company has largely followed its contractual disciplinary procedure for Tina's misconduct, save for the imposition of suspension as the next penalty, rather than dismissal. The sanction of suspension is not provided for in the contractual procedure, so such action is technically a breach of contract by Plinkers. However, since the contractual procedure specifies dismissal as the next stage, Tina is in a better position than she would have been in had the company strictly followed its procedure. She might lodge an appeal against the suspension, or the period of the suspension, on the ground of breach of contract. The ACAS Code states that, before making any decision, the employer should take account of a number of factors, such as the employee's disciplinary and general record, length of service, precedent (how other employees have been treated in similar situations), and 'whether the intended disciplinary action is reasonable under the circumstances' (para. 17).

It should be noted that the statutory disciplinary and dismissal procedures do not apply to Tina because she has not yet been dismissed but only suspended on full pay. Suspension on full pay is specifically excluded from the definition of 'relevant disciplinary action' for the purposes of the statutory disciplinary and dismissal procedures (reg. 4, Employment Act 2002 (Dispute Resolution) Regulations 2004 (SI 2004/752)).

In conclusion, it would appear that Plinkers has committed a breach of contract in suspending Tina. She could appeal to the Managing Director about this, although she would be in a worse position than if the company had strictly followed its own disciplinary procedure. She could also appeal on the ground that the imposition of the dismissal would be unfair or unreasonable in all the circumstances but this appeal is unlikely to be successful, given that the company has very largely followed its procedure and given her a second chance, rather than imposing the dismissal penalty.

(c) Simon

Simon's action in refusing to carry out all his contractual duties is a breach of the express term of his contract of employment. It is also likely to amount to a breach of the implied terms of obedience to lawful orders, co-operation, and trust and confidence (the first two implied terms may be seen as particular examples of the general obligation implied under the last term). Simon's refusal to obey a lawful and reasonable order, i.e. to work normally, may justify summary dismissal if it amounts to a repudiatory breach, i.e. one going to the root of the contract: see *Western Excavating (ECC) Ltd* v *Sharp* [1978] QB 761, CA. In *Laws* v *London Chronicle (Indicator Newspapers) Ltd* [1959] 1 WLR 698, Lord Evershed MR said that 'one act of disobedience can justify dismissal only if it is of a nature which goes to show (in effect) that the servant is repudiating the contract'.

The implied duty of co-operation requires employees to act in such a way as to ensure that nothing is done to obstruct the running of the employer's business. This term was in issue in *Secretary of State for Employment* v *ASLEF (No. 2)* [1972] 2 QB 455, CA, in which employees working to rule during an industrial dispute with a view to disrupting the running of the employer's business were held to be acting with a lack of good faith and therefore in fundamental breach of the implied term in their contracts, even though they were not in breach of any express term. In *ASLEF (No. 2)* Buckley LJ said that the implied term was one 'to serve the employer faithfully within the requirements of the contract'. Similarly, in *Ticehurst v British Telecommunications plc* [1992] ICR 383, CA, BT was not acting unlawfully when it refused to allow Mrs Ticehurst, a manager with the company, to work in circumstances where, because of an industrial dispute, she had withdrawn her goodwill and was refusing to work normally (by refusing to sign a declaration to work normally), with the aim of disrupting the efficient running of the business. Mrs Ticehurst was held to be in breach of the implied term to provide faithful service and, as BT was not required to accept part-performance of the contract, they could refuse to accept any performance and withhold wages.

Therefore, SupaFast has a choice in the face of Simon's offer of partial performance of the contract. It may (i) treat the refusal to work normally as a repudiatory breach; or (ii) accept partial performance and deduct a sum representing the duties not performed (see *Sim v Rotherham Metropolitan Borough Council* [1987] Ch 216) and *Miles v Wakefield Metropolitan District Council* [1987] AC 539)—this is sometimes called the 'part work, part pay' approach; or (3) indicate that it will not accept partial performance and refuse to make any payment to Simon (sometimes called the 'part work, *no pay*' approach: see *Wiluszynski v London Borough of Tower Hamlets* [1989] IRLR 259, CA). In the circumstances, the company has taken the third option, and Simon has no rights to claim against the company.

Further reading

Anderman, S.D., *Labour Law: Management Decisions & Workers' Rights*, 4th edn (London: Butterworths, 2000), chs 3, 7.

Deakin, S., and Morris, G. S., *Labour Law*, 4th edn (Oxford: Hart Publishing, 2005), chs 4, 5.

'Disciplinary and grievance hearings: right to be accompanied—informal oral warnings' (2003) 731 *IDS Brief 3–4*.

'Employment law review 2001: contracts of employment' (2002) 700 *IDS Brief 7–9*.

Ewing, K. D., 'The implications of Wilson and Palmer' (2003) 32(1) ILJ 1–22.

Jones, M., 'Employment Act 2002: statutory dispute resolution' (2003) 8(1) *Employment Law & Litigation 27–32*.

Pitt, G., *Employment Law*, 6th edn (London: Sweet & Maxwell, 2007), chs 4, 6, 8.

'Written reasons for dismissal' (2002) 702 *IDS Brief 14–17*.

6

Unfair dismissal

Introduction

Unfair dismissal is a huge topic. One of the standard textbooks, I.T. Smith and G. Thomas, *Smith and Wood's Industrial Law* 8th edn (Oxford University Press, 2003) spends 129 pages on this topic and there are books devoted to it. The student is likely to become overwhelmed by the detail: not just are there some 40,000 claims each year for unfair dismissal that are unreported, but all those that reach the Employment Appeal Tribunal (EAT) are to be found on its web site. The facts of these cases are often memorable but what the student needs is a firm grasp of the structure of the claim coupled with a knowledge of the basic cases, in particular *Iceland Frozen Foods* v *Jones* [1983] ICR 17 and *British Home Stores* v *Burchell* [1980] ICR 303n. The relevant part of the Employment Act 2002 came into force in autumn 2004, but is scheduled to be abolished during the currency of this book: at the time of writing, it is unknown what, if anything, is to replace it.

Leaving aside automatically fair and automatically unfair dismissals, the authors recommend the following approach:

1. Was the employee qualified to bring a claim for unfair dismissal? The employee must prove that he or she is qualified.

2. If so, was the employee dismissed? The employee must prove that he or she has been dismissed.

3. If so, what was the reason for the dismissal? The reasons are: capability, conduct, redundancy, breach of statute, and 'some other substantial reason'. The employers must prove that they held one of these five reasons.

4. If the employers prove one of the five so-called potentially fair reasons, was the dismissal reasonable? The amendments to the law brought about by the Employment Act 2002 (in force October 2004) are particularly important. If they do not so prove, the dismissal *was* unfair, and the tribunal goes immediately to stage 5.

5. Which remedy is the tribunal to award? The tribunal must look at the remedies in this order: reinstatement (same job back), re-engagement (different job), and

compensation. There is slightly complex law about the award of compensation but the clever student will have a paragraph or two which he or she can write out to answer a question which calls for a discussion of the remedy for unfair dismissal. As the authors have stressed several times in this book, students often miss out remedies but a discussion can hardly ever be inappropriate and the rewards in terms of marks and favourable impression on the examiners will repay the effort!

With that strong framework for analysis in mind, let's see how it can be used in practice.

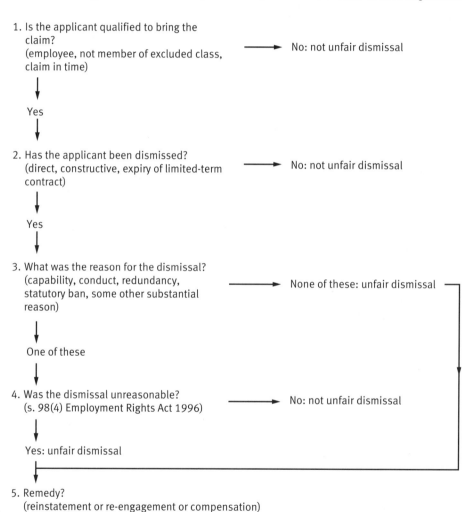

1. Is the applicant qualified to bring the claim?
   (employee, not member of excluded class, claim in time) ———→ No: not unfair dismissal

   Yes

2. Has the applicant been dismissed?
   (direct, constructive, expiry of limited-term contract) ———→ No: not unfair dismissal

   Yes

3. What was the reason for the dismissal?
   (capability, conduct, redundancy, statutory ban, some other substantial reason) ———→ None of these: unfair dismissal

   One of these

4. Was the dismissal unreasonable?
   (s. 98(4) Employment Rights Act 1996) ———→ No: not unfair dismissal

   Yes: unfair dismissal

5. Remedy?
   (reinstatement or re-engagement or compensation)

Figure 6.1: An outline of the five stages of an unfair dismissal case where the applicant has not been automatically unfairly dismissed

Note: The burden of proof is on the employee at stages 1 and 2; is on the employers at stage 3; is neutral at stage 4; and lies on the party who asserts at stage 5 (normally the employee but if the employers assert lack of mitigation, the onus is on them).

Question 1

Alice has worked as the company accountant for a small firm called Jam Ltd for several years. The company's managing director is James A. Milne. One day James sees Alice open the company safe and remove a large sum of money, later found to be £5,000, and put it into her handbag. On his asking her what she was doing, she replied: 'I can't tell you!' He sacked her on the spot. In fact she was giving the money to her ex-husband, Brian, to secure the return of their son, Charles, whom Brian had abducted the previous day.

Would Alice be successful in an action for unfair dismissal?

Commentary

The rubric is restricted to unfair dismissal; therefore, it would be incorrect to discuss wrongful dismissal or any other claim. It is also important to remember that the examiner is looking for legal argument; it does not matter whether the candidate thought that there was an unfair dismissal or not but whether the legal arguments in the answer are acceptable.

The question invites a discussion of unfair dismissal and the subject has to be covered within a set time. Therefore, before entering the exam room, the candidate should know how to tackle a straightforward unfair dismissal question. (By 'straightforward' is meant a claim where the alleged unfair dismissal is neither 'automatically' unfair nor 'automatically' fair.) The answer demonstrates a possible sequence for answering such a question.

Answer plan

- Qualifications for unfair dismissal
- Dismissal
- Reason to dismiss: conduct
- Reasonable dismissal: size and administrative resources of the employers and equity and the substantial merits of the case; 'band of reasonable responses' test, fair procedure; statutory dispute resolution procedures
- Remedy: reinstatement; re-engagement; compensation: basic and compensatory award—quantum and deductions

Suggested answer

Alice must prove that she is qualified to bring an unfair dismissal (UD) claim. It seems that she is an employee of the firm. She is a 'company accountant', a phrase suggestive of permanent employment with Jam; the question also states that she works 'for' the company. Since she has done so for several years, she meets the one year's continuous employment qualifying period for UD. She is not subject to the rules on retirement, in force 1 October 2006, has brought the claim within three months of the effective date of termination (or if that was not reasonably practicable within a reasonable time), and is not a member of an excluded class such as a share fisherperson. Therefore, she is qualified to bring a UD claim: see s. 94 of the Employment Rights Act 1996 (ERA).

The question states that she has been dismissed and that the dismissal has instant effect. She is therefore dismissed within s. 95(1)(a) ERA. The onus of proof of dismissal lies on the applicant.

The reason for dismissal is theft. This constitutes gross misconduct: *Sinclair* v *Neighbour* [1967] 2 QB 279. There may a clause in her contract to similar effect and the ACAS Handbook *Discipline at Work* also so provides in stating that there can be a dismissal without notice for gross misconduct when there is theft from the employers. The burden of proof at this stage lies on the employers and they will have no difficulty.

The next stage is that of the reasonableness or unreasonableness of the dismissal. Since 1980 the onus at this point has been 'neutral'; in other words, no party bears the burden but the tribunal must make up its mind, and fairness is a matter of fact, not of law.

On the facts of the present case the issue of unfairness is the principal difficulty. ERA, s. 98(4) states inter alia that the question whether the dismissal was fair must be determined in accordance with equity and the substantial merits of the case, and regard must be had to the size and the administrative resources of the employers. Several issues arise for comment. Though in the general run of cases the employee should be informed of the allegation against her, there is no need to do so if she is caught redhanded. However, the ACAS Code of Practice *Disciplinary and Grievance Procedures* 2004 recommends among other things the right to reply and the right to appeal. She has not been given the right to reply or to appeal, though it is not expected that in a small firm, as this company is, there will be an elaborate appeals structure: size matters, as s. 98(4), ERA provides. Breach of a Code of Practice is not necessarily fatal to the employers' defence but can be taken into account by the tribunal when assessing reasonableness. Besides the Code tribunals usually follow the guidelines laid down in *British Home Stores Ltd* v *Burchell* [1980] ICR 303n, EAT, which was itself a case of theft. Although the case is only of EAT authority, it has been approved by the Court of Appeal on several occasions including *W Weddel & Co Ltd* v *Tepper* [1980] ICR 286. *Burchell* provides a threefold test:

1. Did the employers believe the reason they gave for dismissal? Here, they did believe that they were dismissing for theft.

2. Did they have 'in mind reasonable grounds upon which to sustain that belief?' Here they did have such grounds because Alice was seen to remove the money.

3. Did they carry out 'as much investigation into the matter as was reasonable in

all of the circumstances of the case?' On the facts an investigation should have revealed the true situation. It may be that the dismissal was unfair for this reason.

The third question is a pointer to the importance of procedural fairness after *Polkey* v *AE Dayton Services Ltd* [1988] AC 344, HL. An otherwise fair dismissal can be rendered unfair when the procedure was unfair unless going through that procedure would be utterly useless or futile. On the facts no investigation was undertaken and no account has been taken of Alice's employment record, which may be exemplary. It should, however, be noted that the Employment Act 2002 to some degree resurrects the rule in *British Labour Pump Ltd* v *Byrne* [1979] ICR 347 that a dismissal which was procedurally unfair will be a fair dismissal if going through a fair procedure would have made no difference to the decision to dismiss. Section 29 of the 2002 Act deals with dismissal for gross misconduct, as occurred here. The employers must give the employee a statement as to why they are dismissing for gross misconduct, detailing the grounds they had at the time of dismissal for thinking that the employee was guilty of gross misconduct. The written document must also contain a statement about the employee's right to appeal. If there is an appeal, the employers must notify the employee of the outcome of the appeal. If s. 29 is not complied with, the dismissal is automatically unfair (new s. 98A of the ERA, inserted by the Employment Act 2002) and the tribunal must make an award of four weeks' pay; if the employers fail unreasonably to follow the statutory procedure, the tribunal may increase the award of compensation by between 10 and 50 per cent. (For further details of the 2004 changes see Question 2.)

Beyond procedural fairness the tribunal must not substitute its own decision for that of the employers: see *Iceland Frozen Foods Ltd* v *Jones* [1983] ICR 17, EAT. Although *Iceland's* 'range of reasonable responses' test came in for criticism just around the turn of the millennium, it was strongly reaffirmed by the Court of Appeal in *HSBC* v *Madden* [2000] ICR 1283. Therefore, if the current employers did dismiss and a reasonable employer on the same facts may have dismissed, the dismissal is fair.

Leaving aside the issue of the statutory fair dismissal procedure, if the employee has been found to be unfairly dismissed, she is entitled to a remedy. The tribunal must explain the potential remedies: reinstatement (same job), re-engagement (similar job), and compensation, which comprises a basic and a compensatory award. The tribunal must look at the remedies in the order stated. Reinstatement within s. 114(1), ERA is possible on the facts. Trust and confidence may remain and the employee may well wish to be reinstated and it does not seem impracticable to reinstate. The tribunal has to take into account any contributory fault by Alice. If reinstatement is not ordered, the tribunal is to consider re-engagement next. It may be that there is not a job similar to that of company accountant in such a small firm. If neither remedy is awarded, the tribunal deals with compensation. The basic award is calculated on the same basis as a redundancy payment (except that years of work under 18 count), subject to a maximum week's pay at the time of writing in late 2007 of £310. There is a formula for working out the total based on age, length of continuous employment (20 years maximum), and the week's pay. The current maximum is £9,300. Misconduct may lead to a reduction in the sum. In addition the compensatory award is calculated under the heads laid down in *Norton Tool Co Ltd* v *Tewson* [1973] 1 WLR 45, NIRC, subject to a maximum of £60,600. This sum is also subject to deductions, in particular in respect of failure to mitigate and contributory conduct.

Summary

While the issue of fairness is one for the tribunal, Alice may well win her claim; if so, she is entitled to a remedy as outlined in the previous paragraph.

Question 2

Outline the changes brought about by the Employment Act 2002 (Dispute Resolution) Regulations 2004.

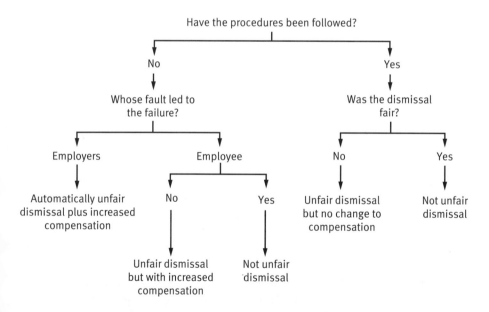

Figure 6.2: The 2004 procedures
Source: Adapted from p. 28 of the DTI's *Guidance on the Employment Act 2002 (Dispute Resolution) Regulations 2004 and the associated provisions in the Employment Act 2002, 2004*

Commentary

Examiners are always keen for candidates to demonstrate that they have a good grasp of recent changes, especially ones which affect one of the core areas of employment law, unfair dismissal, in such a fundamental way. This is also the type of question and answer that can be 'raided', to be used in other unfair dismissal answers including answers to problems.

The answer below seeks to deal with the question set and to place the changes in the context of the previous law. The amended law could be restated in the answer in several possible ways, and the answer below exemplifies only one possible approach. The examination candidate who cannot tackle this question swiftly and acceptably should move on when reading the exam paper but if he or she has a firm understanding of the topic, this is very much a question on which high marks can be scored. Note that, while the 2004 Regulations are scheduled to be repealed during the currency of this book, it is unknown at the time of writing what, if anything, will replace them.

Answer plan

- The Employment Act 2002 as implemented by the 2004 Regulations
- The aim of the Regulations
- The effect on unfair dismissal
- Statutory discipline and dismissal procedure (SDDP); statutory grievance procedure (SGP)
- Meetings and appeals
- Difficulties and exceptions
- Effect on procedural fairness and quantum
- *Polkey*
- Critique

Suggested answer

The law, which affects claims brought to employment tribunals after 1 October 2004 including ones founded on continuing policies, is based on the 2002 Employment Act. The rules are found in s. 32 and Schs 2 and 4 to the Act. There are other practitioner-oriented changes such as amendment to the application form (now renamed the ET 1), but these will not be discussed here. Not every aspect of that statute has been brought into force by the 2004 Regulations (mention should be made of the fact that currently the government does not propose to bring into force the provision that the procedures mentioned below are to form part of the contract of service with consequential effects on remedies) but the aim of the government was very clear: it wanted to reduce the number of applications going each year to the tribunals, over 100,000 in most recent years, and more if one realizes that an application may contain more than one claim, by some 30 per cent. This reduction would save money but it would also be in tune with the desire of the government to divert what would previously have been tribunal cases into other routes for the resolution of disputes; in particular, it wished to resolve claims at the earliest possible opportunity: in this way it was hoped that more employees than before would be reinstated after a grievance.

It might have been expected that with such laudable aims the government would have produced a simple and effective way of diverting applications but as we shall see, the law is complex. It should also be noted that though this answer is one on unfair dismissal, the procedures are much broader than that area of law; employment law claims under the Equal Pay Act 1970, the Sex Discrimination Act 1975, the Race Relations Act 1976, the Disability Discrimination Act 1995, the Employment Equality (Sexual Orientation) Regulations 2003 (SI 1661), and the Employment Equality (Religion or Belief) Regulations 2003 (SI 1660), fall within the 2004 Regulations, as do some other rights e.g. detriment in respect of trade union membership and activities within s. 146 of the Trade Union and Labour Relations (Consolidation) Act 1992 and detriment in respect of the statutory union recognition process in Sch. A1 to that statute, unauthorized deductions from pay, detriment in employment and redundancy payments under the Employment Rights Act 1996, detriment under the National Minimum Wage Act 1998, breach of contracts of employment when heard in employment tribunals under the Employment Tribunals Extension of Jurisdiction (England and Wales) Order 1994, and detriment under the Transnational Information and Consultation of Employees Regulations 1999 (SI 1999/3323). Other aspects of employment law are not covered: a non-exhaustive list includes refusal of employment on the ground that the applicant is or is not a member of a union (TULR(C)A 1992), failure to provide a written statement, failure to provide paid time off for ante-natal care/dependants, parental leave, right to request flexible working, failure to provide written reasons for dismissal (all under the ERA 1996), the right to be accompanied (the Employment Relations Act 1999), and the right not to be less favourably treated or suffer detriment found in the Part-Time Workers (Prevention of Less Favourable Treatment) Regulations 2000 (SI 1551) and in the Fixed-Term Employees (Prevention of Less Favourable Treatment) Regulations 2002 (SI 2034).

The basic approach

The Act introduces two new dispute resolution procedures, the dismissal and disciplinary procedure (DDP) and the statutory grievance procedure (SGP). The procedures apply to claims listed in Sch. 4 to the 2002 Act (see above). It should also be stressed that the changes apply only to employees and not to all workers. Therefore, there is the jurisdictional issue of finding out whether a worker is an employee or not. Workers may well be protected by discrimination law (see Chapter 1 of this book), but they will not fall within the ambit of the Act and Regulations unless they are employees.

The dismissal and disciplinary procedure

The standard DDP applies when the employers are considering dismissal (for any reason including redundancy and including the expiry of a limited-term contract) or if they are contemplating disciplinary action including suspension on no or reduced pay on the ground of conduct or capability (only). The DDP does not apply if the retirement is by mutual agreement or if the retirement is in accordance with the Employment Equality (Age) Regulations 2006 (SI 2006/1031). If the standard DDP applies, the employers must provide the employee with a written statement of the basis for the discipline or dismissal together with an invitation to a meeting (step 1); step 2 is the meeting, after which the employers inform the employee of the decision and of the right to appeal; step 3 is the appeal, after which the employers tell the employee of their decision. There is also a modified DDP: this occurs when the employers have lawfully dismissed the employee without notice for gross misconduct on discovering that misconduct or shortly afterwards, in circumstances in which it was reasonable to do so without investigating those circumstances. 'Lawfully' here means: 'the employers were legally entitled to dismiss without notice'. In that event the employers must provide the statement of the reason for the dismissal and provide an appeal but there is no meeting to discuss the dismissal. If either the standard or as the case may be the modified DDP is not followed by the employers, the dismissal is automatically unfair. It should be stressed that even though the employers have followed the correct DDP, the dismissal may still be unfair, for example because they did not have a potentially valid reason to dismiss or they did not act in a procedurally fair way (see also below). If an employee is dismissed but the decision to do so is reversed on appeal, continuity is preserved.

The statutory grievance procedure

A grievance is defined as 'a complaint by an employee about action which his employer has taken or is contemplating taking in relation to him'. This definition includes complaints by one employee against another (see below). There are problems with this definition. These three are taken from the EOC's website for legal advisers. First, does 'action' cover 'omission'? In another area of employment law the House of Lords held that it did not and 'action short of dismissal' was changed by Parliament to 'detriment' to get round this problem; perhaps that interpretation will be used here. If so, part of the thrust of the SGP will be stultified. Secondly, do actions taken 'by an employer' cover action done by colleagues? Take, for example, harassment by a coworker. The employer may be vicariously liable but can such harassment be 'action which the employer has taken'? The DTI's (now the DBERR's) Guidance 2004, para. 56, assumes that vicarious liability is covered. Thirdly, can the action be said to be taken 'in relation to him' when the employer has a discriminatory policy? A ban on part-time work may be discriminatory against one gender unless justified but it is difficult to say that such a prohibition is action taken against this particular employee.

The *standard* procedure consists of three steps:

1. The employee sends a written copy of the grievance to the employers. There is no template for what the employee is to write but it is suggested that the complaint letter (or email or other form of communication in writing) should be fairly full in order that the employers are appraised of the substance of the complaint.

2. The employers invite the employee to a meeting to discuss the grievance. There is a duty on the employee to take all reasonable steps to attend the meeting. The nature of the meeting is considered below. After the meeting the employers must tell the employee of the decision and the right to appeal, should the employee not be satisfied with the decision.

3. If the employee does not wish to appeal, the employers must be told; if the employee does wish to appeal, the employers must invite him or her to an appeal meeting. The employee must take all reasonable steps to attend the meeting. After the meeting the employers must inform him or her of the outcome.

Discrimination questionnaires are not part of step 1 in the SGP.

The *modified* grievance procedure applies when the employee has ceased employment *and* the employers were not aware of the grievance before the end of employment (or if aware, the SGP had not been initiated before termination) *and* both parties agree in writing to the modified procedure. Facts which fall within all three conditions will probably be rare.

The differences from the SGP are that there is no meeting to discuss the grievance and that there is no appeal. The steps in the procedure are:

1. The employee sends to his or her former employers a statement of the grievance.

2. The employers send their reply to the former employee.

The meeting and the appeal meeting

The Regulations do not provide a timetable for these meetings. Obviously the first meeting cannot take place until the employers have received the grievance and they must have a reasonable opportunity to consider any response. Schedule 2 to the Employment Act 2002 provides that any step taken under the SGP (or the DDP) must be taken without reasonable delay. The same Schedule stipulates that the time and locations of all meetings must be reasonable, that the meetings must be conducted in such a manner that both sides are able to explain their cases and that on appeal the employers' representative should if possible be of a more senior level than the person who was at the initial meeting. If the employee, his or her companion (see below) or the employers could not attend the meeting for a reason unforeseen at the time of arranging the meeting, the employers must invite the employee (and if there is one, the companion) to a meeting. If it happens that for the employee it was not reasonably practicable for unforeseen reasons to attend this meeting, the law deems the parties to have completed the SGP. The effect is that neither party suffers an increase or reduction in compensation received or to be paid. If either party did not attend a rearranged meeting for a reasonably foreseen reason, there is no further duty to attend another meeting and the tribunal may attribute fault, with a consequent effect on the compensation. The procedure is deemed to have been complied with and the effect is that the normal three months' time limit applies (i.e. there is no extension).

If the employee is disabled, the employers must make reasonable adjustments for him or her under the Disability Discrimination Act 1995 as amended.

The right to be accompanied

By s. 10 of the Employment Relations Act 1999 a worker (not just an employee) has the right to be accompanied at a grievance hearing (as well as at a disciplinary or dismissal hearing). The worker may be accompanied by a colleague or by a union official but not, for example, by a lawyer. If the employers refuse to allow the worker to be accompanied, the worker may apply to an employment tribunal. The sanction is an award of up to two weeks' pay, subject to the normal statutory maximum (£310 p.w. from 1 February 2007). If the companion cannot make the meeting, the 1999 Act provides that the employee must propose an alternative date within five days.

Difficulties with the law

There are some problems. First, a constructive dismissal falls within the SGP and not as might have been expected by all employment lawyers within the 'dismissal' part of the DDP. It is for this reason that the statutory grievance procedure has been noted in an answer to a question on unfair dismissal. Secondly, 'disciplinary' within DDP does not include warnings, whether oral or written. Thirdly, there is a possibility of overlaps. For example, if an employee has disciplinary action taken against her which is discriminatory, does she have an SGP on the basis of discrimination or should there be a DDP because there has been a 'disciplinary'? The standard DDP applies to disciplinary action taken on the grounds of conduct or capability but the SGP applies if the action was discriminatory just as it does if the action is taken for any other reason than conduct or capability. Another difficulty is this: if the employee makes a protected disclosure within the Public Interest Disclosure Act 1998 (as inserted in the Employment Rights Act 1996), he or she has a choice of going down the SGP route or the whistleblowers' route: but once the employee has chosen the route, there is no going back.

Exceptions

There are also exceptions to the law. It should be noted that if these exceptions apply, the normal time limits also apply, as indeed does the whole law of unfair dismissal. The principal exceptions to the DDP are:

- oral warnings;
- written warnings;
- suspension on full pay;

- constructive dismissals (as mentioned above: the SGP applies);
- collective redundancies (20 or more employees within 90 days);
- dismissal and immediate re-engagement of a class of employees (e.g. where the employers desire to change the contract of employment);
- most dismissals occurring as a result of industrial action, the exception being where the employers make selective dismissals of those taking part in lawfully organized ('official') action or where the employers have not taken reasonable steps to resolve the industrial action (cf. TULR(C)A ss 237, 238 and 238A, the last as inserted by the Employment Relations Act 1999 and since amended);
- dismissal where the continued employment of the employee would be illegal, but the normal unfair dismissal rules do apply;
- dismissal consequent on a sudden and unforeseen event, but it should be remembered that the normal unfair dismissal rules continue to apply;
- dismissal where the employee or employers have reasonable grounds for the belief that the employee or another may be injured or the employee's or another's property damaged;
- the employee or employers have been harassed and starting or continuing the process would lead to further harassment;
- it is not practicable to commence the DDP, e.g. because of the employee's illness.

The modified DDP applies where the employee has filed an application to the tribunal before the employers have sent him the step 1 letter, a statement of the reason for the discipline or dismissal. In this event there is no adjustment to the compensatory award as detailed below.

The DDP is deemed to have been completed when:

- the employee applies for interim relief within seven days in a case of victimization on trade union grounds;
- the employee appeals to an outside body under an 'appropriate procedure' agreed between an independent union and the management (in this case steps 1 and 2 of the DDP must have been completed).

Since the DDP is deemed to have been completed, the time limit which normally applies in unfair dismissal claims, three months, is extended by a further three months.

The SGP exceptions are mainly the following. In all of them the Regulations deem the SGP to have been completed. First, if the employee has been harassed and has reasonable grounds for believing that starting the SGP or continuing with it would result in more harassment, he or she is deemed to have completed the SGP. However, the process is deemed to have not been completed and the fault for the failure is laid at the employers' door with the effect that if the claim is successful, the amount of compensation will be increased. Secondly, if the employee has reasonable grounds for believing that if he or she started the SGP, the employers would make significant threats to him or her or his or her property or to a third party or his or her property, the SGP need not be used. Thirdly, if the employee has left employment and it is not reasonably practicable to go through the SGP, the procedure does not apply. Fourthly, if the grievance is a collective one, that is, one involving two or more employees and raised by a trade union official (or if there is no recognized union, by the staff representative), the SGP does not apply to those named in the written grievance document. Fifthly, it is not practicable to start the process, as when the employee is seriously ill or the employers' factory is burned down. It should be remembered that a grievance about a dismissal falls within the DDP unless the dismissal was constructive. Where the SGP is deemed to have been completed, the normal three months' time limit for unfair dismissal cases is extended by three months.

Effect of the changes to the law

If the rules apply, a claimant who issues an ET1 will not have his or her claim heard if he or she fails to start the SGP. If the claimant starts the SGP but does not complete it before proceedings commence, the ET will reduce compensation by between 10 and 50 per cent. It must make the 10 per cent reduction and may make a reduction of up to 50 per cent unless it would not be just and equitable to make such a reduction. These uplifts and reductions affect only the compensatory award of unfair dismissal, not the basic award. However, if the employers failed to complete the DDP, the basic award is subject to a minimum award of four weeks' pay. The compensatory award remains subject to the statutory limit even though there has been, say, a 50 per cent increase in the amount which would otherwise have been awarded. The same rules about compensation also apply where the failure to complete the procedure was due wholly or mainly to the employee's failure to comply with the conditions of the SGP or to appeal under the SGP. There is a real difficulty for applicants here. If they bring their claims before the completion of the SGP, their compensation will be reduced. However, if they wait too long, the limitation period may well have elapsed. The normal discretionary extensions to the employment tribunals' power to hear claims after the period has elapsed ('not reasonably practicable' or 'just and equitable' depending on the jurisdiction) continue to apply, so it may be that the tribunals will exercise the discretion to extend the periods in such circumstances.

If the employee brings a claim to which the DDP applies and has completed step 1, the time limit of three months in the case of a claim of unfair dismissal is extended by three months. If the DDP is completed, however, within the normal three month limitation period for unfair dismissal claims, that time limit still applies and is not extended (e.g. to three months after completion). If the DDP applies, but the employee does not complete step 1, the claim is inadmissible.

What about *Polkey?*

If the employers do not complete the DDP, the dismissal is automatically unfair. If, however, they do so comply, but they do not comply with an additional procedure which it would have been reasonable to follow, such as the ACAS Code of Practice on Disciplinary and Grievance Procedures as revised from time to time or the staff handbook, then the dismissal will nevertheless be fair if the employers demonstrate that following such additional procedure would have made no difference to the dismissal *and* that the dismissal is substantively fair. If the DDP is not applicable, the employers can nevertheless seek to convince the tribunal that following any additional procedure would have made no difference. See s. 34 of the 2002 Act, which inserts s. 98A into the 1996 Act.

The written statement

The 1996 Employment Rights Act is amended so that employers have to provide employees with a written statement including their disciplinary rules and the new minimum dispute resolution procedures, no matter how many employees are employed. If the tribunal finds the statement to be inaccurate or incomplete, it must award compensation, and may award two to four weeks' pay (capped in the usual fashion: for the year from 1 February 2007, the limit is £310) where compensation is the remedy awarded, as it normally is in an unfair dismissal claim. If compensation is not a possible remedy, then the tribunal may make a separate award of the same discretionary amount. No award in either case will be made if to do so would in the tribunal's view be unjust or inequitable. See s. 38 of the Employment Act 2002 for details.

Question 3

Erica has worked for some years as a postroom operative for Freddies Ltd. She has come under increasing pressure at home because her husband has left her. She has to look after her young son and her aged mother. Her line manager, George, has noticed that she has been getting slower at her job and, after warning her on several occasions, he dismisses her when she spills coffee over an important document.

Consider Freddies' liability for unfair dismissal, if any.

 ## Commentary

Read the rubric! The question is not about sex discrimination or wrongful dismissal. Any discussion of irrelevant matters will not score marks, will waste time, and will create a bad impression. The question is solely about unfair dismissal.

The answer to many unfair dismissal questions is straightforward but the amount of possible material to include can appear daunting. It is suggested that if the candidate writes something about the five issues normally involved in a problem dealing with non-automatic unfair dismissal, he or she is on the way towards passing and if the topics are considered in a logical manner, he or she is heading for a decent mark. Once the structure is arranged, then comes the hard bit of selecting material to use in the time. One framework is what the authors call 'QDR3': qualifications, dismissal, reason, reasonableness, remedy. Such a structure allows the candidate to fit the material under the various headings and ensures that he or she does not miss a major topic out. (See the flowchart in Figure 6.1.) The authors suggest that subheadings are used: it appears to the examiner that the writer can organize material.

No examiner on undergraduate courses expects calculations of compensation for unfair dismissal, but a good student ought to be able to give an outline of the ways in which the basic and compensatory awards are calculated and the deductions from each award. Writing about these issues is easy and can provide 'easy' marks, especially as not all students do write about the remedy.

Answer plan

- Qualifications
- Dismissal
- Reason: capability
- Written reasons claim
- Fairness of dismissal: *Iceland Frozen Foods* and *Burchell*; s. 98A of the Employment Rights Act 1996
- Remedy

Suggested answer

By s. 94 of the Employment Rights Act 1996 (ERA) all employees are entitled to a remedy for unfair dismissal (UD). This principle is not, however, completely followed through.

Qualifications

The applicant bears the burden of showing that she is qualified to bring a claim. There is little reason to doubt that Erica (E) is an employee. The question states that she has been employed (presumably continuously) for more than one year, the qualifying period for UD. As far as can be seen, she is not excluded for any other reason such as being a share fisherperson or being retired. She has it is assumed brought her claim within the time limit, three months from the effective date of termination, unless to bring it within that time was not reasonably practicable. The conclusion is that she is qualified to claim.

Dismissal

The question explicitly states that she has been dismissed by her line manager. This type of dismissal, which has no accepted name, is sometimes called 'direct', 'express', or 'actual' dismissal and falls within s. 95(1)(a), ERA. Even if she had not been expressly dismissed, the giving of several warnings, if unjustified, could constitute a constructive dismissal: see *Walker* v *Josiah Wedgwood & Sons Ltd* [1978] ICR 744, EAT. A constructive dismissal according to *Western Excavating (ECC) Ltd* v *Sharp* [1978] QB 761, CA, occurs where the employers evince an intention no longer to be bound by the contract or they breach a fundamental term, one of which is the duty of trust and confidence, which is breached by giving unjustified warnings. Since there is an express dismissal, no discussion is needed of any other type of dismissal. The burden of proving dismissal lies on the applicant.

Reason

If the employers cannot prove that they had one of the five potentially fair reasons for UD (six if one includes the special regime for age-related dismissals), they have no defence, and the tribunal will move to the final stage, that of remedy. If the employers can prove one of the reasons, they have not (yet) won because the fourth stage, that of reasonableness, must be considered.

On the facts the employers may seek to show incapability under s. 98(2)(a), ERA: E has been 'getting slower at work' and her spilling the coffee may demonstrate incompetence) or perhaps misconduct (s. 98(2)(b): the question is not clear as to whether or not she deliberately spilt the coffee. (The question says that she 'spills' the drink, not 'knocks over the coffee' but it remains uncertain whether she acted intentionally or recklessly, which may demonstrate misconduct, or whether she was just careless, a form of incapability.) Incapability includes 'skills' (s. 98 (3)), and perhaps the slowness shows a lack of skill.

The reason is 'the set of facts known to the employer or belief held by him which cause him to dismiss the employee': *Abernethy* v *Mott, Hay & Anderson* [1974] ICR 323. If Freddies believe that they have dismissed on a certain ground, that ground is the reason for the purposes of UD. If a sham reason is given, the tribunal can look behind it. If there are two or more reasons, the tribunal has to say which was the principal or motivating cause: *Carlin* v *St Cuthbert's Cooperative Association Ltd* [1974] IRLR 188. In an important decision the House of Lords held that if the employers advance several possible reasons and the tribunal does not accept one or more of them, the employers must prove that the remaining reason was the principal reason: *Smith* v *City of Glasgow DC* [1987] ICR 796. Employers cannot change the reason they give if to do so would not give the ex-employee enough of an opportunity to meet the allegation.

By s. 92, ERA the employers must in response to a request give the former employee the reason for dismissal within 14 days of the request. An unreasonable failure to supply reasons is remedied by the Employment Tribunal's awarding two weeks' pay if the claim is made within three months of dismissal. Unlike compensation for UD there is no cap on the amount of week's pay. The written statement of reasons is admissible in a tribunal (s. 92(5), ERA); and tribunals will draw their own inferences if they find that the reason the employers have given for this purpose differs from that provided for the purpose of defending the UD claim.

Reasonableness

Assuming that the employers can prove one of the five potentially fair reasons, presumably incapability, the tribunal must consider the reasonableness—fairness—of the dismissal, having regard to that reason and to the size and administrative resources of the employers and to equity and the substantial merits of the case. *Iceland Frozen Foods Ltd* v *Jones* [1983] ICR 17 remains a highly important authority. It makes the points that:

1. The tribunal should direct itself by reference to the words of s. 98(4), ERA.

2. It must look at the reasonableness of the employers' conduct, not at the fairness to the employee.

3. It 'must not substitute its decision as to what was the right course to adopt for that of the employer'.

4. It must in most cases apply the 'range (or band) of reasonable responses' test (if this employer dismissed and a reasonable employer may have dismissed, the dismissal is fair, even though another employer might have used a lesser sanction such as demotion, suspension, or loss of pay). This test was abandoned for a brief time in 1999–2000 but orthodoxy was reasserted by the Court of Appeal in *Foley* v *Post Office* [2000] ICR 1283.

5. It must act as an 'industrial jury', determining whether 'the decision to dismiss the employee fell within the range of reasonable responses which a reasonable employer might have adopted'.

When applying the guidelines in *Iceland,* the tribunal should bear in mind the equally famous phrases in *British Home Stores Ltd* v *Burchell* [1983] ICR 303n: did the employers believe the reason they gave? Did they have reasonable grounds for that belief? Did they carry out a reasonable investigation? Here, the employers may have believed the reason they gave for dismissing and may have had in mind reasonable grounds for that belief, but they do not appear to have carried out any investigation, never mind a reasonable investigation. In fact the third part of *Burchell* needs to be read more broadly than articulated by the Court of Appeal: did the employers act in a procedurally fair way? The leading authority was *Polkey* v *AE Dayton Services Ltd* [1988] AC 344, HL: employers had to act in a procedurally fair manner unless it was utterly useless or futile to do so. Had Freddies conducted an investigation, they might well have discovered the true reason for E's slowness: the double burden of work and family life. It would certainly not have been futile to uncover this reason for Freddies could have reacted differently from the way they did, by, say, providing support. *Polkey* overruled the 'no difference' test laid down in *British Labour Pump Ltd* v *Byrne* [1979] ICR 347. By that test, if acting in a procedurally fair manner would not have made any difference to the outcome, dismissal, then the sacking was fair. This test made a comeback in the Employment Act 2002. If Freddies dismiss, and it would not have made any difference to the result had they followed a fair procedure, then if they do follow the procedure stipulated in that statute, the failure to follow the non-statutory fair procedure will not make the dismissal unfair. The statutory fair procedure where there is not a dismissal for gross misconduct comprises three steps: the employer must send out a written statement of the reason for dismissal outlining the basis for that reason with an invitation to attend a meeting; there must be a meeting after which the employer must inform the employee of the reason for any decision and of the right to appeal; if the employee wishes to appeal, there is an appeal hearing. If the statutory procedure has not been followed, the dismissal is automatically unfair: new s. 98A of the 1996 Act, as inserted by the Employment Act 2002. This rule applies even though the employers would have dismissed anyway, had a fair procedure been adopted. The tribunal must award a minimum of four weeks' pay. If the employers do not follow the statutory procedure, the compensatory award must be increased by 10 per cent, unless there are 'exceptional circumstances' rendering it not just and equitable to award that percentage, in which event a tribunal may award such percentage as it thinks just and equitable; it may award an increase of up to 50 per cent if it is just and equitable so to do.

There are a couple of other procedural fairness points which should be mentioned. There was no consultation with E or with her union, if she was a member, perhaps the warnings were not precise enough (or they did not lead to increased supervision or training), and there was no appeal. It should be noted that by the now repealed s. 127A of the ERA, as inserted by the Employment Rights (Dispute Resolution) Act 1998, the compensatory award used to be reduced by up to two weeks' pay if the employee did not go through any internal appeals procedure but s. 127A was repealed when the 2004 procedures came into force.

Remedy

Part of this topic has been dealt with in the context of procedural fairness above.

The primary remedy for UD is reinstatement (same job back); if not, re-engagement in a similar job is the next option. On the facts reinstatement is possible; it may be what E wishes and would not seem impracticable for her to get her old job back. In fact the most common remedy for UD is the third one the tribunal should consider, compensation, which comprises a basic and a compensatory award. The basic award is calculated according to a set formula based on the applicant's age, the maximum week's pay (currently £310), and the length of service. We are not told the exact age of E or how long she has worked at Freddies, but having worked for only 'some years' she is unlikely to obtain anything near the maximum, currently £9,300. The basic award is subject to various deductions including any redundancy payment and any ex gratia payment.

The compensatory award is calculated according to the headings laid down by Sir John Donaldson in *Norton Tool Co. Ltd* v *Tewson* [1973] 1 WLR 45, NIRC: loss to the date of the hearing (including perks and expenses), future loss, loss of employability (see *Vaughan* v *Weighpack Ltd* [1974] ICR 261), loss of pension rights, and loss of accrued rights. Loss means 'economic' loss and does not include, for example, compensation for injury to feelings: *Dunnachie* v *Kingston upon Hull City Council* [2005] 1 AC 226 (HL), approving *Norton Tool*. From that figure are deducted various sums, e.g. for accelerated receipt, contributory fault (s. 123(6), ERA), if the applicant's employment would have ceased anyway (see s. 123(1), ERA, the 'just and equitable' principle), any ex gratia payment, and failure to mitigate. From 1 February 2007, the maximum for this award is £60,600, a figure which since 1999 has increased annually on 1 February in line with the Retail Price Index.

Question 4

Compare and contrast wrongful dismissal and unfair dismissal.

Commentary

This is a straightforward essay question. It is one that may be covered in different ways but should be the sort of question that any student ought to be able to answer. After all, dismissal is one of the core areas of employment law. An examiner would expect that all candidates could do a 'decent' answer and gain a 'decent' mark; the better student will always go for depth. Examiners have different ideas about subheadings in answers to essay questions. Find out what your university or college thinks. The authors believe that subheadings can help to provide a structure—and they ensure that the candidate deals with each subtopic and then moves on, rather than returning to earlier subtopics.

Answer plan

- Source
- Jurisdiction
- Qualifying period

- Limitation period
- Elements of each claim
- Remedies, especially compensation

Suggested answer

Source and consequences

Facts can give rise to both claims. For several reasons it is important to distinguish the claims. If both claims are brought on the same facts, normally the unfair dismissal one is stayed. Wrongful dismissal (WD) is a common law action for breach of contract; unfair dismissal (UD) is a creature of statute, originally the Industrial Relations Act 1971, now the Employment Rights Act 1996 (ERA). One consequence of the different source is that WD was until quite recently only heard in the ordinary civil law courts, the High Court or the county court, the distinction depending largely on the sum claimed, and UD was heard in the employment tribunals (ETs). However, after lengthy debate contractual claims for sums of £25,000 and under may now, as a result of the Employment Tribunals (Extension of Jurisdiction) Order 1994 (SI 1994/1623), be heard in the ETs. There are several caveats. First, the ETs and the ordinary courts have concurrent jurisdiction over such claims; therefore, it is incorrect to speak of the transfer of jurisdiction. Second, ETs can hear claims concerning breaches of the employment contract only if they relate to the termination of the contract, as WD does. They have no jurisdiction over claims arising during the running of the contract. Third, employers can bring counterclaims against their former employee. Fourth, ETs have no power to issue injunctions or declarations. As creatures of statute they do not have the inherent jurisdiction of ordinary courts. Fifth, certain claims relating to termination are excluded: covenants in restraint of trade, duties of confidentiality, copyright and other intellectual property claims, actions concerning living accommodation, and claims in respect of personal injury cannot be heard in ETs, even when they relate to termination of contract. Therefore, for example, a claim that a restraint of trade clause is invalid because the employee has been wrongfully dismissed (see *General Billposting Ltd* v *Atkinson* [1909] AC 118, HL) must be heard in the ordinary courts.

Until recently another difference between WD and UD was that legal aid was available for the former but not for the latter (assistance by means of the green form scheme was available), even when they were dealing with WD actions (though it was available for proceedings before the EAT). Legal aid was available for WD, which remains a contractual action. With the use of conditional fees it seems that such payments are rare in employment tribunals but more research is needed to determine the effect of the abolition of legal aid on WD claims. There was a longstanding debate whether legal aid should be extended to employment tribunals but governments of whatever persuasion set their minds against it largely on the ground of cost (but cf. Scotland). ETs have for a couple of decades been accused of increasing legalism, and more common use of lawyers would lead to further accusations. Certainly when ETs, then called industrial tribunals, began to acquire employment law jurisdictions, the Donovan Committee, the Report of which led to the creation of the law of UD, thought that ETs should be informal as well as speedy and accessible. Certainly informality if not speed may be impeded by the use of lawyers; however, lawyers can also speed up proceedings because they know the law (unlike lay people) and they should be able to sort the relevant from the irrelevant.

Another consequence of WD's juridical base is that the time limit for bringing a claim in the ordinary courts is six years, whereas for UD it is only three months from the effective date of termination, subject to the 'not reasonably practicable' exception, a fairly narrow exception. In legal terms three months is a short period of time. If a lawyer does not submit the form IT 1 (renamed ET 1 from October 2005) in time, he or she is liable to be sued for negligence, i.e. the remedy lies against the adviser, and the UD claim fails. This time limit applies even though the employee is appealing against the dismissal internally. As part of its encouragement of grievance and disciplinary proceedings the government enacted the Employment Act 2002. Tribunals may have to be more flexible about time limits. Part of the government's justification for the revised procedure under the Act was that 64 per cent of the employers and employees had not had a meeting before dismissal and the first that employers often knew of the claim was that they received form ET 1. Unfortunately, these statistics are undermined as they do not take into account the fact that there may have been other methods of contact such as phone calls and emails. For more on fair procedure see below.

Dismissal: wrongful and unfair

A further consequence of WD's being a contractual action is that its foundation is a breach of contract. If there is no such breach, there is no WD. As with other contracts the breach of the contract of employment has to be one of a condition, not of a warranty. The terms 'condition' and 'warranty' are rarely used in employment law but the distinction nevertheless pervades dismissal law. As Lord Evershed MR said in *Laws* v *London Chronicle (Indicator Newspapers) Ltd* [1959] 1 WLR 698, CA, 'a contract of service is but an example of contracts in general, so that the general law of contract is applicable'. One effect of this juridical base is that dismissal is defined in terms of contract law: dismissal must be a breach of a fundamental term. Certain terms will always be fundamental, e.g. the duty to pay wages; others will be warranties; yet others may be innominate terms. For the purposes of WD the dismissal can be express as when the employers say: 'I sack you'; or it can be constructive as occurs when the employers repudiate the contract by evincing an intention no longer to be bound by the contract or they breach a fundamental term, entitling the employee to leave. Both forms of dismissal apply to UD, though repudiation is usually known as constructive dismissal. There is a third type of dismissal applicable to statutory claims only, expiry of a limited-term contract.

For WD if there is a dismissal, it must be 'wrongful'; that is, the employers must have given no notice or insufficient notice. The length of the notice period depends partly on contract, partly on statute. Section 86, ERA states that if an employee has worked for under two years, the length is one week; over 12 years the period is 12 weeks; between two and 12 years the period increases by a week for every year of employment (e.g. the period is five weeks if the employee has worked for the employers for five years). If, however, the contract provides for a lengthier period, that period applies. The contractual term could be either express or implied; if implied, the period is of reasonable length and what is reasonable depends on the facts. Notice periods form one aspect of the 'floor of rights'; they can be added to by contract, but not taken away by contract. However, s. 86(6), ERA provides that notice need not be given if the employers have a cause, a justification, for not giving notice on dismissal. In other words, they may dismiss summarily in certain circumstances. While there is no definitive list of causes, illustrations include theft from the employers (*Sinclair* v *Neighbour* [1967] 2 QB 279), taking industrial action (*Simmons* v *Hoover Ltd* [1977] QB 284), and disobeying a lawful order (*Macari* v *Celtic Football and Athletic Co. Ltd* [1999] IRLR 787). A series of incidents can amount to a cause, as in *Pepper* v *Webb* [1969] 1 WLR 514. Whether there is a justification depends on the facts of each case.

The basis of UD is statutory. Therefore, it is governed by statute. In a case where the dismissal is not automatically unfair, the employee must prove that he or she is qualified and has been dismissed. The burden of proof then switches to the employers to show that they had one of five possible potentially fair reasons: capability, conduct, redundancy, statutory illegality, and some other substantial reason. If the employers cannot prove that the reason they held fell within one of these five reasons, they lose at this stage and the tribunal moves to determine the remedy. If they can, the ET still has to determine fairness, applying s. 98(4), ERA.

Procedure

One of the reasons for the introduction of UD was the failure of WD to remedy a dismissal which was carried out in a procedurally unfair manner. While the emphasis on procedural fairness has changed over the years, until recently the main authority was *Polkey* v *AE Dayton Services Ltd* [1988] AC 344, HL, where it was said that a dismissal was unfair if the employers had not acted in a procedurally fair way even though they would have dismissed anyway, unless to go through a fair procedure would have been futile. The Employment Act 2002 partly reverses *Polkey*. A failure to follow the procedure laid down in that statute makes the dismissal automatically unfair: s. 98A(1), ERA, as inserted by the 2002 Act. (The remedy is four weeks' pay if the ET considers that to be just and equitable: see the inserted s. 112(5), (6), ERA.) For the effect of the compensatory award, see s. 31 of the Employment Act 2002. However, a failure to follow a procedure beyond that laid down in the statute does not in itself make the dismissal unfair, reversing the rule in *Polkey*. For further details see Question 2 of this chapter. But note that the statutory dismissal procedure is scheduled to be abrogated during the currency of this book.

Further distinctions

1. Coverage: WD applies to all those working under a contract; UD applies only to employees, and there are certain exceptions such as domestic servants who are close relatives of the employer.

2. There is no upper age limit in WD. There are special rules governing retirement on age-related grounds found in the Employment Equality (Age) Regulations 2006 (SI 2006/1031), which came into force on 1 October 2006.

3. The qualifying period for non-automatic UD is one year's continuous employment: Unfair Dismissal and Statement of Reasons (Variation of Qualifying Period) Order 1999 (SI 1999/1436). There is no qualifying period for WD.

4. If an employee is dismissed and brings a claim for UD in respect of the reason provided by the employers and wins, the employers cannot as it were retrospectively justify a UD by referring to a good reason to dismiss which they discovered after the dismissal: *W. Devis & Sons Ltd* v *Atkins* [1977] AC 931, HL. However, WD can retrospectively be justified in this way: *Boston Deep Sea Fishing&Ice* Co v *Ansell* (1888) 39 Ch D 339, CA.

5. The remedy for WD, being a contractual action, is damages aimed at putting the claimant in the position she or he would have been in, had the contract been lawfully performed. The primary remedy for UD was intended to be reinstatement, and if not that, re-engagement in a similar job. In fact the remedy most often used is compensation consisting of a basic and compensatory award, the latter calculated according to the heads found in *Norton Tool Co Ltd* v *Tewson* [1973] 1 WLR 45.

6. There is no limit on WD compensation but there is on UD: at the time of writing the basic award is restricted to £9,300 and the compensatory award to £60,600.

7. The compensatory award for UD includes compensation for the manner in which the employee was dismissed, if his or her employability is affected, but there is no such remedy in WD.

Conclusion

The differences between these two remedies derive from the juridical base of each claim. UD was instituted to remedy the defects of WD. However, sometimes it can be seen that UD is restricted too, particularly the financial cap on the compensatory award. For high earners the cap means that losses are not compensated, and there has in recent times been a revival of interest in UD partly for this reason.

Question 5

The courts and tribunals have construed the law of unfair dismissal in favour of employers.
Discuss.

Commentary

Always check the type of questions you may be asked. Some employment law papers consist largely or solely of problems. The question invites a discussion of judicial interpretation of statute, not of the rights and wrongs of the law of unfair dismissal as stated in the Employment Rights Act 1996. Comparisons with wrongful dismissal and redundancy payments are likely to be otiose.

Answer plan

(1) Judicial interpretation of the statute in favour of employees

- Procedural fairness
- Constructive dismissal

(2) In favour of employers

- The definition of 'employee'
- The definition of 'some other substantial reason'
- The 'range of reasonable responses' test

Suggested answer

The Employment Rights Act 1996 (ERA) and its predecessors have received various glosses by courts and tribunals over the years. Sometimes the construing has worked in favour of employees but it may be safely said that there are several aspects of judicial interpretation which reflect a judicial bias towards employers.

Sometimes interpretation is in favour of employees. An example is procedural fairness. There is no reference to this concept in s. 98(4), ERA. While the law has fluctuated (and see the changes made by the Employment Act 2002), a landmark authority was *Polkey* v *AE Dayton Services Ltd* [1988] AC 344, HL. If the employers dismiss in a procedurally unfair way, that sacking will be unfair unless it would have been futile or utterly useless to undertake a fair process. It may be rare for some element of procedural unfairness not to exist on the facts. For example, in *Charles Robertson (Developments) Ltd* v *White* [1995] ICR 349 an employee had been caught stealing on camera. Nevertheless, Holland J in the EAT was of the opinion that a disciplinary interview had to be undertaken when the employee was longserving and the crime was not of a serious nature. *Polkey* marked the high water mark of procedural fairness and the courts and tribunals have retreated somewhat since then. *In Duffy v Yeomans and Partners* [1995] ICR 1 the Court of Appeal held that the dismissing employers need not act in a procedurally fair manner if reasonable employers would not have done so. This ruling is one marking something of a return to the 'no difference' rule in *British Labour Pump Ltd v Byrne* [1979] ICR 347 that if going through a fair procedure would make no difference to the decision to dismiss, procedural fairness was not required. The enactment of the Employment Act 2002 is another twist in the story.

It can be added that sometimes interpretation which seemingly has gone in favour of one side or another has subsequently been reined in. The best example is the judgment of Lord Denning MR in *Western Excavating (ECC) Ltd v Sharp* [1978] QB 761, CA. He defined constructive dismissal as a breach of a fundamental term of the employment contract (or evincing an intention no longer to be bound). This determination, based largely on the words of the statute, overruled a line of authority which had held that it was sufficient that the employers acted unreasonably. Since breach of a fundamental term was thought to be harder to show than unreasonableness, which does not require the employee to prove a breach of contract, it was expected that fewer employees than previously would succeed in their claims. However, the development of implied terms over the last quarter of a century has led to the need for a breach of contract to exist. What would have not seemed a breach, but (merely) unreasonable conduct, may now be a breach of an implied term, particularly that of trust and confidence. Lord Hoffman in *Malik v Bank of Credit and Commerce International SA* [1998] AC 20, HL described this term as a 'default' one, i.e. it applies between all employers and employees unless expressly negated. It is now rare for unreasonable conduct not to be a breach of this or some other implied term. For example, in *Hilton International (UK) Ltd v Protopapa* [1990] IRLR 316, EAT telling off an employee in front of colleagues was a breach of the implied term of mutual respect. The breach must still be of a fundamental term. In *Cantor Fitzgerald International v Callaghan* [1999] ICR 639 the Court of Appeal said that breach even of a basic term such as that of pay could be insufficient to amount to a breach of a fundamental term where the employers had made a mistake or there had been a breakdown in their technology. It may also occur that what the *employee* thinks is a breach of contract is not. The principal example is *Dryden v Greater Glasgow Health Board* [1992] IRLR 469, EAT. The employers introduced a no-smoking policy. The applicant contended that they had done so in breach of contract. The tribunal held that the change was one of policy, not of contract, and therefore there was no breach of contract.

Instances of pro-employer interpretation are rife. Three instances have been chosen: the definition of 'employee', the definition of 'some other substantial reason', and the 'range of reasonable responses' test.

O'Kelly v Trusthouse Forte plc [1984] QB 90, CA is an example of a decision which could have been used to extend the protection of employment law to workers at risk but the court chose not to do so. 'Regular casuals' who worked when asked were held not to be employees despite the fact that they were not in business on their own account and were under the control of their managers as to how they went about their work. It was said that there was no mutuality of obligation. However, they had no other job and would have lost offers of jobs from the employers had they refused them. They were economically dependent on the employers. The court could have ruled them to be employees, particularly as another category of workers were definitely self-employed, namely, those who came in on rare occasions; the workers at issue were much more like the full-time permanent staff.

The term 'some other substantial reason' (SOSR) is undefined in the statute. It does, for example, include dismissal at the behest of a customer (e.g. *Dobie* v *Burns International Security Services* [1985] 1 WLR 43) and reorganizations in the interest of efficiency which are not for redundancy (e.g. *Hollister* v *National Farmers Union* [1979] ICR 542). Even unilateral changes by management to contractual terms can be SOSRs, as in *RS Components Ltd* v *Irwin* [1973] ICR 535. These cases demonstrate the width of the category of SOSR and show that even when the employers act in breach of contract there may still be a SOSR. The courts could have restricted SOSR to matters similar to the other four potentially fair reasons. After all the reason has to be 'some other' reason, and lawyers should interpret this phrase *ejusdem generis* with the previous items in the list. Similarly, the reason must be a 'substantial' one but sometimes the reason has not been very substantial. The Court of Appeal in *Kent CC* v *Gilham* [1985] ICR 227 held that a reason was not substantial only when it was 'trivial or unworthy', a very low hurdle. For example, when dealing with dismissal for efficiency gains, the EAT in *Chubb Fire Security Ltd* v *Harper* [1983] IRLR 311 asked whether the employers had a reasonable belief that dismissing the employee would be more beneficial to them than the detriment it would be to the employee. It will be strange if an employer did not so believe when dismissing in the interests of efficiency. Besides these criticisms the class of SOSR may be attacked for not being a closed category and for covering instances of dismissal not in accord with modern mores (or even the truth). *Saunders* v *Scottish National Camps Ltd* [1981] IRLR 277 illustrates both points. The employers dismissed a male homosexual because they believed that such a person was more predatory towards children than was a male heterosexual. The Court of Session held that the employers had a SOSR despite the lack of supporting evidence.

Finally, the 'range of reasonable responses' test found in *Iceland Frozen Foods Ltd* v *Jones* [1983] ICR 17 gives a large degree of discretion to employers. If reasonable employers may have dismissed on the instant facts and these employers did, then the dismissal is unfair, no matter whether the members of the employment tribunal think that the dismissal was unfair. There is no reference to this test in s. 98(4), ERA, and over the years the test has come in for trenchant criticism. Nevertheless, it still remains the test despite favouring employers and one might have thought that the purpose of the law of unfair dismissal was to favour dismissed employees!

As can be seen the courts and tribunals have not uniformly been pro-employer but it is suggested that the number of pro-employer judgments outweigh the pro-employee judgments.

Question 6

Mick has worked for Frosty Ltd, a painting and decorating firm run by Liam, for many years. He does the joinery work. One day another employee, Kevin, tells Liam that he knows as a fact that Mick has been doing a 'foreigner' for his aunt; that is, working in his time for himself using Frosty's materials and not attempting to gain the customers for the firm. Liam put a phone call through to the aunt, who stated that Mick had done the work. Liam dismisses him with instant effect. Liam later makes enquiries of the firm's clients and finds that Mick has done such work on many previous occasions.

Jane was employed some months ago on a one-year contract as a painter. Liam has found that quite a lot of the work has been defective and repairs have been quite expensive. Liam tells Jane that her contract will not be renewed when the term expires.

Ivan, who joined the firm some years ago as senior contracts negotiator, was injured in a car accident a short while ago. While the injuries are not serious and Ivan is expected to recover completely very soon, Liam decided that he could not wait any longer for Ivan to get better and he sacked him, replacing him with Hetty. He gave Ivan the correct length of notice. Ivan complained bitterly in the meeting he had with Liam before being dismissed that Liam should have let him have a friend to plead his case and that Liam should not have acted without a medical report.

Advise Frosty Ltd. Assume that the provisions of the 2002 Employment Act do not apply.

Commentary

This is a question about dismissal, and there may be both unfair dismissal and wrongful dismissal. Note, however, that unless the dismissal is for an inadmissible reason, in respect of Jane there will be no unfair dismissal because she has not been employed by Frosty for one year continuously and that in relation to Ivan there is no possibility of a wrongful dismissal because the correct length of notice has been provided.

The provisions of the 2002 Act came into force in October 2004. To avoid repetition they are dealt with in the other questions which examine unfair dismissal.

Answer plan

- Mick

  - Wrongful dismissal: summary dismissal, breach of the implied duty of faithful service, breach of fundamental terms and the non-provision of notice, the effect of after-discovered reasons

  - Unfair dismissal: the different effect of after-discovered reasons, potentially fair reasons including qualifications, dismissal and misconduct, the s. 98(4) ERA 1996 test and procedural fairness, remedies including deductions

- Jane

- Unfair dismissal: qualifications, expiry of a limited-term contract is a dismissal, illness is incapability (and possibly frustration: see Ivan, below)

- Ivan

  - Illness may be frustrating event; if not, it is incapability for the purposes of unfair dismissal

  - Right to be accompanied

  - Wrongful dismissal: forum

Suggested answer

Mick

Mick is dismissed 'with instant effect'; therefore, there is a possibility of wrongful dismissal because the correct length of notice has not been provided by Frosty. However, he has breached the duty of fidelity, the implied term which provides that an employee must serve his or her master in good faith. Breach of this term is a breach of a fundamental term, entitling the employers to dismiss summarily. Where there is such a breach there is no wrongful dismissal and s. 86(6) of the Employment Rights Act 1996 (ERA) provides that no statutory period of notice need be given when the employee is in breach of such a term. Even if one act of moonlighting is not such a breach and therefore one which justifies the failure to give the correct length of notice of dismissal, the discovery post-dismissal that Mick has done many similar jobs retrospectively validates an otherwise wrongful dismissal: *Boston Deep Sea Fishing & Ice Co* v *Ansell* (1888) 39 Ch D 339, CA. Mick therefore has no claim for wrongful dismissal.

In relation to unfair dismissal, a potentially fair reason to dismiss discovered after the dismissal does not retroactively make fair that which would otherwise be unfair but compensation may be reduced: *W Devis & Sons Ltd* v *Atkins* [1977] AC 931, HL. Mick is qualified to bring such a claim: he is an employee, as the facts state ('another employee'); he has worked for several years, i.e. more than the one-year qualification period laid down in the Unfair Dismissal (Variation of Qualifying Period) Order 1999 (SI 1999/1436); he does not belong to an excluded category such as share fisherpersons; presumably he is below the normal retiring age and he has brought the claim within the prescribed period, three months, unless it was not reasonably practicable to bring the claim within that period. The burden of proving that he is qualified lies on Mick. He must also prove that he has been dismissed within s. 95, ERA. On the facts there is a 'direct', 'express', or 'actual' dismissal. At that point the burden switches to Frosty to prove that they have a potentially fair reason, which on the facts will be conduct, one of the five reasons laid down in s. 98, ERA. Their argument at this point is that by doing 'foreigners' he has so misconducted himself that it is reasonable to dismiss him. Section 98(4) ERA 1996 provides that the tribunal must take into account the size and administrative resources of Frosty and must decide according to equity (meaning fairness, not the rules of equity) and the substantial merits of the case. The employers must act within the bounds of reasonableness responses: *Iceland Frozen Foods Ltd v Jones* [1983] ICR 17, EAT, which the Court of Appeal confirmed in *HSBC Bank plc v Madden* [2000] ICR 1283. The tribunal must also apply the tests laid down in *British Home Stores Ltd v Burchell* [1980] ICR 303n, EAT, as often approved by the Court of Appeal: did Frosty genuinely believe that Mick did the misconduct in question? (Here they did, relying on what another employee had told Liam.) Did they have reasonable grounds for that belief? (Here it can be said that they did not form their belief negligently because they checked the facts; therefore, they had reasonable grounds.) And did they conduct such an investigation into the misconduct as the facts reasonably warranted? It is suggested that this third part of the test may lead to a finding of unfair dismissal. *Polkey v AE Dayton Services Ltd* [1988] AC 344, HL provided that employers had to act in a procedurally fair manner unless it was utterly futile so to do. The coming into force of the Employment Act 2002 affected this proposition. See Question 2 in this chapter and see also the ACAS Code of Practice No. 1, *Disciplinary and Grievance Procedures*. The 2004 version takes into account the 2002 Act. Perhaps if Frosty had held such an investigation, they might have discovered all kinds of reasons for Mick's doing the work. For example, perhaps his aunt did not allow non-family into her house; perhaps she could not afford the prices charged by companies but Mick did the work for free. If the sacking was unreasonable within s. 98(4), ERA, the tribunal must look at the remedies. (These are discussed elsewhere in this chapter and are not repeated here.) When the tribunal is making deductions, there should be one for contributory fault known at the time of dismissal (s. 122(2), ERA in respect of the basic award and s. 123(6), ERA in respect of the compensatory award) and in respect of the fact that Frosty found other dismissible instances of misconduct post-dismissal. That type of fault is taken into account in the general 'just and equitable' sum provision found in s. 123(1), ERA. See *Tele-Trading Ltd v Jenkins* [1990] IRLR 430, CA for this distinction. The deduction under s. 123(6) should be made before that in s. 123(1) because a deduction under the former may affect what is just and equitable under the latter: *Rao v Civil Aviation Authority* [1994] ICR 495, CA.

Jane

The expiry of a limited-term contract is deemed by statute (s. 95(1)(b), ERA) to be a dismissal for the purposes of the law of unfair dismissal if it is not renewed. Here the contract will not be renewed. Therefore, there is the possibility of a claim for unfair dismissal. In that event the law stated when discussing Mick applies here too, e.g. qualifications (when the contract expired, Jane would have one year's continuous employment as required by the Regulations noted above), the reason for the dismissal (here capability), reasonableness of dismissal including procedural fairness, and remedy. It is quite likely that Jane has been unfairly dismissed because on investigation, which does not appear to have occurred, Frosty might have found that she was untrained or unsupervised or both. Further discussion of incapability occurs below: illness is deemed to be incapability by s. 98(3), ERA.

There can be no claim for wrongful dismissal because the non-renewal of a fixed-term contract does not constitute a dismissal for the purposes of that action.

Ivan

Ivan is dismissed for incapability arising out of injuries caused in a car accident. As stated above illness is deemed to be incapability. It is suggested that the contract has not been frustrated by the injuries for, although injuries may be a frustrating event, the facts do not demonstrate that performance of the contract is radically different from that which the parties agreed. Accordingly, the dismissal is a true dismissal, not one which could be called a reaction to the events which amounted to frustration. In that event as with the other two employees the law of unfair dismissal comes into play. Ivan appears to be qualified and he has been dismissed. There has been no consultation, which will render the dismissal unfair (*East Lindsey DC* v *Daubney* [1977] ICr 566, EAT), unless consultation would have made no difference to the result: *Taylorplan Catering (Scotland) Ltd* v *McInally* [1980] IRLR 53, EAT. It is suggested that Liam has been too precipitate in not consulting and in not waiting for a medical report. Liam also does not seem to have conducted any enquiry or sought alternative employment for Ivan, though no job need be created for him: *MANWEB* v *Taylor* [1975] ICR 185, DC. The normal remedies are available.

If the request to be accompanied was a reasonable one, Ivan may bring a claim to the tribunal. Failure by employers to accord this right is compensated by up to two weeks' pay: ss. 10–11, Employment Relations Act 1999. However, this right is restricted to being accompanied by a colleague or trade union official, not by a friend. The three months' time limit applies with the usual 'not reasonably practicable' exception.

Since the injuries are not likely to last for a year the Disability Discrimination Act 1995 does not affect the current law as applied to the facts.

Depending on the length of employment ('some years') Ivan will be entitled to the correct length of notice under statute or under contract, depending on which is the longer. Since that notice has not been given, there is also a wrongful dismissal action available. Claims are made in the ordinary courts or if the claim is for below £25,000, is not one of the claims excluded from the jurisdiction of the employment tribunals, and is on termination of the contract of service, in the employment tribunal. Since the claim may well be for damages equivalent to only a few weeks' notice, despite the concurrent jurisdiction the claim may well be brought before the latter forum.

Question 7

ANSWER BOTH PARTS

(a) 'The tribunals have striven to apply the Employment Act 2002 (Dispute Resolution) Regulations 2004 (SI 2004/3426) in such a way that justice has not been thwarted by the wording of the Regulations but interpretation has sometimes been stymied by the wording of the Regulations.'

Discuss. [60%]

AND

(b) The Department for Business, Enterprise and Regulatory Reform (DBERR), previously the Department of Trade and Industry (DTI), is engaged in a consultation process with a view to abolishing the 2004 Regulations, as recommended by the Gibbons Report. Why did the Gibbons review come to the conclusions that it did and which recommendations has it proposed to take the place of the Regulations? [40%]

Commentary

The question is in two parts and both must be tackled. If, say, half the marks are allocated to each part of the question then, if you answer one part at first class level but do not answer the second part, you are heading for a fail. For example, assume that the marker has allocated 50% of the total marks to (a) and 50% to (b): if the candidate answers one part only, then immediately 50% of the marks are lost; a first class answer (70%) to the other part will result in only a mark of 35%, a fail. Some law schools add at the end of each sub-question the amount of marks allocated to each part and, if so, you should allocate approximately the same proportion of your total answer to each part.

Part (a) does not ask for an outline of the law (on which see **Question 2** in this chapter) except in so far as a summary of the Regulations is needed to understand the tribunals' interpretation of the Regulations. If you do not know your cases, you should not tackle this question. Part (b) looks to an exposition of the Gibbons Report on dispute resolution. Again, a general outline of the Regulations will not in itself gain many marks.

In order to guide the reader through the answer the authors recommend using sub-headings even in essay-style answers (contrary to what the reader may have been taught at school).

Answer plan

- The standard and modified statutory discipline and dismissal procedures including the uplifts
- The effect of s. 98A(2) of the Employment Rights Act 1996
- The standard and modified statutory grievance procedures
- The Gibbons Review (2007) with an outline of the major recommendations.

Suggested answer

(a)

Introduction

Though there have been no decisions of the Court of Appeal or House of Lords (or of the Court of Session in Scotland) on the 2004 Regulations and though several aspects of them have not received judicial construction (such as the interpretation of the modified statutory discipline and dismissal procedure), the Employment Appeal Tribunal (EAT) has delivered a good number of judgments on their interpretation. It is the objective of this answer to see whether or not the tribunals have been obliged to construe the Regulations in such a manner that the words of the Regulations do not impede justice, which after all is stated to be the 'overriding objective' of employment tribunals.

Statutory discipline and dismissal procedures (SDDPs)

The SDDPs apply only when the employers are contemplating disciplinary action or dismissal. Employers who commence capability proceedings against an employee do not contemplate dismissals, even though the end of the process may be a dismissal: *South Kent College* v *Hall* EAT/0087/07. Therefore, the law on SDDPs does not apply.

The SDDPs do not apply in certain other circumstances, one of which occurs when the employee is constructively dismissed within s. 95(1)(c) of the Employment Rights Act 1996. In that event the Statutory Grievance Procedures (SGPs) apply. However, in turn SGPs do not apply if the employers are contemplating 'actual' dismissal. Where the employee resigns because she knows that she will shortly be dismissed, it was said *obiter* in *Brock* v *Minerva Dental Ltd* [2007] ICR 917 (EAT) that neither the SDDPs nor the SGPs apply.

When the standard SDDPs do apply, cases from the EAT stress that Step 1, the letter, is very easy for the employers to deal with. In one of the landmark authorities, *Alexander* v *Bridgen Enterprises Ltd* [2006] ICR 1277, Elias P. stated:

> ... the employee simply needs to be told that he is at risk of dismissal and why. In a conduct case this will be ... the nature of the misconduct in issue, such as fighting, insubordination or dishonesty. In other cases it may require no more than specifying, for example, that it is lack of capability or redundancy.

This is a minimal requirement, and one made even more so by the decision in *Draper* v *Mears Ltd* [2006] IRLR 869 that the letter need not specify on its face to, for instance, the alleged misconduct but it may refer, as here, to 'last Tuesday's events'. On the previous Tuesday the employee had been caught redhanded and he knew in that context what 'last Tuesday's events' were. The case of *Patel* v *Leicester City Council* EAT/0368/06 stresses the minimal nature of the requirement that the employers send the employee a letter. The employers were dissatisfied with the employee's performance and they put her on a redeployment register; they sent her a letter saying that she would be dismissed if they could not find her another post. The

EAT held that this letter constituted step 1 of the SDDPs even though it was by no means certain that she would be dismissed and indeed the employers were seeking to redeploy her.

Step 2, however, requires more than step 1 because the employers must tell the employee of the 'basis' of the reason for dismissal. Again *Alexander* is helpful. Elias P said that in a misconduct case all that was needed was that the employee knew what she was being accused of so that she could put her side of the story. In a redundancy scenario, as *Alexander* was, the employers must explain why redundancies are needed and why the employee is at risk of being made redundant. On the facts of the case, employees had been told the criteria for selection for redundancy but not their scores under those criteria and the EAT held that they had been automatically unfairly dismissed. However, the employee must be given a reasonable opportunity to respond to criticism and providing her with the case against on the morning of the hearing did not give her such an opportunity: *Bowen* v *Millbank Estate Management Organisation* EAT/0032/07. Accordingly the dismissal was automatically unfair, and it made no difference that she was allowed after the meeting to make representations that the panel took into account before reaching its decision.

Step 2 was widely construed in favour of the employers in *Patel*, above. The employee asked for a meeting with her employers and she raised the question of why they were taking so long to redeploy her. The EAT held that this meeting constituted step 2 despite the meeting being at the request of the employee and despite the meeting covering issues other than possible dismissal.

Draper v *Mears*, above, demonstrates that if the employee has sufficient information to meet the allegation, there is no need for step 1 and step 2 to be in sequence.

The SDDPs must be restarted where the employee is undergoing a disciplinary and new accusations are made during the SDDP: *Premier Foods Ltd* v *Garner* EAT/0389/06, a pro-employee decision.

According to the Regulations the employers must give the decision to dismiss 'after the meeting'. However, the EAT held in *Dugdale plc* v *Cartlidge* EAT/0508/06 that it was not a failure by the employers to abide by step 2 if they announce their decision at the end of the meeting. Here the EAT is seeking to get round the drafting of the Regulations in order to promote a common-sense interpretation of the Regulations. The effect, however, is to construe the provision in the employers' favour.

Step 3 is the appeal. Perhaps surprisingly, if the employee does not avail herself of the appeal stage of the SDDPs, she may and almost certainly will receive reduced unfair dismissal compensation because she is at fault for not completing the relevant SDDP. Moreover, the appeal must be made without unreasonable delay. What is unreasonable is a question of fact for the employment tribunal and the issue of whether a delay of six months was unreasonable was remitted to the tribunal in *Patel*, above; see also *Khan* v *Home Office* EAT/0026/06.

'A procedure'

Where the employers comply with the SDDPs, the next issue concerns the effect of s. 98A(2), which stipulates that a failure to follow 'a procedure' does not of itself make the dismissal unfair provided that the employers show that they would have dismissed if they had followed the procedure. 'A procedure' means any procedure (*Kelly-Madden* v *The Manor Surgery* [2007] ICR 207 (EAT) following *Alexander*, above, and disapproving *Mason* v *Governing Body of Ward End School* [2006] ICR 1128 (EAT)). Therefore, to comply with s. 98A(2) the procedure need not be in writing or be in any way formal. The effect of placing the burden of proof on the employers was demonstrated by the EAT decision in *YMCA Training* v *Stewart* [2007] IRLR 185. The employment tribunal found that the claimant stood a 60 per cent chance of being dismissed. The EAT held that the effect of finding that the employers were more likely than not to dismiss rendered the dismissal fair. It is not just the compensation is reduced by the percentage chance of being dismissed.

The uplifts for failure to comply with the SDDPs

Section 31 of the Employment Act 2002 governs increases and decreases in compensation where one party has failed to follow the correct statutory procedure. The EAT in *Metrobus Ltd* v *Cook* EAT/0490/06 held that the uplift for non-compliance with the SDDPs was penal in nature and on the facts an increase of 40 per cent was justified where the employers were in serious default of their obligations. A serious default would be for example a refusal to start on the SDDPs process or a refusal to hear an appeal. Contrariwise, the EAT in *Bainbridge* v *Redcar & Cleveland BC* [2007] IRLR 494 reduced a 5 per cent uplift to a 0 per cent one when the meeting between the parties would have been useless because they were involved in an equal pay claim and it would not have been possible to reach any decision without the employees' solicitor being present. This was therefore not just one of those exceptional cases where an increase of under 10 per cent was appropriate but one where a nil uplift was awarded because any meeting was futile.

It should be noted that compensation can still be reduced for contributory fault (and under the principle in *W. Devis & Sons* v *Atkins* [1977] AC 971 (HL)) even if the effect is to reduce the amount awarded to nothing: *Ingram* v *Bristol Street Parts* EAT/0601/06, *obiter*. The effect is therefore that any uplift is made nugatory.

Statutory grievance procedures

The standard SGP

The EAT has read the requirement for there to be a grievance widely, an interpretation in favour of employees. For example, it is sufficient that the employee is complaining about something, and the document in which the employee is complaining need not be called a grievance: *Galaxy Showers Ltd* v *Wilson* [2006] IRLR 83. A request for flexible working may constitute a grievance: *Commotion Ltd* v *Rutty* [2006] ICR 290. A resignation letter can be a 'grievance': *Shergold* v *Fieldway Medical Centre* [2006]

ICR 304; so too can a solicitor's letter before action (*Mark Warner Ltd* v *Aspland* [2006] IRLR 87 and even a 'without prejudice' letter (*Arnold Clark Automobiles Ltd* v *Stewart* EAT/0052/05). The employee need not have written the letter herself: *Mark Warner*. In the case of a dyslexic employee a grievance was made when he told his manager of his grievance and the latter wrote it down. There is no need to use the employers' grievance form: *Thorpe* v *Poat* EAT/0503/05. However, an ET 1, a claim form, is not a grievance for the purposes of the SGP: *Gibbs* v *Harris* EAT/0023/07. Similarly, a discrimination questionnaire such as one in respect of disability is not a grievance: *Holc-Gale* v *Makers Ltd* [2006] ICR 462.

A related question is this: if there is a grievance, what does that grievance cover? In *Canary Wharf Management Ltd* v *Edebi* [2006] ICR 719 the EAT held that a grievance about the physical conditions of work did not cover disability discrimination. As Elias P. put it: 'If the statement cannot in context fairly be read even in a non-technical and unsophisticated way as raising the grievance that is the subject-matter of the . . . complaint, then the tribunal cannot hear the claim.' However, the tribunal does have jurisdiction when the complaint in writing did not refer to an equal pay grievance but that complaint had to be read in light of a previous conversation about equal pay between the employee and a manager of the employers: *Serco Group* v *Wild* EAT/0519/06. The authorities are not clear-cut on whether a grievance can cover matters after the complaint was brought. Perhaps the most reasoned case is *Galaxy Showers*, above, where the EAT held that where the grievance was a letter threatening resignation if the employers did not act as the employee required, he would resign, the tribunal had jurisdiction over the constructive dismissal when the employee did resign.

The cases are not definite as to whether the SGP must be used when one of the respondents is not the employers but, for instance, is a line manager. The (Scottish) EAT said in *Bissett* v *Martins* EAT(S)/0022/06 that the SGP did not apply and the EAT sitting in London is divided: *Odoemelam* v *Whittington Hospital NHS Trust* EAT/0016/06 agreed with the EAT in Scotland but another division of the EAT disagreed in *London Borough of Lambeth* v *Corlett* EAT/0396/06.

The modified SGP

Unlike the complaint in the standard SGP, the modified SGP requires the employee to set out the basis of the grievance. In *Bradford City Council* v *Pratt* [2007] IRLR 192 EAT the employee had brought a grievance about equal pay; she then resigned, and agreed that her grievance should be treated under the modified SGP. However, on her claim form she did not note who her comparators were. The EAT upheld the contention of the employers that she had not laid down the basis of her grievance; therefore, the tribunal did not have jurisdiction. Because the date for bringing the claim had now passed, the employee could not bring another claim and she lost her case. This case is an illustration of how the drafting of the Regulations have prevented justice from being granted—the technicalities have defeated the expectation of justice.

(b)

Introduction

The committee chaired by Michael Gibbons reported in March 2007 (*Better Dispute Resolution: A Review of Employment Dispute Resolution in Great Britain*, URN 07/755) and what was then the DTI immediately issued a public Consultation Paper basically requesting argument in favour of and contrary to the proposals with a deadline for responses in June 2007. At the time of writing the outcome of the consultation process is not known but it is expected that the Government does intend to abolish the 2004 Regulations, and it has already announced that there will be an Employment Simplification bill in the 2007–08 Session of Parliament and this bill could be the vehicle for the abolition. However, come what may, there is very little chance of the repeal taking place before some time in 2009 (i.e. during the currency of this book) and, in particular it is uncertain whether s. 98A(2) of the Employment Rights Act 1996, as inserted by the Employment Act 2002, will be retained or replaced. This subsection provides that a dismissal may be fair even when the employers have acted in a procedurally unfair manner by not following rules of procedure (such as their own) which differ from the statutory minimum found in the 2002 statute and the 2004 Regulations.

The recommendations of the Gibbons Review

In his foreword Gibbons wrote:

> The headline recommendation is the complete repeal of the statutory dispute resolution procedures set out in the 2004 Dispute Resolution Regulations. I also present a suite of complementary recommendations which, in aggregate, are genuinely deregulatory and simplifying. If implemented, they should reduce the complexity of the current system and reduce costs to business and employees. They uphold and preserve all existing employee rights and ensure access to justice.

The Report considered that the intention behind the 2004 Regulations was 'sound' but that the implementation of that intention had been 'inappropriately inflexible and prescriptive'. The aim had been to increase early resolution but the result had been that formal processes had come to be used when less formal ones would have led to earlier resolution. The review noted the following problems with the Regulations:

1. They 'exacerbate and accelerate disputes' because the parties concentrate on getting the SGPs and SDDPs correct rather than focus on settling the dispute amicably.

2. 'complexity drives users to seek legal advice earlier with associated increased costs' (for example, is a complaint made on a 360 per cent feedback form a grievance?).

3. 'the Regulations are not relevant to all situations' (an example was the appeal stage in small businesses where the appeal could not be heard by a person who heard the original complaint but also noted were situations in which there were

multiple claimants, where it was burdensome to go through the process for each individual claimant, and cases where both disciplinary action and grievances were taking place at the same time e.g. an allegedly discriminatory discipline procedure: in such instances it was not always clear whether both the SGP and the SDDP had to take place).

The tribunals also were not helpful in this regard. 'The overwhelming view of those the Review spoke to was that tribunals are increasingly complex, legalistic and adversarial making them a daunting experience for many.' (para. 1.41) Sometimes, indeed, the Regulations were inappropriate, e.g. on the expiry of a limited-term contract and on redundancy. Any proposals for reform had to be simpler and less prescriptive while keeping to the objective of resolving workplace disputes as early as possible in order to reduce disruption to businesses and to employees' careers and to save money: the Report noted that 42 per cent of respondents to a survey (DTI, *Employment Rights at Work—Survey of Employees* (2005)) reported a problem at work within the last five years and that the cost of defending an employment tribunal claim was some £9,000: PricewaterhouseCoopers/BRE *admin burdens measurement exercise* (2003). The latest figure for legal fees is £4,360: DTI, *Survey of Employment Tribunal Applications* (2005). Gibbons recommended also

1. Purely monetary disputes should be dealt with swiftly without the need for a tribunal hearing, perhaps by a legally qualified adjudicator acting under the supervision of a tribunal chair.

2. The advice via the web, guidance, and a helpline provided to all parties should be improved.

3. In-house alternative dispute resolution mechanisms such as mediation should be encouraged.

4. A free early resolution service should be established by the government and that should include mediation.

5. The fixed periods of ACAS conciliation should be abolished.

6. The behaviour of the parties should be reflected in costs orders.

7. The claim and response form should be simplified.

8. Employment tribunals should be given power to deal with cases involving multiple claimants.

9. The situations in which tribunal chairs may sit alone should be reviewed so that lay members should sit only when they add value.

10. Time limits should be unified.

11. Powers to deal with weak and vexatious cases should be reconsidered so that the tribunals use them consistently.

12. And, finally, employment law should be simplified (!).

Further reading

Collins, H., *Justice in Dismissal* (Oxford: Clarendon, 1992).

Ewing, K. D., 'Remedies for breach of the contract of employment' [1993] CLJ 405.

Pitt, G., 'Justice in Dismissal: a reply to Hugh Collins' (1993) 22 ILJ 251.

Smith, I. T., and Thomas, G., *Industrial Law*, 8th edn (Oxford: Oxford University Press, 2003), ch. 8, pp. 494–622.

7

Statutory redundancy payments and consultation procedures

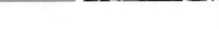

Introduction

The law relating to redundancy is a major topic within any employment law course. Questions on this area are favourites of examiners and often arise, either as part of unfair dismissal law, i.e. issues concerning unfair selection for redundancy, inadequate consultation/failure to consult, etc. (see Chapter 6), or as questions focusing on the technical definition of redundancy, the right to a redundancy payment, and so on. This chapter deals with the law on statutory redundancy payments, and the consultation procedures surrounding this area. There may be other legal issues surrounding *contractual* redundancy payments and procedures which should also be borne in mind when dealing with the *statutory* right to redundancy payment.

Students should be aware of the following issues in this area: the qualifying period of continuous employment required in order to claim a statutory redundancy payment; the technical definition of redundancy in the Employment Rights Act 1996 (ERA); questions concerning 'work of a particular kind' and the case law there under; 'bumped' redundancies; whether suitable alternative employment has been considered or offered; the statutory trial period when considering suitable alternative employment; the calculation of the statutory redundancy payment (note that the 'tapering provisions', formerly within s. 162(4) of the ERA, were repealed by the Equality (Age) Regulations 2006).

In order to qualify for a statutory redundancy payment an employee must have two years of continuous employment ending with the 'relevant date', which is the equivalent of the Effective Date of Termination (EDT) in unfair dismissal law: ERA, s. 155. An awareness of the provisions on termination with and without notice, and the termination of limited-term contracts is necessary (ERA, s. 145), together with the effect on the relevant date that such dismissals will have. The statutory minimum notice periods under s. 86, ERA may be added to the period of continuous employment where no notice has been given, in the absence of repudiatory conduct by the employee which would justify summary dismissal: ERA, s. 145(5).

The technical definition of redundancy set out in the ERA has caused courts and tribunals much trouble over the years. Section 139 of the Act may be summarized as defining redundancy as (1) closure of the business—actual or proposed (s. 139(1)(a)(i)); or (2) closure of the business—actual or proposed—in the place where the employee was employed (s. 139(1)(a)(ii)); or (3) cessation or diminution—actual or expected—of the requirements of the business for employees to carry out work of a particular kind (s. 139(1)(b)(i)); or (4) cessation or diminution—actual or expected—of the requirements of the business for employees to carry out work of a particular kind in the place where the employee was employed: s. 139(1)(b)(ii).

Clearly, (1) above is what the layman would regard as a typical and straightforward case of redundancy. The definition in (2) requires a consideration of the place where the employee was employed (mobility clauses may have to be considered to determine this question), whereas the situations described in (3) and (4) focus upon the concept of 'work of a particular kind'. The situation described in (4) concerns the two concepts of 'work of a particular kind' *and* the place where the employee was employed.

In the past, the issue of whether there has been a cessation or diminution of 'work of a particular kind' involved a discussion of the 'job function test' and the 'contract test' (see *Nelson* v *BBC (No. 1)* [1977] IRLR 148, CA, and *Cowen* v *Haden* [1983] ICR 1, CA and the decisions in *Safeway Stores plc* v *Burrell* [1997] IRLR 200, EAT and *Murray* v *Foyle Meats Ltd* [1999] IRLR 562, HL. In *Murray,* the House of Lords approved the decision in *Burrell. Murray* establishes that both the 'job function test' and the 'contract test' are now defunct (the House of Lords stated that the statutory wording should be applied, and no more). Although the determination of the place where the employee was employed is a factual one, the contract may be important in giving an indication of where the employee worked (see *High Table Ltd* v *Horst* [1998] ICR 409, CA) although it may be significant that the employee in fact worked in only one place, despite a mobility clause in the contract (see *Bass Leisure* v *Thomas* [1994] IRLR 104).

Students should understand the concept of a 'bumped' redundancy, as established in *Gimber* v *Spurrett* (1967) 2 ITR 308, IT, and *Elliott Turbomachinery Ltd* v *Bates* [1981] ICR 218, EAT, a concept now firmly established in *Burrell* (and approved in *Murray,* although neither case concerned bumping), which emphasized that the question is whether the need for *employees* generally has diminished or ceased, not the need for *this particular employee* bringing the redundancy claim.

Employers must consider whether suitable alternative employment is available for redundant employees and offer it to the employee: ERA, s. 141(1). There may be a problem concerning what constitutes suitable alternative employment. It may not be suitable alternative employment if the job offered involves a significant drop in status (see *Taylor* v *Kent County Council* [1969] 2 QB 560, QBD), or a reduction in pay (see *Tocher* v *General Motors Scotland Ltd* [1981] IRLR 55, EAT). An employee who unreasonably refuses an offer of suitable alternative employment, or unreasonably terminates the new contract while working during the statutory trial period of four weeks, loses his right to a statutory redundancy payment: ERA, s. 141(2), (3), (4).

Redundant employees whose contracts are renewed or who are re-engaged on terms where the capacity and place of work, and the other terms and conditions, do not differ from those of the previous employment are regarded as not dismissed, so no right to claim a redundancy payment arises: ERA, s. 138(1); employees who are offered suitable alternative employment within four weeks of the dismissal for redundancy, the terms of which differ (wholly or in part) from those of their previous job have a statutory trial period of four weeks in which to decide whether or not they consider the job to be suitable: ERA, s. 138(2), (3). Termination of the contract during this period by either employee or employer does not affect the employee's entitlement to claim a statutory redundancy payment, and the date of the original dismissal is the relevant date: ERA, s. 138(2), (4). Contractual trial periods may be provided for, in which case the statutory trial period would begin after the expiry of the contractual trial period: see *Turvey* v *C. W. Cheney & Son Ltd* [1979] ICR 341.

The statutory redundancy payment is calculated in a similar way to the basic award in unfair dismissal compensation, i.e. it depends upon the employee's age, length of continuous employment, up to a maximum of 20 years (s. 162(3)), ending with the 'relevant date', and gross wage (subject to the current statutory maximum—from 1 February 2007 this was £310 although you should note that this figure generally goes up each year in line with annual inflation-linked percentages: see ERA, ss. 210–19. The calculation is done on the following basis:

1. One and a half weeks' pay for each year of continuous employment which consists wholly of weeks in which the employee was not below the age of 41.

2. One week's pay for each year of continuous employment which consists wholly of weeks in which the employee was not below the age of 22.

3. Half a week's pay for each year of continuous employment not falling within the preceding paragraphs (employment before the eighteenth birthday is not taken into account: ERA, s. 211(2).

(Note the repeal of the provision (formerly, ERA, s. 156) that an employee aged over 65 (or the normal retiring age) could not claim a redundancy payment if, before the relevant date, he or she had reached the normal retiring age operating in the business for employees holding that employee's position, if it was below 65 (where the same retiring age applied to that position, whether held by a man or a woman), or, in any other case, the age of 65.)

If the employer wishes to avoid a successful unfair dismissal claim by reason of redundancy, it is necessary to ensure that a fair procedure has been adopted, including giving reasonable warning of the impending redundancy, and engaging in individual consultation with the relevant employee(s): see *Williams* v *Compair Maxim Ltd* [1982] IRLR 83. Reasonable time off must be given to the employee who is under a redundancy notice to allow them to look for alternative employment: ERA, s. 52(1). The statutory dismissal and disciplinary procedures (DDP) should also be complied with, unless the redundancy falls within certain exceptions, such as sudden closure of a business or where the collective consultation provisions apply (see TULRCA 1992, s. 188).

The Trade Union and Labour Relations (Consolidation) Act 1992 (TULRCA) stipulates statutory consultation and notification procedures which must be observed where the employer intends making collective redundancies, i.e. at least 20 employees redundant at the same establishment within 90 days or less. This collective consultation concerning 'affected employees' must take place with either trade union officials (where there is a recognized trade union), or employee representatives (where there is not). The 'affected employees' include not only those to be dismissed, but any others who may be affected by measures taken in connection with those dismissals, e.g. a reorganization.

Where it is proposed to dismiss more than 100 employees within 90 days or less, consultation must take place at least 90 days before the first dismissals take effect, and in any other case at least 30 days before the first dismissals take effect: TULRCA, s. 188(1A). Failure to comply with the statutory requirements may lead to the employer being liable to pay each redundant employee a 'protective award' during the 'protected period' (of up to 90 days), with no statutory ceiling on a week's pay: TULRCA, ss. 189, 190.

Finally, it should be noted that there are notification requirements applicable to collective redundancy situations, whereby the employer must give written notification to the Department of Trade and Industry (DTI): TULRCA, s. 193.

Question 1

Lite Bikes Ltd, a manufacturer of bicycles of all kinds, announced a week ago that it intended making some of its employees redundant over the next two weeks. After the announcement, the following events occur:

Eric, whose job title is 'bicycle operative—hand-painting technician', has been engaged on hand painting expensive, hand-made, lightweight racing bikes since he started work for the company. The company has decided to automate the painting of these bikes, and Eric is instructed to join other bicycle operatives working in the bicycle-frame brazing workshop. Eric feels that he would not be using his skills in the brazing workshop, so he refuses to transfer to the brazing workshop, on two-thirds of the wage he is currently paid. He is dismissed for this refusal, following the completion of the statutory DDP. He wishes to claim a redundancy payment. At the time of his dismissal, he had worked for Lite Bikes Ltd for 103 weeks. Advise Eric as to his right, if any, to a statutory redundancy payment.

Commentary

It is important to note that this question requires an answer confined to a discussion of issues concerning *entitlement* to claim a statutory redundancy payment. Answers straying into a general discussion of unfair dismissal law on the redundancy ground will not attract marks for such a discussion.

This question raises a number of issues concerning redundancy. It is necessary to discuss the following issues: whether Eric has the required qualifying period of continuous employment to claim a redundancy payment; whether he is in fact redundant within the Employment Rights Act 1996 definition (some reference to the contract test/function test debate is necessary, together with a discussion of the approach set out by the EAT in *Safeway Stores plc* v *Burrell* [1997] IRLR 200, and approved by the House of Lords in *Murray* v *Foyle Meats Ltd* [1999] IRLR 562); and whether he has been dismissed for redundancy purposes.

Answer plan

- Discuss whether Eric has sufficient continuous employment to claim redundancy, taking into account the statutory minimum notice period.

- Consider the other provisions relating to entitlement to claim a statutory redundancy payment: the technical definition of redundancy; the two tests—the 'job function' test and the 'contract' test, and the recent case law interpreting the redundancy provisions, i.e. *Burrell* and *Murray*.

Suggested answer

In order to claim a statutory redundancy payment, an employee must have two years' continuous employment by 'the relevant date': Employment Rights Act 1996 (ERA), s. 155. Under the ERA, s. 145, where a contract of employment is terminated by notice, the relevant date is the date on which that notice expires. Where the contract is terminated without notice, the relevant date is the date the termination takes effect and, for limited-term contracts, it is the date when the term expires. Eric has only 103 weeks of continuous employment at the time of his dismissal but, since he has been summarily dismissed, he may add on the minimum statutory period of notice of one week, under s. 86 (ERA, s. 145(5)) to give him the required two years of employment by moving the relevant date to the expiry of the contractual notice period. This right under s. 86 applies only where there has been no repudiatory conduct by Eric (ERA, s. 86(6)), so the question is whether his refusal to transfer constitutes such conduct. The answer to that question hinges upon whether Eric is redundant, and effectively dismissed on that ground. There is also the question of whether his refusal to transfer precludes him from claiming a statutory redundancy payment (assuming that the job offered is suitable alternative employment). However, where a reference is made to an employment tribunal for a statutory redundancy payment, there is a statutory presumption where an employee has been dismissed by his employer that he is, unless the contrary is proved, dismissed by reason of redundancy for the purposes of a statutory redundancy claim: ERA, s. 163(2). It is for the employer to prove that his dismissal was for a reason other than redundancy or that Eric is barred from making such a claim for some other reason.

Under the ERA, s. 139(1)(b)(i), an employee is dismissed by reason of redundancy, 'if the dismissal is wholly or mainly attributable to—the fact that the requirements of that business...for employees to carry out work of a particular kind...have ceased or diminished or are expected to cease and diminish'. Clearly, there is or will be no requirement for employees to hand-paint bicycles. The issue is whether the contractual provision that Eric may be required to work elsewhere in the factory and on other duties means that he is not redundant. This raises the question of whether his hand-painting job is 'work of a particular kind', and whether the job in the brazing workshop is the same kind of work and involves no change in the nature of the job (employees are expected to adapt to changing methods of working: see *North Riding Garages Ltd v Butterwick* [1967] 2 QB 56; *Cresswell v Board of the Inland Revenue* [1984] IRLR 190).

Until recently, there have been two approaches to testing whether a redundancy has arisen under the statutory definition: the 'job function test' and the 'contract test'. Under the former, the approach was to consider what an employee *was actually doing* (see *Chapman v Goonvean and Rostowrack China Clay Co Ltd* [1973] ICR 310, CA); whereas, under the latter, the approach was to consider what the employee *could be required to do under the contract of employment*. *Nelson v BBC (No. 1)* [1977] IRLR 148, CA, provides an application of the contract test: a producer/editor working in the Caribbean Service of the BBC, who, under the terms of his contract could be required to work in any capacity in any country, and who rejected the offer of alternative work, was held not to be redundant when the Caribbean Service was closed down (see also the Court of Appeal's decision in *Cowen v Haden* [1983] ICR 1).

In *Safeway Stores plc v Burrell* [1997] IRLR 200, the EAT stated that both the contract test and the function test were incorrect approaches, distorting the statutory language. A three-stage process was required, asking the following questions:

1. Was the employee dismissed? If so,

2. Had the requirements of the employer's business for employees to carry out work of a particular kind ceased or diminished or were they expected to cease or diminish? If so,

3. Was the dismissal of the employee...caused wholly or mainly by the state of affairs identified at stage 2 above?

The EAT said that at stage 2, 'The only question to be asked is: was there a diminution/cessation in the employer's requirement for *employees* to carry out work of a particular kind, or an expectation of such cessation/diminution in the future (redundancy)? At this stage it is irrelevant to consider the terms of the applicant employee's contract of employment' (EAT's emphasis). This reasoning was approved by the House of Lords in *Murray v Foyle Meats Ltd* [1999] IRLR 562, in which it was stated that both the function test and the contract test are an unnecessary gloss on the statute.

Applying the *Burrell* approach to Eric's case, stage 1 has been satisfied (he has been dismissed). If, as seems likely, hand-painting bicycles is 'work of a particular kind', then there is clearly a cessation in the requirement for this kind of work, due to the introduction of automation. On the causation point in stage 3, it is necessary to establish the link between the dismissal and the cessation in requirements for work of a particular kind. Here, it seems that, in the absence of a contractual provision allowing it to do so, the employer's instruction to transfer constitutes a unilateral variation of the contract, and Eric's refusal to transfer would not amount to repudiatory conduct, barring him from claiming a redundancy payment: ERA, s. 140. If the transfer is an offer of alternative employment, it seems unlikely that, because of the drop in salary and the very different work being offered, it is suitable alternative employment (ERA, s. 141), so Eric's refusal is not unreasonable. He would not, therefore, be prevented from claiming a redundancy payment on this ground.

Question 2

Geraldine has worked as a cleaner for Kwik Kleen Ltd for the last three years, during which time she has been assigned by the company to the central London office of Marston & Douglas Investments Ltd, carrying out cleaning work for the company. Last month, Marston informed Kwik Kleen that it no longer required their services as it was providing its own in-house cleaning operations. Geraldine has a clause in her contract which states, 'You may be required to transfer to another location within a reasonable daily travelling distance of your existing place of work.' Kwik Kleen does not invoke this clause but instead dismisses Geraldine, after following the statutory DDP. Advise Geraldine as to her entitlement to claim a statutory redundancy payment.

 ## Commentary

This question concerns Geraldine's entitlement to claim a statutory redundancy payment: the key issue here concerns the place where the employee was employed under s. 139(1)(b)(ii), in particular the geographic or function test, as opposed to the contract test, and the relevant case law. It requires a discussion of the effect of the mobility clause on the question of the place where Geraldine was employed.

 ## Answer plan

- Discuss the redundancy provisions in relation to the place where the employee was employed; the 'geographic' and 'contract' tests as against the current position.
- Consider the effect of the mobility clause.

Suggested answer

In order to claim a statutory redundancy payment, Geraldine must establish that she is redundant under the definition in the Employment Rights Act 1996 (ERA), s. 139(1)(b)(ii), i.e. that the dismissal is 'wholly or mainly attributable to' the fact that the requirements of the business 'for employees to carry out work of a particular kind *in the place where the employee was employed*... have ceased or diminished or are expected to cease or diminish' (emphasis added). The central issue in Geraldine's case is how to determine the place where she was employed.

There are at least two ways of determining this issue, i.e. by applying the 'contract test' or the 'factual' or 'geographic test', and, until recently, different courts and tribunals applied one or other of these tests to determine such questions. The former test looked at where the employee could be required to work under her contract, while the latter test focused on the factual aspect of the geographical area within which the employee actually worked. Widely different answers could be reached, depending on which test was used. For example, in *Sutcliffe* v *Hawker Siddeley Aviation Ltd* [1973] ICR 560, NIRC, Mr Sutcliffe, who worked at RAF Marham, was instructed to move to another RAF station, RAF Kinloss, when Marham closed. A mobility clause in his contract provided that he could be moved anywhere in the UK, but he refused to transfer. The court held that the place where he was employed meant the place where he could be required to work under the contract, rather than the place where he in fact worked. As there was work at RAF Kinloss, he was not redundant. Similarly, in *United Kingdom Atomic Energy Authority* v *Claydon* [1974] ICR 128, NIRC, Mr Claydon was employed at the Atomic Energy Authority's (AEA) establishment in East Anglia, under a contract containing a provision that he could be transferred to any of the AEA's establishments in the UK. When the AEA asked Mr Claydon to transfer to its Aldermaston site because they no longer had any need for him in East Anglia, he refused, and the AEA did not invoke its rights under the mobility clause. Instead, they dismissed him and he claimed a redundancy payment. The National Industrial Relations Court (NIRC) followed *Sutcliffe* in applying the contract test, under which his 'place of work' was nationwide, and looking nationally at the AEA's establishments, there was no redundancy, so the dismissal was not by reason of redundancy. However, the NIRC did state that, had the AEA invoked its right to order Claydon to transfer, any refusal on his part to do so would allow the employer to lawfully dismiss him for breach of contract.

The EAT in *Bass Leisure Ltd* v *Thomas* [1994] IRLR 104 preferred the factual or geographic test rather than the contract test, although it stated that on either test the applicant in the instant case won. Mrs Thomas was based at her employer's Coventry depot, from where she travelled to various public houses collecting the takings from fruit machines. On the closure of its Coventry depot, Mrs Thomas was instructed to base herself in Birmingham (some 20 miles away), pursuant to a contractual mobility clause (this contained two qualifications: first, that the employer should take account of the employee's domestic circumstances; and, second, that, judged objectively, the alternative place of work must be suitable). Mrs Thomas agreed to try the new arrangements but found that they did not suit her, so she left and claimed constructive dismissal and a redundancy payment. The EAT held that the correct test to apply was the geographic test, making a factual enquiry 'taking account of the employee's fixed or changing place or places of work, and any contractual terms which go to evidence or define the place of employment' but excluding any mobility clause from consideration. Under this test, she had been constructively dismissed (because the employer had not satisfied the two requirements indicated above, and was therefore in breach of contract) by reason of redundancy.

Bass was approved by the Court of Appeal in *High Table Ltd* v *Horst* [1997] IRLR 513, CA. Mrs Horst and other waitresses were employed by High Table as silver service waitresses at Hill Samuel's London office. Although their contracts stated, 'it is sometimes necessary to transfer staff...to another location', they had in fact worked only at the Hill Samuel office. When Hill Samuel decided to reorganize its catering, they needed fewer waitresses working longer hours, and High Table dismissed all three waitresses. Applying the geographic or factual test, the Court of Appeal found that the waitresses had all been employed, as a matter of fact, at the Hill Samuel offices, and, as there was a reduced need for waitresses there, they were all redundant. Peter Gibson LJ (with whom Hobhouse and Evans LJJ agreed) stated, 'If an employee has worked in only one location under his contract of employment for the purposes of the employer's business it defies common sense to widen the extent of the place where he was so employed, merely because of the existence of a mobility clause'.

Applying this factual enquiry approach to Geraldine's case, it would appear that, since she has been working at Marston's London office (and nowhere else) for the last three years, she is redundant as there is a redundancy situation *at that place*, resulting in her dismissal. Therefore, she may claim a statutory redundancy payment by notice in writing, within six months of the relevant date: ERA, s. 164.

Question 3

Ted works for Yarrow Developments Ltd, a construction company. Ted has worked for Yarrow for six years as an administrator in its Site Administration Department, and was given notice of dismissal and allowed to work his contractual notice period of ten weeks. The statutory DDP were complied with. He has been told by Yarrow that the reason for the dismissal is that Ken, who works in the company's Accounts Department, is being transferred from that department into Ted's job. As a result of reorganization and computerization, the Accounts Department has reduced its work force from five to three. When Ken still has five more weeks of his notice to work, Sure & Trusty Construction Ltd, Yarrow's wholly owned subsidiary, offers Ted a position in its Direct Sales Team based in offices some five miles from Yarrow's offices, commencing immediately upon the expiry of his notice with Yarrow. The job involves direct marketing of the company by way of telephone calls to prospective customers. The job involves slightly longer working hours (43 hours per week, rather than the 40 hours per week Ted was working) and a lower salary (£23,000 per annum, rather than the £25,000 Ted was earning). Ted, who has two weeks of his notice remaining, seeks your advice as to whether to take the job offered by Sure & Trusty, or whether he may claim a statutory redundancy payment.

Advise Ted.

Commentary

In this question, a consideration of the law relating to 'bumped' employees is required, specifically, whether such employees are dismissed by reason of redundancy and may therefore claim statutory redundancy payment. Further, it requires a discussion of whether the job offer from Sure & Trusty constitutes suitable alternative employment, and, if so, whether Ted might be held to have unreasonably refused it, thereby losing his right to claim a redundancy payment. Since Ted has been working for six years, no question arises as to whether he has the requisite period of qualifying employment.

Answer plan

- Discuss whether there has been a reduction of work of a particular kind.
- Consider the issue of 'bumped' redundancies.
- Discuss whether suitable alternative employment has been offered by an associated employer, and the statutory trial period.
- If suitable alternative employment has been offered, discuss whether there has been an unreasonable refusal of this by Ted.

Suggested answer

It would appear from the facts that a redundancy situation has arisen in Yarrow's Accounts Department in that, owing to the reorganization/computerization, there is clearly a reduction in the need for employees to carry out work of a particular kind: ERA, s. 139(1)(b)(i). However, rather than dismiss Ken, the company has decided to dismiss Ted, i.e. Ted has been 'bumped' out of his job to make way for Ken. May a bumped employee claim that he been dismissed by reason of redundancy? Established case law suggested that such employees could so claim: see *W Gimber & Sons Ltd* v *Spurrett* (1967) 2 ITR 308, HC; *Elliott Turbo Machinery Ltd* v *Bates* [1981] ICR 218, EAT. In such situations, the employee is dismissed not because of a reduction or cessation of *his* work, but rather because of a reduction in the need for another employee's work, and the wording of the Employment Rights Act 1996 (ERA) supports this view (the s. 139 requirements are fulfilled where there is a cessation or reduction in the need for *employees* to carry out work of a particular kind, and this need not necessarily be the dismissed employee's work). There must, of course, be a causal connection between the dismissal and the redundancy, but in Ted's case this is established.

This approach was questioned in *Church* v *West Lancashire NHS Trust* [1998] IRLR 4, where the EAT, applying the 'contract test', held that the concept of bumped redundancies was unsound, and that an employee was redundant only where there was a reduction in the need for the dismissed employee's work. However, the bumped redundancy concept was approved by the House of Lords in *Murray* v *Foyle Meats Ltd* [1999] ICR 827, so the EAT decision in *Church* can no longer be considered to be good law. Further, the House of Lords in *Murray* approved the approach of the EAT in *Safeway Stores plc* v *Burrell* [1997] IRLR 200, in which the EAT approved *Gimber* and *Elliott* and stated 'In our judgment the principle of "bumped" redundancies is statutorily correct.'

It would appear that Ted may claim a statutory redundancy payment, but the next issue is whether Sure & Trusty's job offer constitutes an offer of suitable alternative employment under ERA, s. 141(1)(b). The offer must be made by the original employer or an associated employer (ERA, s. 146(1)), it must take effect either on the ending of the original contract or no more than four weeks thereafter (ERA, s. 141(1)), it must be either on the same terms and conditions or suitable employment in relation to the employee (s. 141(3)), and it may be either oral or in writing (s. 141(1)). Clearly, Sure & Trusty's offer is for a job to commence on the ending of Ted's contract with Yarrow, but is Sure & Trusty an associated employer? Under ERA, s. 231(a), any two employers are to be treated as associated, if 'one is a company of which the other (directly or indirectly) has control'. 'Control' means voting control by a majority of shares: see *Hair Colour Consultants Ltd* v *Mena* [1984] ICR 671; *South West Launderettes Ltd* v *Laidler* [1986] ICR 455). As Sure & Trusty is a wholly owned subsidiary of Yarrow, Yarrow therefore has direct control of it, and so Sure & Trusty is an associated employer of Yarrow.

Where, as in Ted's case, the alternative work is not on the same terms and conditions as the original contract the employee has a statutory right to a trial period of not more than four weeks to decide whether the alternative employment is suitable for him (ERA, s. 138(2)), although this period may be extended for re-training, by agreement (ERA, s. 138(3)(b)(ii)). Therefore, if Ted takes up the offer of alternative employment, he would have four weeks to decide whether or not he wanted to continue in the new job. If he decided against continuing in the new job and terminated it (or gave notice to do so) for a reason connected with the difference between the original contract and the new one, he would be treated as dismissed on the date of the termination of his original contract by reason of redundancy: ERA, s. 138(2), (4).

The next question is whether the job offered constitutes *suitable* alternative employment. If it does, and Ted unreasonably refuses it at the outset or during the statutory trial period, he would lose his right to claim a statutory redundancy payment: ERA, s. 141(2), (3), (4). If he accepts it, he is treated as not having been dismissed, and his continuity of employment is preserved, so that the period of employment with the previous employer counts: ERA, s. 213(2). The job offered differs considerably in that, it involves (i) a different job title and different duties, (ii) longer working hours, (iii) a lower salary, and (iv) a different location, five miles from his current work base. The suitability of the alternative job and the reasonableness of the refusal are two separate questions, the first to be determined objectively, the second assessed subjectively, i.e. depending on factors personal to the employee (see *Cambridge & District Co-operative Society* v *Ruse* [1993] IRLR 156, CA, where a manager of a butcher's shop was offered the post of manager in a supermarket butchery department, which he tried but left during the trial period because he considered it beneath his dignity to work under the store manager: held, a reasonable refusal).

It may be the case that personal factors might mean that Ted could reasonably refuse the job, and the cases are but illustrations of the principle. Changes in pay, hours, and status are important considerations. In *Taylor* v *Kent County Council* [1969] 2 QB 560, QBD, the High Court held that a former head teacher of ten years' standing, who was offered a job, on the same headmaster's salary, in a pool of supply teachers had reasonably refused the offer of alternative employment, on the ground of loss of status (it was 'quite unsuitable'). In *Tocher* v *General Motors Scotland Ltd* [1981] IRLR 55, the EAT held that the reduction in earnings and loss of status justified the employee's rejection. It seems likely that the drop in pay, the longer hours, the different location, and the different position offered would all be factors inclining to the view that this is not suitable alternative employment. There may also be factors arising from Ted's personal circumstances which would mean that any refusal on his part would be reasonable.

In conclusion, the advice to Ted is that he has nothing to lose by taking the job immediately his current contract of employment terminates, since he has the benefit of the statutory trial period of four weeks in which to decide whether he wishes to continue in the new job. If, during the trial period, he decides not to proceed with the new job, it seems likely that he would not lose his right to claim a statutory redundancy payment on the ground that the alternative work offered was not suitable, or that his refusal to take it was reasonable, for the reasons discussed above.

Question 4

Plimshot Electrical Supplies Ltd is a company employing 120 employees, operating from its only premises in Workton. Today, it received information by fax from Wizzo Inc., its parent company in the USA, that Wizzo would cease funding Plimshot. Plimshot has been entirely reliant upon this funding to keep the business going. As a result of the severe financial difficulties Plimshot is facing because of Wizzo's news, it took the decision to dismiss all its work force and close down the business. It proposes to start dismissing employees from next week, with 25 employees to be dismissed in the first week, followed by the remaining employees three weeks later. There is a recognized independent trade union, the Electrical, Plumbing and Allied Trades Union (EPATU), to which all of its employees belong. Plimshot seeks your advice as to the correct redundancy dismissal procedure to follow. Advise Plimshot.

Commentary

A number of issues concerning collective redundancies arise in this question. The answer must cover the company's obligations as regards: information and consultation procedures (both individual and collective); allowing employees time off to look for work; notification requirements to the Department of Trade and Industry (DTI); and the possibility of unfair dismissal claims from employees. Since the company is in severe financial difficulties, there may be an issue as to securing actual payment of statutory redundancy payment if it goes into insolvent liquidation or defaults in payment.

Answer plan

- Discuss individual and collective redundancies, in particular the provisions concerning information and consultation procedures, and any defences available for failing to consult; consider also protective awards.
- Consider the provisions relating to time off to look for work while under a redundancy notice.
- Discuss the notification requirements to the DTI.
- Discuss the potential unfair dismissal claims, and the possibility of claiming a statutory redundancy payment if the company goes into insolvent liquidation.

Suggested answer

As Plimshot intends closing down the business entirely, this is a classic example of one of the three main redundancy dismissal situations, i.e. closure, actual, or intended, of the business as a whole: Employment Rights Act 1996 (ERA), s. 139(1)(a)(i). As its only base is Workton, no question arises under ERA, s. 139(1)(a)(ii) (closure of the business in one place, where the business has other places of establishment). Plimshot will be potentially liable for unfair dismissal if it fails to follow the correct procedure concerning information and consultation prior to dismissal, at both the collective and individual level. Broadly, this means that Plimshot should give as much warning as possible of the impending redundancies and consult with affected employees and, where there is one, a recognized trade union (there is an obligation to consult with employee representatives where there is no recognized trade union: see Trade Union and Labour Relations (Consolidation) Act 1992 (TULRCA), s. 188(1B)(b)).

At the collective level, the company has statutory obligations to inform and consult EPATU, the recognized trade union, about the dismissals. Section 188(1) of TULRCA places an obligation on employers who are 'proposing to dismiss as redundant 20 or more employees at one establishment within a period of 90 days or less' to consult with 'appropriate representatives of any employees who may be affected by the proposed dismissals or may be affected by measures taken in connection with those dismissals'. Clearly, all three conditions ((i) 20 or more employees; (ii) at one establishment; (iii) within 90 days or less) are satisfied here. In Plimshot's case, the 'appropriate representatives' would be those of the recognized independent trade union, EPATU: TULRCA, s. 188(1B)(a). Consultation must take place 'in good time', subject to minimum periods: TULRCA, s. 188(1A). These periods are: 'where the employer is proposing to dismiss 100 or more employees' within 90 days or less, at least 90 days 'before the first of the dismissals takes effect': 'otherwise, at least 30 days before the first of the dismissals take effect': TULRCA, s. 188(1A). In *Junk* v *Wolfgang Kuhnel* (C-188/03) [2005] IRLR 310, the ECJ held that, under Directive 98/59/EC, collective consultation must take place before notice of dismissal is given to any employees. This interpretation means that, under s. 188, the words 'proposing to dismiss' mean 'proposing to give notice of dismissal' (see also *Leicestershire CC* v *Unison* [2005] IRLR 920, EAT).

Section 188(4), TULRCA states that the information to be provided for the purposes of consultation must be in writing and state, inter alia: the reasons for the proposed redundancies; the numbers and descriptions of those employees to be made redundant; the total number of employees of that description employed at the establishment; the proposed method of carrying out the dismissals, having regard to any agreed selection procedure, and the timing of them. The consultation, to be undertaken 'with a view to reaching agreement with the appropriate representatives', must include consultation about ways of '(a) avoiding dismissals, (b) reducing the numbers of employees to be dismissed, and (c) mitigating the consequences of the dismissals': TULRCA, s. 188(2).

It should be noted briefly that, as Plimshot is to make all 120 of its employees redundant, it is caught by the Information and Consultation Directive (Directive 2002/14/EC, implemented in the UK by the Information and Consultation of Employees Regulations 2004 (SI 2004/3426) ('ICER')) because the Regulations apply (from April 2007) to companies with 100 or more employees (and to companies with 50 or more employees, from April 2008). Under the ICER, employers must provide employee representatives with information about the undertaking concerning, inter alia, (i) any threat to employment, and (ii) any decisions likely to lead to substantial changes in work organization or contractual relations. It must also consult with the representatives about these matters. The EAT has power to impose a maximum penalty of £75,000 against employers who fail to comply with the ICER (reg. 23(2)). Clearly, the proposed dismissals affect both of these areas and Plimshot has breached these statutory obligations.

If it proceeds with the proposal to dismiss employees, Plimshot will be in breach of these statutory consultation requirements, as it proposes to start dismissing employees from next week, with 25 employees to be dismissed in the first week, followed by the remaining 95 employees three weeks later. However, there is a defence under TULRCA, s. 188(7) where 'special circumstances' make it 'not reasonably practicable' for the employer to comply with the consultation requirements under that Act. In this case, the employer must 'take all such steps towards compliance with that requirement as are reasonably practicable in those circumstances'.

Here, it would appear that it is not reasonably practicable for Plimshot to comply, given the sudden withdrawal of crucial funding by its parent company in the USA, but Plimshot should still do what it can towards meeting the requirements, so as to comply with the requirement to take all reasonably practicable steps towards compliance: TULRCA, s. 188(7). For example, it should inform the EPATU officials immediately of the proposed redundancies, and consult with them in compliance with s. 188(2), although, given the circumstances, there is probably little that can be done to avoid the dismissal, or reduce the numbers affected, or mitigate the consequences. However, the union should be given information concerning the proposed method of carrying out the dismissals, the selection procedure, and the timing of them (the question might be, 'Why are 25 employees to be dismissed in the first week, with the others to be dismissed three weeks later?'), since it may be able to suggest ways to mitigate the effects of the redundancies. The question of whether Plimshot has sought or will seek financial assistance from elsewhere would also arise.

As to the sudden financial crisis, this may be sufficient to constitute 'special circumstances'. In *Clark's of Hove* v *Bakers' Union* [1978] ICR 1076, CA, the employer dismissed nearly all of the 380 employees and ceased trading on the same day owing to financial difficulties over the last few months. Once the directors realized that alternative funding could not be secured, they immediately dismissed the employees. The Court of Appeal held (in considering predecessor legislation couched in similar terms to TULRCA, s. 188) that, on the facts, the circumstances here were not special (insolvency, per se, is not a special circumstance) but Geoffrey Lane LJ stated: 'if . . . sudden disaster strikes a company, making it necessary to close the concern, then plainly that would be a matter which was capable of being a special circumstance: and that is so whether the disaster is physical or financial'.

The EPATU, on behalf of affected employees, may apply to the employment tribunal for a protective award on the ground that the employer failed to comply with the consultation requirements, and a declaration to that effect: TULRCA, s. 189. The complaint must be presented either before the date of the last of the dismissals or within three months of that date (the tribunal has a discretion to extend that time limit where it considers that it was not reasonably practicable to present the complaint within the three-month period: s. 189(5)). Plimshot may raise the defence set out in TULRCA, s. 188(7), already discussed. A protective award is a monetary award made where the consultation requirements have not been complied with, and where the defence available is not accepted by the tribunal. It relates to the specified employees who have been or will be made redundant over the protected period, up to 90 days (the protected period is what the tribunal considers to be just and equitable, bearing in mind the seriousness of the employer's failure to comply: TULRCA, s. 189(4)(b)). Every employee to whom the protective award applies is entitled to a week's pay for the protected period, with no upper limit on the amount of a week's pay. If Plimshot fails to pay the award, the employee(s) affected may present a complaint to the employment tribunal within three months of the date of the failure to pay: TULRCA, s. 192(1).

In addition to the consultation requirements, Plimshot must notify the Department of Trade and Industry (DTI) in writing of the dismissals, at least 30 days before the first dismissal takes effect (where between 20 and 99 employees are to be made redundant); the period of notice is at least 90 days where 100 or more are to be made redundant: TULRCA, s. 193. The 'special circumstances' defence (discussed above) applies, in which case Plimshot must take such steps as are reasonably practicable in the circumstances: s. 193(7). Failure to comply may lead to conviction and a fine of up to level 5 on the standard scale in a magistrates' court (s. 194(1)), currently £5,000.

In addition to the collective consultation requirements, Plimshot should be aware of the possibility of unfair dismissal claims on the redundancy ground from qualifying employees, i.e. generally, those with one year's continuous employment: ERA, s. 108(1). However, given the circumstances, it is unlikely that these would succeed.

Plimshot must allow affected employees with the relevant qualifying period of continuous employment reasonable paid time off during working hours to look for other work, or to make arrangements for training for future employment, before the expiry of the notice period: ERA, s. 52(1). The qualifying period is two years of continuous employment by the date on which the notice of termination is due to expire, or the date by which the statutory notice period, had it been given, would have expired, whichever is the longer: ERA, s. 52(2). The maximum amount of pay in these circumstances is 40 per cent of a week's pay. Employees who are not allowed such time off, or who are not paid for the time taken off, may apply to an employment tribunal for the appropriate remuneration: ERA, s. 54(4).

Finally, Plimshot may go into insolvent liquidation before paying redundancy payments and the protective award (if made). Both of these payments (along with wages, accrued holiday pay, and payment for time off) constitute preferential debts under the Insolvency Act 1986, s. 386 and Sch. 6, so that any such payments (up to £800) payable in respect of the four-month period immediately preceding the insolvency of the employer are given precedence over other creditors' claims. In addition, where an employer is insolvent and has failed to pay, inter alia, a statutory redundancy payment, employees may apply to the Secretary of State for payment out of the National

Insurance Fund: ERA, ss. 166–7. The employee may also claim other guaranteed debts from the Secretary of State to be paid out of the National Insurance Fund, such as eight weeks' arrears of pay (which includes payment for time off to seek work when under a redundancy notice), subject to the statutory limit on a week's pay (ERA, ss. 182–9), which from 1 February, 2007 is £310.

Further reading

Collins, H., Ewing, K. D., and McColgan, A., *Labour Law: Text and Materials* (Oxford: Hart Publishing, 2002), ch. 8, pp. 859–68, ch. 10.

'Employee consultation: Part 1: collective consultation about mass redundancies' (2003) 704 IRLB 2–16.

Honeyball, S., and Bowers, J., *Textbook on Labour Law*, 8th edn (Oxford: Oxford University Press, 2006), ch. 9.

McDonald, K., 'Employee consultation: Part 1: collective consultation about mass redundancies' (2003) 768 *IRS Employment Law* 46–60.

Nickson, S., 'In practice' (2002) 98 *Employment Lawyer* 19.

Pitt, G., *Employment Law*, 6th edn (London: Sweet & Maxwell, 2007), chs 5 and 9.

Sandison, K., 'Redundancies: EAT rules on duty to consult' (2002) 32 (Jul/Aug) ELJ, 21–4.

Sargeant, M., *Employment Law*, 2nd edn (Harlow: Pearson, 2003), ch. 10.

Smith, I. T., and Thomas, G., *Industrial Law*, 8th edn (London: LexisNexis, 2003), ch. 8, section 3, ch. 9.

8

Discrimination

Introduction

The original position of English law was that employers could reject job applicants, refuse to promote workers, and dismiss them for any reason whatsoever including discriminatory ones, without redress. By the middle of the twentieth century some of the discriminatory laws against women had been repealed. Laws forbidding racial discrimination came on to the statute book in the mid-1960s but current law dates from the mid-1970s. The Sex Discrimination Act 1975 and the Race Relations Act 1976, both as amended, the former particularly by EC law, for a long time were the sole statutes in this area but they were joined by the Disability Discrimination Act in 1995 (DDA), which has also been amended. Laws against discrimination on the grounds of sexual orientation, and religion or belief came into effect in late 2003. Question 1 looks at the effect of EC law on sexual discrimination law. Question 2 draws out the different law on disability discrimination. The third question involves both discrimination and equal pay, these being issues which are often set together. This chapter concentrates on sex, race, and disability. Equal pay itself forms a separate chapter in this book (Chapter 9). Age discrimination law came into effect in late 2006 and is mentioned where relevant.

At the beginning it is worth stating that laws on sexual and racial discrimination tend to be very similar and in general they should be construed alike. They both cover direct and indirect discrimination, though for the moment the definition is different in relation to indirect discrimination on grounds of colour and nationality, and victimization, though racial discrimination also covers segregation. Both have exceptions, 'genuine occupational qualifications', though the list is shorter in respect of racial discrimination than sexual discrimination. Note also that discrimination on the ground of race or ethnic or national origins also has 'genuine occupational requirement' as exceptions to the anti-discrimination principle.

Disability discrimination is somewhat different. Unlike in racial and sexual discrimination, disability-related discrimination may be justified by the employers. However, direct discrimination cannot be justified: s. 3A(4) of the DDA: there is no law of indirect disability discrimination but there is a law of 'reasonable adjustment', which is the functional equivalent of indirect discrimination. Employers no longer have a defence of justification to this type of disability discrimination.

The authors recommend ending answers to problem questions with something on remedies, where marks are often easily scored (and students often miss out this topic). Students should be able to outline compensation, recommendations, and declarations. The tip is: learn a paragraph or two on remedies for discrimination which can be used in just about any context!

Question 1

Consider the effect EC law has had on sexual discrimination law.

Commentary

This question is of the textbook style; if you know your law, you should be able to answer this question and gain a decent mark. You need to structure your answer carefully. It is suggested that subheadings may be helpful to guide the examiner through your answer. The question is drafted to exclude race discrimination and equal pay but one or two comparisons would be helpful — and may score marks!

Answer plan

- The definition of 'sex' to include transsexuals (but not homosexuals)
- Switching of the burden of proof
- Definition of indirect discrimination (now in its third formulation)
- Free-standing right not to be sexually harassed
- Justification for indirect discrimination
- Pregnancy as direct discrimination
- Removal of the financial limit on compensation for sex discrimination

Suggested answer

The Sex Discrimination Act 1975 (SDA) was drafted not in reliance on EC law, the Equal Treatment Directive 76/207 (ETD), but using United States law as a template. The then Home Secretary, the late Roy Jenkins, was persuaded to have the statute drafted to cover both disparate treatment (direct discrimination) and disparate impact (indirect discrimination) rather than just having it cover the former in order to root out what may be called hidden discrimination. The UK joined the EEC, as it then was, in 1973 and for several years, it can be argued, UK law was in advance of EC law. In particular, in the context of equal pay the ECJ extended the concept of indirect discrimination to EC law in *Jenkins* v *Kingsgate (Clothing Productions) Ltd* [1981] 1 WLR 972. Nowadays EC law is likely to be in advance of UK law.

'Sex'

The English statute was originally restricted to 'biological' men and women: *White* v *British Sugar Corp* [1977] IRLR 121, IT. The ECJ, however, in *P* v *S* [1996] IRLR 346 held that it was sexually discriminatory to dismiss a transsexual who was undergoing gender reassignment. This decision was applied by the EAT in *Chessington World of Adventures* v *Reid* [1997] IRLR 556, which construed the SDA in conformity with the ETD. The SDA was itself amended by the Sex Discrimination (Gender Reassignment) Regulations 1999 (SI 1999/1102). What has not occurred, however, is the extension either of the ETD or the SDA to homosexuals: see *Grant* v *South-West Trains* [1998] ICR 449 (on equal pay) and the 'gays in the military' cases, which were withdrawn from the ECJ and put before the European Court of Human Rights. The reasoning of the ECJ was that there had to be a comparison between male homosexuals and female ones and since both were treated in the same way, there was no discrimination. The Directive on the equal treatment in employment 2000/78 extends protection to homosexuals from December 2003 with various exceptions including genuine occupational requirements: the Employment Equality (Sexual Orientation) Regulations 2003 (SI 2003/1661) transpose this part of the Directive.

Burden of proof and definition of indirect discrimination

The EC Directive 97/80, often called the Burden of Proof Directive, came into force in the UK in October 2001. The enacting instrument was the Sex Discrimination (Indirect Discrimination and Burden of Proof) Regulations 2001 (SI 2001/2660). These Regulations amended the definition of indirect sex (but not race) discrimination. In respect of the burden of proof there was not much change. English law placed the burden of proving justification on employers already. No change to the burden of proof as to justification was made by the Employment Equality (Sex Discrimination) Regulations 2005 (SI 2005/2467) transposing the Equal Treatment Amendment Directive 2002/73. The so-called Race Directive 2000/43/EC was transposed into English law by the Race Relations Act 1976 (Amendment) Regulations 2003 (SI 2003/1626). The Regulations amended the burden of proof and the definition of indirect discrimination but only for matters covered by the Directive: race and ethnic or national origin. Therefore, the old definitions continue to apply to discrimination on grounds of colour and nationality, a complex and unnecessary law.

The 2001 Regulations also amended the definition of indirect discrimination. For there to be such discrimination, before 2001 there had to be a requirement or condition with which fewer women than men could comply, which was to the applicant's detriment and which the employers could not justify. One difficulty was the high hurdle of 'requirement or condition'. A well known example is *Price* v *Civil Service Commission* [1977] 1 WLR 1417. The Civil Service refused a woman of 35 a job because for that job there was an age limit of 17 to 28. Although women between those ages could physically apply, they may in practice have been prevented from doing so by giving birth and rearing children. It was held that the age bar was a requirement or condition and therefore potentially the applicant had a claim. If the employers had expressed the ages as a preference, that would not have been a requirement or condition and the applicant would not have had a sex discrimination claim. An example from the cases is *Falkirk Council* v *Whyte* [1997] IRLR 560, EAT sitting in Scotland. The employers stated that one of the desirable qualities for applicants for a certain post was to have supervisory experience. In England the Court of Appeal in *Perera* v *Civil Service Commission (No. 2)* [1983] ICR 428 stated that 'requirement or condition' meant a 'must'; a qualification for the job, here being a barrister or solicitor, was a 'must', a requirement, but being able to communicate well in English was only a desirable quality and therefore not a 'requirement or condition'. If the applicant was turned down for that reason, she or he had no claim. In fact, the EAT in *Falkirk* held that 'requirement' had to be read broadly to include desirable qualities in order to comply with EC law, which was at odds with cases like *Price*. The law on indirect racial (but not nationality or colour) discrimination is as a result of the 2001 Regulations in line with *Falkirk*. What is now needed is a 'provision, criterion or practice', a reduced hurdle for applicants. If a desirable quality constitutes a 'practice', there is the possibility of a case. The law of sexual indirect discrimination was brought into line with that of racial discrimination by the EE(SD) Regs 2005 implementing the Equal Treatment Amendment Directive 2002/73 with effect from 1 October 2005. There has to be a provision, criterion, or practice '(i) which puts or would put women at a particular disadvantage when compared with men; (ii) which puts her at a disadvantage; and (iii) which he cannot show to be a proportionate . . . means of achieving a legitimate aim.'

Harassment

The SDA did not originally refer to sexual harassment. However, *Porcelli* v *Strathclyde RC* [1986] ICR 564, Court of Session, held that harassment is direct discrimination because a man would not treat another man in the way that he treated the woman. However, in *Mac Donald* v *Advocate General for Scotland* [2003] UKHL 33 it was held that *Porcelli* went too far. The fact that the harassment was sexually based did not mean that there was direct discrimination. The reason for the harassment must be the sex of the victim: unpleasant treatment of a woman is not itself sexual harassment, though it is evidence of it. The EC has become increasingly interested in harassment. As a result of the study by Michael Rubenstein, *The Dignity of Women at Work* (1987), the Commission issued a Recommendation in 1991 and a Code of Practice in 1992. In the Recommendation it defined harassment as 'unwanted conduct of a sexual nature or other conduct based on sex affecting the dignity of men and women at work, including conduct of superiors and colleagues'. The EAT in *Wadman* v *Carpenter Farrar Partnership* [1973] IRLR 374 said that employment tribunals should use this definition. The Equal Pay Amendment Directive was transposed into English law in late 2005. It brings the law of sexual harassment into line with racial harassment law which was redefined as 'unwanted conduct which has the purpose or effect of (a) violating [a worker's] dignity or (b) creating an intimidating, hostile, degrading or offensive environment...' by the 2003 Regulations, which inserted s. 3A(1) into the Race Relations Act 1976 to comply with the 2000 'Race' Directive. However, as noted above, these Regulations apply only to race and national or ethic origins and not to colour and nationality in respect of which the 1976 definition continues to apply. The EE(SD) Regs 2005 came into force on 1 October 2005. We have now to distinguish between harassment 'on ground of sex' and harassment 'of a sexual nature'.

Justification

The width of the employers' defence in English law has varied across the years. For employees the nadir was reached in the judgment of Eveleigh LJ in *Ojutiku* v *MSC* [1982] ICR 661, CA: '—acceptable to right-thinking people as sound and tolerable reasons'. The ECJ's higher standard, set in *Bilka-Kaufhaus GmbH* v *Weber von Hartz* [1986] ECR 1607, is that there must be a real need for the difference, the practice must be appropriate to fill that need, and the practice must be necessary to achieve that end. The ECJ has held that generalizations are insufficient to constitute a justification: *R* v *Secretary of State for Employment ex parte Seymour-Smith* [1999] IRLR 253 (government contended that the then two-year qualifying period for unfair dismissal encouraged recruitment, but no facts and figures were deployed to support that assertion). The ECJ does give states more margin of appreciation than it gives to non-state organizations but the standard is higher than that in *Ojutiku*. The 2005 Regulations define justification as 'a proportionate...means of achieving a legitimate aim', a phrase that is becoming common across discrimination law.

Pregnancy

The SDA, s. 5(3) states: 'A comparison in the cases of persons of different sex or marital status under s. 1(1)...must be such that the relevant circumstances in the one case are the same, or not materially different, in the other'. Originally when applying s. 5(3) it was held that discrimination against pregnant women was not sex discrimination because there were no similarly situated men (*Turley* v *Allders Department Stores Ltd* [1980] ICR 66, EAT): men could not become pregnant. The EAT later, however, held in *Hayes* v *Malleable WMC* [1985] ICR 703 that a pregnant woman could be compared with an ill man. This decision was the subject of trenchant criticism; pregnancy is not an illness and unlike illness it may be planned. Finally the House of Lords referred the issue to the ECJ, which ruled in *Webb* v *EMO Air Cargo (UK) Ltd* [1994] ECR I-3537 that discrimination on the ground of pregnancy *was* discrimination per se. There was no need for a male comparator. Section 5(3) was disapplied to that extent. The law was settled by the EE(SD) Regs 2005: discrimination on the ground of pregnancy *is* sex discrimination. The government stressed that this change was solely 'for the purposes of legal clarity', and no change in the width of the law was intended. Note also the Pregnant Workers Directive 92/85 and *Brown* v *Rentokil Ltd* [1998] ECR I-4185, ECJ: dismissal on the ground of pregnancy/childbirth up to the end of maternity leave is discrimination; after the end of that leave a woman suffering a pregnancy/childbirth-related illness is to be compared with a sick man.

Remedies

The ECJ ruled in *Marshall* v *Southampton and South West Hampshire AHA (No. 2)* [1993] ICR 893 that the financial cap on awards for sex discrimination and the lack of interest on awards were in breach of the EC law principles that national measures implementing EC law must be sufficiently powerful and effective to achieve the objective of that law and any loss must be recompensed in full. English law was amended by the Sex Discrimination and Equal Pay (Remedies) Regulations 1993 (SI 1993/2798) to comply with EC law. In turn the maximum limit on race discrimination awards was lifted by the Race Relations (Remedies) Act 1994.

In conclusion it may be seen that over the years EC law has led to many changes to the SDA itself and to the case law implementation of the Act.

Question 2

Nigel is the supervisor of area reps for Bigco plc. His job is to go round all the reps every month and check on their performance. While he was on holiday abroad he caught a rare disease, which made him blind in one eye and only partially sighted in the other. As a result he cannot drive out to all the reps, many of whom work miles away from public transport. Bigco dismisses him for incapacity in that he cannot perform his job.

Oliver, who is one of the security guards at Bigco's main offices, has been living as a woman for several years. He has recently undergone gender reassignment surgery. Bigco dismissed Oliver, who now calls herself Olivia, because neither the male nor the female employees wish to share the lavatories with her.

Prue, who is aged 48, applies for a job as receptionist with Bigco. The application is rejected because she was not a school-leaver, as was stated in the job advert.

Advise Bigco as to its liability for disability and sex discrimination.

 Commentary

This is a three-part question and unless the candidate can attempt all three parts he or she is likely to fail. The tip is: it is much easier scoring marks at the bottom of the mark range than it is near the top. Therefore, it is much easier to score three forties and pass than it is to score two sixties (on the assumption that each part of the question is worth equal marks). If you cannot answer any one of the parts, do a different question! Some examiners put the amount of marks next to each part: if so, spend approximately the proportionate amount of time on each part. For example, if the Oliver/Olivia part is worth 20 per cent of the marks, spend about one-fifth of your time dealing with that part. Because there is not much law on gender reassignment, less time needs to be spent on that topic than on disability discrimination.

As always, read the rubric. There is a possibility of other claims but the question is restricted to discrimination. Any mention of, for example, unfair dismissal is a waste of time, does not score marks, and creates a poor impression.

 ## Answer plan

- Nigel
  - Disability discrimination: physical or mental impairment, substantial and long-term adverse effect, ability to carry out normal day-to-day activities
  - Defining and applying the law
  - Less favourable treatment
  - Possible justification of direct disability discrimination provided that the justificatory reason is material and substantial
  - Failure to make reasonable adjustments as disability discrimination, the adjustment must be reasonable, the examples in the Act of reasonable adjustments
  - Forum, time limit and remedies
  - The former exception, repealed in 2004, of employers who employ fewer than 15 workers
- Oliver/Olivia
  - The Equal Treatment Directive and transsexuals
  - Sex Discrimination (Gender Reassignment) Regulations 1999
  - Vicarious liability, time limit, remedies
- Prue
  - Age discrimination is according to the question not required
  - Sex discrimination: effect of the 2001 Regulations, detriment, justification, remedies

Suggested answer

Nigel

Nigel may well be disabled within the meaning of s. 1(1) of the Disability Discrimination Act 1995 (DDA). Does he have a 'physical or mental impairment which has a substantial and long-term adverse effect on his ability to carry out normal day-to-day activities'? Partial sightedness is undoubtedly a physical impairment on the present facts. It has a 'substantial' effect: 'substantial' means simply 'more than minor' or 'more than trivial': *Goodwin* v *Patent Office* [1999] ICR 302, EAT, and since Nigel can no longer drive, his lack of sight is of substantial effect. The effect is long term, which is defined as lasting more than a year or reasonably likely to last for more than a year or if the claimant is likely to die within that period, the rest of his or her life. The effect is certainly adverse because Nigel can no longer drive. By Sch. 1 a disability does affect day-to-day activities if it affects inter alia eyesight, as here. 'Day-to-day' means the activities which the claimant does outside work (*Goodwin*), e.g. in one case putting rollers into her hair, but things done at work cannot be excluded if they are part of normal day-to-day activities out of work, as driving is: *Law Hospital NHS Trust* v *Rush* [2001] IRLR 611, Court of Session. Here Nigel's day-to-day activities are affected. The employment tribunal would no doubt hold Nigel to be disabled. None of the exceptions such as alcohol addiction, hay fever, kleptomania and pyromania found in the Disability Discrimination (Meaning of Disability) Regulations 1996 (SI 1996/1455) applies. It should be noted that the decision as to whether an applicant is disabled within the meaning of the statute is for the tribunal, not for the medical staff who give evidence: *Abadeh* v *British Telecommunications plc* [2001] ICR 156, EAT.

Since Nigel is disabled, the question becomes one of seeing whether he has been treated less favourably than others to whom the reason does not apply and whether the employers can justify that treatment. Bigco would not have sacked others since the others would not have been partially sighted (see *Clark* v *Novacold Ltd* [1999] ICR 951, CA) (to be precise there is no 'like for like' comparison as there is in the Sex Discrimination Act 1975 and the Race Relations Act 1976 but rather the dismissed worker is compared with a worker who has not been dismissed, not with a non-disabled worker who has not been dismissed) and he has been dismissed on the ground of his disability. Bigco has dismissed him, which by the DDA is a form of unfavourable treatment. Unlike in the law of sexual and racial discrimination, direct discrimination, which is the form of discrimination which occurs when the employers treat a worker less favourably than they treat or would treat another, in the law of direct disability discrimination can be justified (DDA, (s. 3A(5))) but disability-related discrimination may be justified: s. 3A(1), (3). Differential treatment is justified only if in the circumstances of the particular case the justification is material and substantial. 'Substantial' bears the same meaning as it does in s. 1(1), DDA, 'more than minor', a much criticized low hurdle for the employers to surmount. The circumstances which are relevant ('material') are those which pertain to both the worker and the employers: *Baynton* v *Saurus General Engineers Ltd* [2000] IRLR 375, EAT. A somewhat similar recent case is *Jones* v *Post Office* [2001] IRLR 384, CA. The applicant was a mail delivery driver. When he had a heart attack as a result of diabetes, he was, following standard policy, taken off driving duties. The court held that where there was medical evidence and a properly conducted risk assessment, the tribunal should not substitute its own decision for that of the employers if the reason for the dismissal is material and substantial. Applying this authority, the tribunal in the present case would find the dismissal justified.

That does not complete the question on Nigel, for there is another form of discrimination, the failure to make reasonable adjustments to amend physical features or other arrangements (DDA, s. 4A, as renumbered by the Disability Discrimination Act 1995 (Amendment) Regulations 2003 (SI 2003/1673) with effect from October 2004). This failure must be one which places the disabled person at a substantial disadvantage in comparison with non-disabled workers. It is for the employers to adjust, not for the disabled worker to suggest means of accommodating his or her disablement. The adjustment must be reasonable and in that equation matters such as cost, practicability, and whether any adjustment could avert the adverse effect are important, and the Act gives examples of adjustments such as reallocating duties, transferring to an existing job vacancy, modifying equipment, and providing supervision. Perhaps the employers could have moved Nigel to another job, which would have been a reasonable adjustment, though most of the other adjustments would not be possible for a blind person. The adjustment would also seem to be reasonable. If so, Bigco is in breach of the duty and therefore discriminates. It should be noted that indirect discrimination as exists in sex and race discrimination law does not form part of disability discrimination law.

If Nigel has a successful claim, he should apply to the employment tribunal within three months of the act, unless the tribunal finds it just and equitable to extend the limitation period (see s. 17A). If successful, the tribunal may award the normal discrimination remedies: declaration, recommendation, and compensation, which is awarded on the tort basis (DDA, s. 8(3)). The last includes compensation for injury to feelings. There is no maximum award.

One final matter: the Act used not to apply to those who employed fewer than 15 workers (this exemption was repealed in 2004).

Oliver/Olivia

Under the Equal Treatment Directive 1976 discrimination against a worker on the grounds of gender reassignment is discrimination of the ground of sex: *P* v *S* [1996] ICR 795, ECJ. The Sex Discrimination Act 1976 was consequently amended by the Sex Discrimination (Gender Reassignment) Regulations 1999 (SI 1999/1102). The effect of the amendment is to make direct discrimination against transsexuals unlawful. The revised statute applies to those who have undergone surgery under medical supervision, as here, and the complainant must have been treated by the employers less favourably than they treat or would treat another who has not undergone such surgery. The employers are vicariously liable in the usual employment law fashion: see *Tower Boot Co Ltd* v *Jones* [1997] ICR 254, CA, a race discrimination case.

The claim must be brought before the tribunal within three months of the last act of discrimination subject to the 'just and equitable' exception as above. The remedies are the same as in disability discrimination: see above. Similarly, there is no maximum amount of compensation which can be awarded.

Prue

Laws on age discrimination deriving from Council Directive 2000/78 establishing a general framework for equal treatment in employment and occupation did not apply in the UK until 2006. There is a Code of Practice, *Age Diversity in Employment,* issued by the Department for Education and Employment but it is not legally binding. The question explicitly refers only to discrimination on the grounds of disability and sex; therefore, discussion of age is not required. Prue's best route to a remedy is to argue that age discrimination can be indirect sex discrimination contrary to the 1976 statute. The first thing to do is to see why Prue was excluded from the job. Until the Act's definition was amended in 2001 by the Sex Discrimination (Indirect Discrimination and Burden of Proof) Regulations 1999 (SI 1999/2660), an age bar was a 'requirement or condition' (*Price* v *Civil Service Commission* [1977] 1 WLR 1417, EAT) because it was a 'must', an essential attribute: *Perera* v *Civil Service Commission (No. 2)* [1983] ICR 428, CA. The current definition is to be found in the Employment Equality (Sex Discrimination) Regulations 2005, SI 2005/2467, amending the SDA. In the amended Act there is even less doubt that the bar is a provision, criterion, or practice. Moving to the second element in indirect discrimination, we can argue that fewer women than men can comply with the policy or practice because in practice more women than men tend to be out of the labour market because they are having or rearing children. Statistical evidence would be helpful to the applicant's case. The third element is detriment. The policy is to Prue's detriment because she cannot get the job. The onus of proving the policy, the pool for comparison, and detriment lies on the claimant. The burden of proof then switches to Bigco; unless it can prove that the policy is justified, it loses. This test of justification, which was laid down in *Weber von Hartz* v *Bilka-Kaufhaus* [1986] ECR 1607, ECJ, is much higher than the test for justification in disability discrimination (see above) and demands: the means must serve a business need, they must be appropriate to satisfy that need, and they must be necessary to achieve the fulfilment of that need. It is suggested that Bigco will not be able to justify restricting access to the job of receptionist to school leavers, though the company may try to argue that 'one cannot teach an old dog new tricks'.

In the event that Prue can show indirect sex discrimination, her remedy lies in the employment tribunal, to which she must apply in the usual way for discrimination cases (see above) and she will receive the normal discrimination remedy or remedies (see above too). Compensation for unintentional indirect sex (but not race) discrimination was permitted by the Sex Discrimination and Equal Pay (Miscellaneous Amendments) Regulations 1996 (SI 1996/438), repealing s. 66(3) of the 1975 Act, which tribunals had held to be inconsistent with the Equal Treatment Directive. As with all discrimination statutes there is no financial limit to the award of compensation: Sex Discrimination and Equal Pay (Remedies) Regulations 1993 (SI 1993/2798).

In conclusion it is suggested that all three will be able successfully to claim that they have been discriminated against by Bigco but for varying reasons.

Question 3

Doris is employed full-time as a welder at Bloggs Ltd, a ship-repairing firm which has its dry dock in Newcastle. She works a 40-hour week and receives reduced price meals in the staff canteen. She earns £21,000 per year. Colin is employed by Bloggs Ltd as a full-time occupational nurse at the same dry dock. He earns £18,000 per year. He does not receive subsidized meals but is part of the pension scheme, is provided with a car, and has part of his mortgage costs paid for by the company. Colin claims equal pay with Doris.

George, who is blind, is employed by the firm as a telephonist. The company has recently updated its phone equipment and has as a consequence dismissed George. He wishes to bring a claim for disability discrimination.

Hussain is a Muslim who works for Bloggs Ltd. He is called a 'black bastard' by his supervisor, Amy. He claims that he has been discriminated against on the ground of race.

Advise Bloggs Ltd.

Commentary

Part questions on equal pay and discrimination are often set together. The question does not look difficult and can be answered by any student quite swiftly. Candidates should always remember that they should write something about remedies: the remedy in the first section, that on equal pay, is obvious but candidates often miss out on remedies for discrimination.

It is also worth remembering the main differences between disability and race/sex discrimination. Disability-related discrimination can be justified (but direct discrimination can no longer be justified), whereas it cannot be for the other types; there is no law of indirect discrimination in respect of disability whereas there is for the other two; but in disability there is a duty of reasonable adjustment, which does not exist for race/sex discrimination; positive discrimination is encouraged in respect of disabilities but except for narrow exceptions not for race/sex discrimination; and usually there is a need for a comparator in race/sex cases but not for disability ones (see *Clark* v *Novacold Ltd* [1999] ICR 951, CA). Note also the differences between race and sex discrimination: compensation is not payable for indirect racial discrimination but is for indirect sexual discrimination; since the amendment in the Sex Discrimination (Indirect Discrimination and Burden of Proof) Regulations 2001 (SI 2001/2660) in force October 2001 (and see the Employment Equality (Sex Discrimination) Regulations 2005 (SI 2005/2467), further amending the SDA), there no longer is a need for a 'requirement or condition' in sex discrimination (a practice or policy suffices), whereas the established law remains for race discrimination on the grounds of colour or nationality, but discrimination on grounds of colour and ethnic or national origins is covered by the amended RRA which adopts the revised SDA definition of indirect discrimination; and there is the strange difference in respect of what might be called 'transferred discrimination': if the employers dismiss the worker, a white one, for refusing an instruction not to admit blacks to a slot machine arcade, they are liable for racial discrimination (*Showboat Entertainment Centre Ltd* v *Owens* [1984] 1 WLR 384, EAT, which the Court of Appeal approved in *Wethers field Ltd* v *Sargent* [1999] ICR 425, because the dismissal is 'on racial grounds' with in s. 1(1)(a) of the Race Relations Act 1976; however, if a woman were dismissed for refusing to obey an instruction to ban men, the employers would not be liable for sex discrimination because the discrimination would not be 'on the ground of her sex' within s. 1(1)(a) of the Sex Discrimination Act 1975. The *Showboat* line of authority came under criticism at the employment tribunal stage in *Redfearn* v *Serco Ltd* [2005] IRLR 744 but the Employment Appeal Tribunal under Burton J (P) strongly upheld it.

Answer plan

- Colin
  - Equal pay: female comparator, modes of claiming ('like work', work rated as equivalent, equal value), when to raise defence, employment tribunal or independent expert?, each contractual term analysed, justifications, remedy (the 'equality' clause), claim in time
- George
  - Disability discrimination: less favourable treatment, definition of disability, duty of reasonable adjustment, defence of justification, remedies
- Hussain
  - Racial discrimination: religion and race ('ethnic origins'), indirect discrimination and the defence of justification, 'but for' causation, actual and hypothetical comparators, racial harassment, detriment, vicarious liability and the employers' defence, remedies. Note that the question does *not* invite a discussion of religious discrimination

Suggested answer

Colin

Colin is claiming equal pay. His comparator is Doris, a woman, as the legislation demands, though the choice of female is his: *Ainsworth* v *Glass Tubes Ltd* [1977] ICR 757. He is not doing the same or broadly similar work as she is doing ('like work' within s. 1(2)(a) of the Equal Pay Act 1970), and there does not seem to be any job evaluation survey (s. 1(2)(b)). Therefore, his sole mode of achieving equal pay is through an equal value claim: s. 1(2)(c), Equal Pay Act 1970 (EqPA) as inserted by the Equal Pay (Amendment) Regulations 1983 (SI 1983/1794), the result of the UK government's being taken before the European Court of Justice by the Commission.

The Act provides that work is of equal value if the applicant's work is 'in terms of the demands made on [him] (for instance, under such headings as effort, skill and decision) of equal value to that of a [woman] in the same employment'. If the tribunal considers that there are no reasonable grounds for concluding that the work is of equal value, the claim will fail at that stage. A material factor defence must normally be raised at this juncture: Employment Tribunals (Constitution and Rules of Procedure) (Amendment) Regulations 1994 (SI 1994/536). If the case proceeds, the tribunal may either refer it to an independent expert drawn from a list kept by ACAS or (since the Sex Discrimination and Equal Pay (Miscellaneous Amendments) Regulations 1996 (SI 1996/438)) determine the case itself. If a report is prepared by an expert, that report is not binding on the tribunal: *Tennants Textile Colours Ltd* v *Todd* [1989] IRLR 3. The parties may use their own expert. The tribunals use a 'broad brush' approach to determining equal value and may find work to be such even though the two types are not precisely equally ranked under the headings found in s. 1(2)(c), EqPA. An equal value claim cannot be stopped if there are possible male comparators engaged on like work or work rated as equivalent: *Pickstone* v *Freemans plc* [1989] AC 66, HL, and therefore the potential for the 'token male' defence has been squashed.

A famous example of a successful equal value claim is *Hayward* v *Cammell Laird Ltd* [1988] AC 894, HL, where a female canteen worker won equal pay with male joiners, painters, and thermal insulation engineers at a shipbuilding company, facts somewhat similar to the present ones. The Lords were of the opinion that each term has to be considered, not the overall job package. Therefore, it is irrelevant that Colin has a better pay package—pension, mortgage, car—than does his female comparator. This approach was also adopted by the ECJ in *Barber* v *Guardian Royal Exchange Assurance Group* [1991] 1 QB 344.

If there is equal value, employers have a possible defence if they prove that the difference in pay was 'genuinely due to a material factor which is not the difference of sex' (s. 1(3), EqPA). Among the potential justifications are longer service, higher output, different location (such as London weighting), and better qualifications (*NAAFI* v *Varley* [1977] 1 WLR 1490, red-circling (*Snoxell* v *Vauxhall Motors Ltd* [1978] QB 11), and preserving the wages of newcomers (*Rainey* v *Greater Glasgow Health Board* [1987] AC 224, HL). Checks would have to be made to see whether any of these exceptions applied on the facts: some certainly do not, e.g. the parties work at the same location.

If the claim is successful, an 'equality clause' is inserted into Colin's contract: s. 1(1), EqPA. His less favourable term on pay is revised upwards to make it no less favourable than Doris's. In turn Doris could bring an equal pay claim to make the terms in her contract which are less favourable than those in Colin's contract equal. By s. 2(4), EqPA the claim must be brought within six months of leaving work (however, cf. *Preston* v *Wolverhampton Healthcare NHS Trust* [2001] 2 AC 415, ECJ). The remedy is damages or back pay previously limited to two years (s. 2(5)) unless there has been deceit by the employers: *Levez* v *Jennings (Harlow Pools) Ltd* [1999] ICR 33, ECJ. When that case returned to the EAT, the limit was disapplied as being contrary to EC law found in Art.

141, ex Art. 119, of the EC Treaty. The time limit is now six years except when the employers deliberately concealed the relevant information or when the worker could not be reasonably expected to have brought a claim, in which event there is no limit: Equal Pay Act (Amendment) Regulations 2003 (SI 2003/1656).

George

This employee has been dismissed and seeks a remedy for disability discrimination. That form of discrimination comes under the Disability Discrimination Act 1995 (DDA) and is prohibited when the employers treat disabled staff less favourably than others on the ground that the worker is disabled. Disability is defined in the statute as physical or mental impairment which has a substantial and long-term impact on the claimant's ability to perform normal day-to-day activities (DDA, s. 1). 'Substantial' simply means 'not minor'; 'long-term' means lasting for 12 months or more (or for the remainder of the worker's life, if less than 12 months); and day-to-day activities include memory, dexterity, and mobility. Also included are those workers who suffered a relevant disability in the past. To come to the facts, blindness is a physical disability, George is personally affected in his day-to-day activities, and the problem is a long-term one—indeed, it looks permanent. There is impairment, here of sight, one of the disabilities on the list, and it has a substantial effect on George's day-to-day activities by definition. It can therefore be said that George is disabled. Was he treated less favourably? It may be that the firm could have found him another job or otherwise treated him better than it did. If the definition is satisfied, the company is liable for disability discrimination.

Employers are also under a duty to make reasonable adjustments to the workplace (DDA, s. 4A) when the disabled are at a substantial disadvantage in comparison with non-disabled workers. 'Substantial' again means 'not minor'; whether the adjustment would be reasonable depends on matters such as cost and the employers' finances. The Act provides a non-exhaustive list of reasonable adjustments such as modifying equipment and reallocating work duties. Failure to make such adjustments is discrimination: DDA, s. 4A, read together with s. 3A(2) and (6).

To disability discrimination on the ground of failure to make reasonable adjustments there is a defence of justification. The burden of proof is on the employers: DDA, s. 5(1)(b). Paragraph 4(6) of the Code of Practice issued by the Disability Rights Commission, which tribunals have to take into account, states that justification is available only when the reason for the discrimination relates to the individual worker and the reason is not trivial. It has to be said that this test is not a difficult one for employers to satisfy. One way of persuading the tribunal that the employers have the defence is to have conducted a risk assessment, taking into account the medical evidence: see *Jones v Post Office* [2001] IRLR 384, CA.

If George is successful, the tribunal may award compensation, which is not financially limited and could be substantial, make a declaration, and make a recommendation. These remedies are the same as in sex and race disability.

Hussain

It should be said first that the question is restricted to race discrimination and does not apply to religious discrimination, the law on which came into force in December 2003. The Race Relations Act 1976 (RRA) does not expressly apply to religions, such as Islam here. However, if the activating cause is 'colour, race, nationality, or ethnic or national origins' (s. 3(1)), discrimination is covered. See *Seide* v *Gillette Industries Ltd* [1980] IRLR 427, EAT for Jews and *Mandla* v *Dowell Lee* [1983] 2 AC 548, HL for Sikhs. There are conflicting decisions whether Muslims are covered by the famous definition of 'ethnic origins' found in the speech of Lord Fraser in *Mandla*: a long shared history, a cultural tradition, plus other relevant factors such as a shared geographical origin, a common language, a common religion, and a common literature. In any event the discrimination on the facts seems to arise from colour ('black') and possibly from race or even nationality or national origins (e.g. Hussain may hail from Bangladesh).

The RRA prohibits direct and indirect discrimination and the defence of justification applies only to the indirect variety as in sex discrimination but unlike disability-related discrimination. On the facts the disparate treatment is because of Hussain's colour (etc.). It is therefore on the ground of race within RRA, s. 3(1). But for his race he would not have been so treated: see, for example, the non-employment case of *James* v *Eastleigh BC* [1990] 2 AC 751, HL. Accordingly, the employer seems to have treated him less favourably than it treats or would treat (hypothetical comparisons are possible, unlike in equal pay claims) a white person and has thereby discriminated against him. The supervisor would not, it is thought, use similar language to a white person. This conclusion is subject to what is sometimes known as the 'bastard' defence, which enquires whether Amy behaved similarly to all workers.

The term 'harassment' did not appear in the Act as originally drafted but it became accepted that racial harassment is direct discrimination provided it is on the grounds of the victim's race: see *MacDonald* v *Lord Advocate for Scotland* [2003] UKHL 33 on sexual harassment. For a campaign of racial harassment see *Tower Boot Co Ltd* v *Jones* [1997] ICR 254, CA. One act of harassment is sufficient: *Bracebridge Engineering Ltd* v *Derby* [1990] IRLR 3, EAT.

Employers are under a duty not to discriminate in employment (RRA, s. 4(2) or by dismissing (s. 4(2) also). The former covers putting someone at a disadvantage. A racial insult is capable of being a detriment: *de Souza* v *Automobile Association* [1986] ICR 514, CA.

If the supervisor discriminates, the employer is vicariously liable (RRA, s. 32) subject to a defence. *Tower Boot* shows that the tortious principle of vicarious liability does not apply in discrimination law; instead the tribunal should apply ordinary language to see whether Amy's conduct was done in the course of employment. As Waite LJ put it in *Tower Boot,* if the tort test were the one to be applied, 'the more heinous the act of discrimination, the less likely it will be that the employers would be liable'. Indeed, whichever test is applied, the narrower tort one or the wider discrimination one, Amy did speak in the course of employment—at work, and it was done by a supervisor to a lower ranked worker. The employer has a defence (RRA, s. 32(3)) if it can prove that it took 'reasonably practicable' steps to prevent a co-worker doing the discriminatory act. The employer's knowledge of the act is irrelevant. A policy of investigating all racial complaints is one way of showing that the employer took such steps. A case law illustration is *Marks & Spencer plc v Martins* [1998] ICR 1005, CA, where the firm had an equal opportunities policy, complied with the Commission for Racial Equality's Code of Practice on selection procedures, and included in the interview panel someone with an interest in recruiting from the ethnic minorities. The court held that the employer was not vicariously liable.

If Hussain succeeds, the normal discrimination remedies are available. The tribunal may make a declaration that he has been unlawfully discriminated against, may make a recommendation as to the employer's future conduct (not an order: *Ministry of Defence v Jeremiah* [1980] ICR 87, CA), and may award compensation, which is assessed using tort principles (*Ministry of Defence v Cannock* [1984] ICR 918) and covers loss of earnings and compensation for injured feelings. There is no cap on the award. The latter is often the largest part of the award, and the minimum for injured feelings is around £750. Compensation for psychiatric harm may be included: *Sheriff v Klyne Tugs (Lowestoft) Ltd* [1999] ICR 1170, CA. Aggravated damages may be awarded as part of injury to feelings. They are available when the employers have acted maliciously or oppressively or the employee has been humiliated or distressed. Exemplary damages are not awardable: *Deane v LB of Ealing* [1993] ICR 329, EAT. Compensation in race cases has been creeping up over time, though the median was £6,640 according to the latest (2005–06) *Annual Report* of the Employment Tribunals Service.

Question 4

Discuss the exceptions to the principle of equal treatment on the ground of age found in the Employment Equality (Age) Regulations 2006 (SI 2006/1031).

 Commentary

The Age Regulations, which purport to transpose the Framework Equality Directive 2000/78, came into force on 1 October 2006. They apply to workers (and not just employees), there is no qualifying period and no upper limit to compensation, and they apply to workers of all ages. The Regulations apply not just to actual age but also to perceived age. They are, however, notable for the width of the exceptions, one of which is already being challenged.

Answer plan

- Direct discrimination may be justified by the employers
- 'Genuine and determining occupational requirement'
- Retirement (the emphasis is on discrimination but other areas of law, unfair dismissal and redundancy payments, have to be considered)
- Recruitment
- The national minimum wage
- Redundancy payments and the basic award
- Long-service entitlements
- Pensions

Suggested answer

Introduction

The Employment Equality (Age) Regulations 2006 to some extent follow the accepted method of dealing with discrimination in the workplace. There are provisions on direct discrimination, indirect discrimination, victimisation, harassment, the burden of proof and remedies that are largely common across the six 'strands' of Anglo-Welsh discrimination law. The provisions apply before, during and after employment. However, what sets discrimination on the ground of age apart is the number and width of the exceptions to age equality, in particular the fact that direct (and not just indirect) age discrimination may be justified.

Direct discrimination

It had come to be almost axiomatic that direct discrimination cannot be justified. For example, if employers treat a female worker worse than a male one on the ground of sex or a black worker worse than a white one on the ground of race, there is sexual or racial discrimination respectively and the employers have no defence of justification. However, direct age discrimination like disability-related discrimination may be justified by the employers. The definition of justification is laid down in the 2000 Directive: the discrimination must be 'objectively justified by a legitimate aim, and the means of achieving that aim [must be] appropriate and necessary' (Art. 2(2)(b), a formulation deriving from the ECJ decision in *Bilka-Kaufhaus* v *Weber von Hartz* [1986] ECR 1607). The transposition of the concept into English law is by the phrase 'a proportionate means of achieving a legitimate aim', which must of course be read in line with the Directive. The burden of proof is on the employers. There is a non-exhaustive list in the Regulations as to when direct discrimination is justified: for instance, it will be justifiable for the employers to stipulate that workers must serve a reasonable period before retirement or to fix a maximum age of recruitment when workers must undergo a good deal of training.

'GOR'

The 2006 Regulations also provide an exception when 'possessing a characteristic relating to age' is a genuine and determining occupational requirement. Perhaps the most obvious example is modelling. Acting is sometimes thought to be another example but since by definition actors act, it is difficult to see why an actor playing say a young boy must actually be young.

Retirement

Regulation 30 states that a retirement at 65 or above that age is neither age discrimination nor unfair dismissal provided that the employers comply with s. 98Z of the Employment Rights Act 1996 (ERA) as inserted by the 2006 Regulations. Before the enactment of s. 98Z employers could retire those aged 65, or those who were older than the employers' normal retiring age if higher than 65, without being subject to an unfair dismissal claim. Section 98Z provides for a 'default retirement age' of 65. If the worker retires at this age (or higher), provided that the employers comply with the statutory procedure contained in s. 98Z, the dismissal is not unfair. It should be noted that the statutory dismissal procedures do not apply to dismissal on retirement. The Government promises to review the default retirement age in 2011. To say the least, the English notion of the default retirement age is controversial in that it breaches the principle of non-discrimination on the ground of age and is at the time of writing being challenged by way of judicial review by Heyday, a branch of Age Concern.

Where the employers' normal retirement age is below 65, they have to justify that age objectively: reg. 3. The usual definition of objective justification, as noted above, and the usual burden of proof apply. If the employers cannot justify setting a retirement age below 65, the dismissal will not be treated as a dismissal through retirement: ERA s. 98ZE, as inserted by the 2006 Regulations.

If the dismissal takes place before the normal retirement age (or where there is no normal retirement age, the employee is dismissed before the age of 65), it is not by reason of retirement (s. 98ZC) and it will be deemed to be unfair because the employers have not proved a potentially fair reason to dismiss. In that event, the statutory dismissals procedure does apply and a failure on the part of the employers to comply with that process will lead to automatic unfair dismissal and the uplift of compensation (see the chapter on Unfair Dismissal).

In order to avoid both an age discrimination and an unfair dismissal claim employers must go through the procedure laid down in Sch. 6 to the 2006 Regulations. The employers must inform the employee in writing of the date of retirement between 12 and six months before the retirement date and must inform him or her of the right to request to continue in employment. If the employee wishes to continue in employment, he or she must inform the employers in writing of her decision between six and three months of retirement and the information must include whether he or she wishes to stay on indefinitely or for a certain fixed period. The employers must next arrange a meeting with the employee, who may be accompanied in the normal way. The employers must consider the request to work on and must give their decision as soon as is reasonably practicable, but there is no duty on them to provide reasons whatever they decide (cf. the so-called 'business' reasons for refusing a request for flexible working as found in s. 80G of the ERA). If this procedure is followed, the dismissal will not be unfair and there will be no breach of the age discrimination law.

Recruitment

There is an exception in respect of recruitment not just where the worker is over 65 but also where he or she is within six months of 65.

National minimum wage (NMW)

The NMW has three age bands (16–17, 18–21, and over 21) to which different levels of the NMW are accorded. By definition, therefore, the NMW is age-related. However, the Government has by reg. 31 granted an exception from the NMW in the 2006 Regulations.

Redundancy payments (RP) and the basic award

The Government has swept away the restriction on the lower and upper age for these ways of gaining compensation for the loss of a job and similarly the tapering provisions when the employee was over 64 have also been abolished. However, and contrary to its original proposals, the Government has by reg. 33 retained the age-related multiplier that determines the quantum of the RP and the basic award for unfair dismissal. Therefore, the employee will still receive different amounts of RP and basic award depending on whether he or she is aged under 21, over 41, or between those two ages. The Government's original intention of having a multiplier of '1' no matter what the age seems to have been negated by the non-regression clause in the Directive. It should be noted that the maximum of 20 years' service continues to apply.

Long-service entitlements

Sometimes employers grant extra entitlements to long-serving workers. An example is that a worker may get an extra day's holiday if he or she has worked for the employers for ten years. The Government has exempted long-service entitlements lasting for up to five years from the Age Regulations. However, entitlements based on length of service must be justified by the employers if they last for more than five years. The employers must prove that what they have done 'fulfils a business need..., for example, by encouraging the loyalty or motivation or rewarding...experience...'.

Pensions

Almost by definition pensions are based on age but the 2006 Regulations exempt age-related discrimination in respect of pensions.

Conclusion

The 2006 Regulations have many exemptions and exceptions, some of which do not seem congruent with the Directive, though some (such as the ability to justify direct discrimination) are. It will be fascinating to see how the Government attempts to justify age discrimination in respect of the default retirement age, and commentators are suggesting that any mandatory retirement age is contrary to the Directive.

Further reading

There is an overwhelming amount of published material. Among recommended books and articles are:

Barnard, C., *EC Employment Law* 2nd edn (Oxford: Oxford University Press, 2000)

Barnard, C., Deakin, S., and Kilpatrick, C., 'Equality, non-discrimination and the labour market in the UK' [2002] IJCLLIR 129.

Bell, M., 'Beyond European labour law: reflections on the EU Race Equality Directive' (2002) 8 ELJ 384.

Clarke L., 'Harassment, sexual harassment and the Employment Equality (Sex Discrimination) Regulations 2005' (2005) 35 ILJ 161.

Clayton, G., and Pitt, G., 'Dress codes and freedom of expression' [1997] EHRLR 54.

Dickens, L., 'Beyond the business case: a three-pronged approach to equality action (1999) 9 HRM Jo 9.

Ellis, E., *EC Anti-discrimination Law* (Oxford: Oxford University Press, 2005).

Fredman, S., *Discrimination Law* (Oxford: Oxford University Press, 2001).

Fredman, S., 'Equality: A new generation' (2001) 30 ILJ 145.

Hepple, B., Coussey, R., and Choudhury, T., *Equality: A New Framework* (Cambridge: University of Cambridge Centre of Public Law, 2000).

Morris, A., and O'Donnell, T., *Feminist Perspectives on Employment Law* (London: Cavendish, 1999).

Sargeant, M., 'The Employment Equality (Age) Regulations 2006: a legitimisation of age discrimination in employment' (2006) 35 ILJ 209.

Smith, I. T., and Thomas, G., *Industrial Law*, 8th edn (Oxford: Oxford University Press, 2003), ch. 5, pp. 267–325, 359–402.

Vickers, L., 'Is all harassment equal? The case of religious discrimination' [2006] CLJ 579.

Wintermute, R., 'Recognising new kinds of direct discrimination; transsexualism, sex orientation and dress code' (1997) 60 MLR 343.

Women and Equality Unit, *Equality and Diversity: Making it Happen* (London: WEU, 2002).

9

Equal pay and family rights

Introduction

Questions on equal pay are popular with examiners. Equal pay issues may arise in questions where sex discrimination issues are also involved. Alternatively, equal pay may form the basis of an entire question on its own.

Equal pay

The equal pay legislation is an aspect of sex discrimination law. The Equal Pay Act 1970 (EqPA) covers sex discriminatory provisions within the contract of employment, i.e. it relates to *all contractual terms,* not only pay. Where there is discrimination on the ground of sex concerning matters outside *contractual* terms, then the Sex Discrimination Act 1975 (SDA) must be used. So, if a woman complains that she was not interviewed, or was subjected to sexual harassment within her employment, her application would be based on the SDA. However, if the claim relates to contractual rights such as pay, benefits, holidays, etc., then it must be brought under the EqPA. (Note that the Race Relations Act 1976 covers pay.)

When considering domestic legislation, it is important to have in mind the relevant provisions of EC law, i.e. Art. 141 (ex Art. 119) of the EC Treaty, which enshrines the principle of equal pay, and the Equal Pay Directive (Directive 75/117/EEC). Article 141 is directly effective where 'there is direct and overt discrimination which may be identified solely with the aid of criteria based on equal work and equal pay' (see *Defrenne* v *SABENA* [1976] ECR 455, ECJ). This Article and the Equal Pay Directive may be relied upon by domestic courts when they construe the Equal Pay Act, i.e. they must take a purposive approach to the interpretation of EC law.

When preparing for examination questions on equal pay, students should ensure they have adequate knowledge (of the legislation and the relevant case law) of the following areas:

- What constitutes 'pay' for these purposes.
- The equality clause in s. 1, Equal Pay Act 1970.

- The three bases upon which an equal pay claim may be founded, i.e. like work, work rated as equivalent, and work of equal value (EqPA, s. 1(2)(a), (b), (c) respectively).

- The problems concerning selection of an appropriate comparator.

- The 'genuine material factor' defence (EqPA, s. 1(3)).

- The time limits within which such claims must be brought.

- Remedies where an equal pay claim is successful, including the period for which arrears may be claimed.

For the purposes of an equal pay claim, 'pay' is given a wide definition: it has been taken to include travel concessions (*Garland* v *British Rail Engineering Ltd* [1982] IRLR 111, ECJ), sickness pay (*Rinner-Kuhn* v *FWW Spezial-Gebaudereinigung GmbH & Co KG* [1989] IRLR 493, ECJ), and pensions payments arising from compulsory redundancies (*Barber* v *Guardian Royal Exchange Assurance Group* [1990] ECR I-1889, ECJ).

Where employment contracts do not already contain one, an equality clause is implied into them (EqPA, s. 1(1)), where the claimant is employed on like work, work rated as equivalent, and work of equal value. Any term of the claimant's contract that is less favourable to her than a term in her male comparator's contract is modified so as not to be less favourable. If her contract does not contain a term conferring a benefit on her which is in the male comparator's contract, then her contract is deemed to include one: EqPA, s. 1(2)(a), (b), (c). Every term is considered individually, rather than considering the overall terms of the contract (see *Hayward* v *Cammell Laird* [1988] IRLR 257, HL). A successful claim means that the claimant is awarded the same terms as her comparator, and not more or less than equal pay, no matter how 'unfair' the pay is.

It is important to understand the three bases upon which an equal pay claim may be founded, i.e. like work, work rated as equivalent, and work of equal value: EqPA, s. 1(2)(a), (b), (c) respectively. Like work means the same or broadly similar work: EqPA, s. 1(4). Different responsibilities may mean that the work is not like work (see *Eaton Ltd* v *J. Nuttall* [1977] IRLR 71). Jobs with a broadly similar nature may be taken to be 'like work': see *Capper Pass Ltd* v *Lawton* [1977] ICR 83.

Work rated as equivalent must be so rated under a job evaluation study (JES), i.e. the female applicant's job must have been given the same value as her male comparator's under a sufficiently objective and analytical JES (EqPA, s. 1(5)), and see *Bromley* v *H and J Quick Ltd* [1988] IRLR 456, CA.

Work of equal value claims depend upon a finding that, although the applicant is not engaged upon like work or work rated as equivalent, it is work of equal value, in terms of the demands made upon her, under such categories as, 'effort, skill, and decision' to that of her male comparator in the same employment: EqPA, s. 1(2)(c). Where a complaint is made to a tribunal concerning an equal value claim, the tribunal may appoint an expert from an independent panel to determine a report on the equal value issue: see EqPA, s. 2A(1), as amended by the Sex Discrimination and Equal Pay (Miscellaneous Amendments) Regulations 1996 (SI 1996/438), and *Commission* v *United Kingdom* [1982] IRLR 333, ECJ.

It is essential that the applicant selects the correct comparator of the opposite sex who is in the same employment. In *Lawrence* v *Regent Office Care Ltd* [2002] IRLR 822, ECJ, the ECJ held that former local authority employees who were outsourced to a contractor were not able to claim their former colleagues as comparators, since they now worked for a private contractor and were not in the same employment. Therefore, there was no 'single source', i.e. no single body which is responsible for the pay inequality, and which could restore equal treatment.

As well as a contemporary comparator, a predecessor or a successor (relying on Art. 141) may be selected, although this may present severe evidential problems: see *McCarthy's Ltd* v *Smith* [1980] IRLR 210, ECJ; *Diocese of Hallam Trustee* v *Connaughton* [1996] IRLR 505.

The genuine material factor (GMF) defence to an equal pay claim involves establishing that the pay differential between the applicant and her comparator was not tainted with sex discrimination: EqPA, s. 1(3). For example, where the difference in pay came about through the operation of permissible factors, such as market factors, it does not infringe the legislation. If there is sex discrimination involved, the employer must go on to objectively justify the pay difference: see *Strathclyde Regional Council* v *Wallace* [1998] IRLR 146, HL; *Rainey* v *Greater Glasgow Health Board* [1987] IRLR 26, HL.

An equal pay claim must be made to an employment tribunal within six months of leaving the relevant employment, although this may be extended in cases where the employer deliberately concealed any fact relevant to the claim or the applicant was under a disability during the normal six-month period: EqPA, s. 2(4) and 2ZA. This time limit has been held by the House of Lords to comply with EC law: see *Preston* v *Wolverhampton Healthcare NHS Trust (No. 2)* [2001] IRLR 237, HL. Originally, s. 2(5) of the Equal Pay Act 1970 stipulated that an equal pay award of remuneration or damages could only be made in respect of two years prior to the institution of proceedings. In *Levez* v *T H Jennings (Harlow Pools) Ltd (No. 2)* [1999] IRLR 764, the ECJ held that this was contrary to EC law in that it prevented a full and effective remedy being given, in breach of what is now Art. 141, and the Equal Pay Directive. The period for arrears of pay under an equal pay claim may now go back six years, with a longer arrears date in concealment and disability cases (EqPA, s. 2ZB).

Family rights

Family rights questions may involve any one or more of a range of rights, such as maternity and parental leave; time off for dependants; and a number of new rights within the Flexible Working legislation introduced by various regulations, the main provisions of which are briefly discussed below.

From 6 April 2003, a number of new rights came into force under the Flexible Working (Procedural Requirements) Regulations 2002 (SI 2002/3207), and the Flexible Working (Eligibility, Complaints and Remedies) Regulations 2002 (SI 2002/3236). These allow qualifying employees (those with at least six months' employment), inter alia, parents of children aged under 6 (or under 18 if disabled) rights ensuring that requests for flexible work arrangements (e.g. job sharing, homeworking, etc.) are not rejected without good cause. From 6 April 2007, these rights are extended to employees with responsibility for caring for (i) spouses and partners (including civil partners), (ii) adult relatives (as defined in the legislation), (iii) adults living at the same address as the employee.

Employers may refuse a request for flexible working on certain grounds. For example, (i) the burden of additional costs, (ii) the detrimental effect on ability to meet customer demand, (iii) the inability to reorganize work among existing staff: Employment Rights Act 1996 (ERA), s. 80G(1)(b).

Apart from these, employees will have the right to apply to an employment tribunal for compensation and/or an order that the employer reconsider the refusal to allow flexible working. Compensation will be subject to a maximum of eight weeks' pay (capped at £310 per week—so the maximum award is £2,480).

Qualifying employees will have the right not to be dismissed or subjected to a detriment for exercising or proposing to exercise rights under the new arrangements: ERA, ss. 47D, 104C.

In addition, the Work and Families Act 2006 introduced new rights (from 1 April 2007) concerning maternity leave for qualifying employees, which abolishes the need to have been continuously employed for 26 weeks before the expected week of childbirth and allows the employee 52 weeks of maternity leave. In addition, legislation has been introduced that extends statutory maternity pay (SMP), statutory adoption pay and maternity allowance from 26 weeks (six months) to 39 weeks (nine months). A further extension of these payments for 52 weeks is proposed by the end of the current Parliament, i.e. by Spring 2010 at the latest. A new paid paternity leave right of up to two weeks' leave also came into effect on 6 April 2003, with pay at the same standard rate as SMP. Statutory paternity leave may be taken at any time up to eight weeks after the birth or placement for adoption.

New adoption leave rights are also available from 6 April 2003. Subject to certain conditions, anyone with 26 weeks of continuous employment may take up to one year in adoption leave (ERA, ss. 75A–75D; Paternity and Adoption Leave Regulations 2002 (SI 2002/2788)). Statutory adoption pay is available for the first 39 weeks (the rate from 1 April 2007 is £112.75), with the remaining weeks (if taken) unpaid.

Question 1

Supa Kool Fashions Ltd is a company employing 20 employees. Provide the advice sought by the following employees:

(a) Rowena, the company's new Marketing Director, who was appointed three weeks ago, has discovered that Tom, her immediate predecessor, was paid £75,000 per annum, whereas she is paid £60,000 for carrying out the same duties. She has also discovered that Charles, who was the Marketing Director but left 12 months ago, was paid £78,000.

(b) Rose, a secretary, is paid a basic rate of £7.50 per hour for a 40-hour week. She wishes to claim equal pay with Harry and Will, two maintenance men, who are paid £8.50 per hour as a basic rate for a 40-hour week. Rose receives luncheon vouchers to the value of £5 per week, which the men do not receive, plus six weeks' holiday per annum, whereas the men receive only five weeks' holiday.

Advise Rowena and Rose, who want to bring equal pay claims against the company.

Commentary

The situations in this question require a discussion of the Equal Pay Act 1970 (EqPA), and relevant case law, with reference to EC law where necessary. Since the examiner has split the question into two parts, your answer should adopt the same approach, and you should deal with each situation in turn. The specific issues arising from the facts in each section are:

(a) Rowena

The issue here is whether, for the purposes of an equal pay claim, Rowena may compare herself with a predecessor who held the same position in the company, and if so, whether she may choose Charles or Tom.

(b) Rose

The question requires a discussion of equal value claims and, specifically, whether, despite the fact that she is on a lower hourly rate, the benefits she receives, which the men do not enjoy, affect her claim.

Answer plan

- Rowena
  - Discuss whether, in Rowena's equal pay claim (based on like work), she may select a predecessor comparator. If so, may she choose Charles or Tom?
  - Does the employer have any defences?
- Rose
  - Discuss whether the equal value claim is affected by the fact that, overall, the terms in the comparators' contracts are less favourable than those in Rose's.
  - Does the employer have a genuine material factor defence?

Suggested answer

These equal pay claims must be brought under the Equal Pay Act 1970 (EqPA), which came into force on 29 December 1975. Provisions of EC law, principally Art. 141

EC Treaty and the Equal Pay Directive (Directive 75/117), may also be relied upon in order to construe the domestic legislation, and to challenge inconsistent provisions of domestic legislation.

The EqPA is a part of domestic sex discrimination law, and it applies to all *contractual* terms (for claims concerning *non-contractual benefits*, the Sex Discrimination Act 1975 must be used). Under the EqPA, the person with whom an applicant wishes to compare themselves is known as the 'comparator' (the choice of comparator is left to the applicant: *Ainsworth* v *Glass Tubes and Components Ltd* [1977] ICR 347, EAT). The successful applicant will be deemed to have an equality clause included in their contracts, by virtue of EqPA, s. 1(1), which means that any less favourable term in the applicant's contract is treated as modified so as not to be less favourable: EqPA, s. 1(2)(a). It is vital that the applicant selects a person of the opposite sex in the same employment, since the equality clause will only operate where the comparator was in the same employment (EqPA, s. 1(2)), so contemporaneous employment is required under the EqPA (but not under Community law—see the discussion of *Macarthys Ltd* v *Smith* ([1980] IRLR 210, ECJ, below.

(a) Rowena

In Rowena's case, the issue is whether she may use as a comparator her predecessors, and, if so, whether she is restricted to Tom rather than Charles. The Court of Appeal in *Macarthys Ltd* v *Smith* [1979] ICR 785 held that the EqPA requires contemporaneous employment of the comparator, who is employed on like work, work rated as equivalent or work of equal value: EqPA, s. 1(2)(a), (b), (c). Mrs Smith took up her post as trainee manageress of the stockroom in January 1976, and became manageress in March 1976. She claimed equality with her male predecessor who had left in October 1975, and who had been paid £10 per week more than she. Although the EAT allowed her claim under the EqPA, it did so by interpreting the Act in accordance with former Art. 119 (new Art. 141) of the Treaty, which, under European Court of Justice (ECJ) jurisprudence, permitted a comparator who had recently been in the same employment. Although the Court of Appeal had rejected this interpretation of the EqPA, the ECJ held that Community law allowed a comparator who was a predecessor ([1980] IRLR 210, ECJ (see also *Albion Shipping Agency* v *Arnold* [1982] ICR 22, EAT: Mrs Arnold could not succeed under the EqPA but was successful under former Art. 119 (new Art. 141), unless objective justification could be established, i.e. that factors other than sex discrimination explained the difference in pay).

The only problem for Rowena might be that she has two predecessors in view. On the *Macarthys* principle, there would appear to be no difficulty in using Tom as a comparator, since he was in the same post only three weeks earlier, but Charles is not her *immediate* predecessor, as he left 12 months ago. This might create formidable problems for Rowena in proving that he is a suitable comparator, not least because the time gap may mean that objective justification arguments succeeded, e.g. there may have been a different labour market at the time. Finally, assuming that she is carrying out the same duties as Tom, she would seem to have a strong claim, unless the employer raises the defence of genuine material factor under EqPA, s. 1(3).

(b) Rose

In order to claim equal pay with Harry and Will, Rose will have to bring an equal value claim under EqPA, s. 1(2)(c). This is used where the claimant is not engaged on like work or work rated as equivalent but work that is of equal value under such headings as, for example, effort, skill, and decision. Rose will not be successful with her equal value claim where a valid job evaluation study has been conducted in which the conclusion was that her male comparators are not doing work of equal value: EqPA, s. 2A(2).

It might be argued by the employer that, looked at overall, Rose's total remuneration package is better than that of Harry and Will, on the ground that, although she receives a lower basic hourly rate for the same 40-hour working week, she has the benefit of one extra week of holiday, plus luncheon vouchers, which they do not receive. This argument was used by the employer in *Hayward* v *Cammell Laird Shipbuilders Ltd* [1988] ICR 464, HL. Julie Hayward was a cook in the employer's canteen whose work was found by an industrial tribunal to be of equal value to that of her male comparators who were craftsmen in the company (a painter, a joiner, and an insulation engineer). Although her basic pay and overtime rates were less favourable, her overall remuneration package was comparable to theirs (she received sickness benefits, holiday pay, and paid meal breaks, which the men did not receive). The House of Lords held that she could succeed in her claim. Their Lordships held that the correct approach under the EqPA was to examine the claimant's contract clause by clause, and to compare each clause in it with that in the male comparator's. If there was found in the man's contract a term benefiting him but no corresponding term in the woman's contract, then that term would be treated as included in hers.

In *Barber* v *Guardian Royal Exchange Assurance Group* [1990] IRLR 240, the ECJ, considering what is now Art. 141 EC Treaty (ex Art. 119), confirmed that the term-by-term approach was correct because 'if the national courts were under an obligation to make an assessment and a comparison of all the various types of consideration granted, according to the circumstances of men and women, judicial review would be difficult and the effectiveness of Article [141] diminished as a result' (at para. 34). Their Lordships in *Hayward* acknowledged that this term-by-term approach could lead to 'leap-frogging' claims, i.e. men and women claiming parity with each term of their contract, thereby improving their contractual benefits overall, but the genuine material factor defence in EqPA, s. 1(3) was available to them (the defence was not raised in *Hayward*). Section 1(3) of the EqPA states that the equality clause shall not operate where the employer proves that the variation between the women's contract and the man's 'is genuinely due to a material factor which is not the difference in sex'. This means that the employer must identify a factor, untainted by sex discrimination, which explains the difference in pay.

In conclusion, it would appear that Rose may bring an equal value claim, with Harry and Will as her male comparators, although she may be met with the genuine material factor defence, i.e. the employer may show that the less favourable term in Rose's contract is due to the presence of other more favourable terms (see also *Leverton* v *Clwyd* CC [1989] IRLR 28, HL).

Question 2

Dee-Zine Ltd is an interior decor company. Samantha is a designer working in the company's Design Department where, due to an upturn in demand and an acute shortage of designers available in the job market, the company has had to recruit designers from outside, on a temporary basis, on six-month contracts. In order to attract these recruits, the company has agreed to pay them £4,000 a year more than the existing designers receive, as an incentive for them to move from their current jobs.

Samantha, who is paid £20,000 per annum, has discovered that Rebecca and Tom, two designers recently recruited, earn £24,000 per annum. Samantha wishes to bring an equal pay claim, using Rebecca and Tom as her comparators.

Melanie is a fabric checker in the company's warehouse earning £16,000 per annum. There are seven other fabric checkers, of whom Tim, the only man working in the fabric checker section, also earns £16,000 per annum. Melanie wishes to bring an equal pay claim, comparing herself with Rick, a male sales assistant in the company's Sales Department, who earns £18,500 per annum. Melanie has discovered that the pay difference between her and Rick has been constant over the last four years, the period for which she wants to claim.

Advise Samantha and Melanie on their equal pay claims.

Commentary

Samantha's claim will be based on the fact that she is engaged on like work with Rebecca and Tom (EqPA, s. 1(2)(a)) but receives lower pay. The issues arising here are: whom she may choose as valid comparators, and whether there is a genuine material factor defence (GMF) under the Equal Pay Act, s. 1(3).

In Melanie's claim, the issues are whether the fact that a man works alongside her will defeat her equal value claim, whether Rick is an appropriate comparator, whether there is a GMF defence available to the employer, and whether she may claim for the whole four-year period.

As well as a discussion of the relevant provisions of the EqPA, your answer should include a discussion of any relevant EC law, particularly Art. 141 (ex Art. 119) EC Treaty.

Answer plan

- Samanatha
  - Discuss whether Samantha is engaged on like work; discuss whether she has chosen valid comparators.
  - Discuss whether there is a genuine material factor defence.
- Melanie
  - Consider whether the fact that a male employee works on the same work as Melanie will defeat her claim.
  - Is Rick an appropriate comparator?
  - Is there a genuine material factor defence applicable?
  - May Melanie claim for the whole four-year period?

Suggested answer

Samantha

It would appear that Samantha is employed on exactly the same job as her comparators, Rebecca and Tom, which means that she would claim under the Equal Pay Act (EqPA), s. 1(2)(a), the like work provision, which is defined in s. 1(4): 'A woman is to be regarded as employed on like work with men if...her work and theirs is of the same broadly similar nature, and the differences (if any) between the things she does and the things they do are not of practical importance.' According to the EAT in *Waddington v Leicester Council for Voluntary Services* [1977] ICR 266, the correct approach is, first, to ask whether the woman's job is the same as or broadly similar to that of the male comparator, and second, if the answer is 'yes', the tribunal should then proceed to consider whether any differences are of practical importance as regards terms and conditions of employment (and it is for the employer to prove that the differences (if any) are of practical importance: *Shields* v *E. Coomes (Holdings) Ltd* [1978] ICR 1159, CA). However, the EqPA, requires a comparator of the opposite sex (s. 1(2)), so Samantha would not be able to select Rebecca as a comparator.

Assuming that Samantha is engaged on the same work as Tom, and that any differences between her contract and his are of no practical importance, the next issue is whether the employer has a genuine material factor (GMF) defence under EqPA, s. 1(3) which is not the difference in sex, otherwise the equality clause will operate: EqPA, s. 1(1). The factor must be 'genuine' in the sense that it is not a sham or pretence, and 'material' in the sense of 'significant and causally relevant': see *Strathclyde Regional Council* v *Wallace* [1998] ICR 205, HL. In like work or work rated as equivalent claims, the GMF *must* be a material difference between the woman's case and the man's (EqPA, s. 1(3)(a)), whereas for equal value claims it *may* be (EqPA, s. 1(3)(b)).

In *Rainey* v *Greater Glasgow Health Board* [1987] ICR 129, HL, the NHS in Scotland, when setting up a prosthetic service within the NHS, decided to pay employees directly recruited from the NHS on the agreed scale, the Whitley Council scale, but in order to ensure adequate staffing levels, they had to recruit prosthetists from the private sector, where they were paid more. Therefore, the NHS offered higher pay to those recruited from the private sector. All of the private sector recruits were men, whereas all but one of the NHS recruits were women. Mrs Rainey, who had been recruited on Whitley Council rates, claimed equal pay with a man recruited from the private sector. The House of Lords agreed with the EAT and the Court of Session that the GMF defence had been made out, and dismissed Mrs Rainey's appeal.

The House of Lords in *Rainey* held that the GMF must be objectively justified. According to the ECJ in *Bilka-Kaufhaus GmbH* v *Weber von Hartz* [1987] ICR 110 (a case on ex Art. 119 of the Treaty) objective justification means that the factor(s) must (i) correspond to a real need on the part of the employer; (ii) be necessary to achieve the objective in question; and (iii) be proportionate to that objective ('the principle of proportionality'). An objective balance must be struck between the need of the employer and the discriminatory impact on the claimant.

On the issue of justification, the House of Lords has held that, once the employer has established that the factor relied upon in the GMF defence is genuine, i.e. not a sham, and is not related to sex, it does not have to go on to show that the factor relied upon is objectively justifiable (see *Strathclyde Regional Council* v *Wallace* [1998] IRLR 146; *Glasgow City Council* v *Marshall* [2000] IRLR 272, HL). However, the EAT in *Sharp* v *Caledonia Group Services Ltd* [2006] IRLR 4 held that in such circumstances objective justification was necessary, i.e. even where the factor is not tainted with sex discrimination. In taking this approach, it was following its understanding of the ECJ's ruling in *Brunnhofer* (Case C-381/99) [2001] ECR I-4961. However, the Court of Appeal in *Armstrong* v *Newcastle-upon-Tyne NHS Trust Hospital* [2006] IRLR 124 followed *Wallace* and *Marshall*, although it seems that the law in this area is subject to some doubt.

It would appear that in Samantha's case, the employer has a strong GMF defence under EqPA s. 1(3), on the same lines as the 'market forces' defence offered by the employer in *Rainey*. It should be noted that, although the GMF defence in Samantha's case is likely to succeed, when the reason for maintaining the pay disparity has disappeared, so does the objective justification under s. 1(3)—see *Benveniste* v *University of Southampton* [1989] IRLR 122, CA, where financial constraints meant that the applicant was placed on a lower salary point on the lecturers' scale than normal (a GMF defence); she succeeded because the financial constraints had ended and so the s. 1(3) defence no longer applied. However, the employer here could argue that this is simply a temporary measure, evidenced by the fact that the incoming designers are engaged on six-month contracts.

Melanie

Although the EqPA s. 1(2)(c) means that a woman can only bring an equal value claim where she is not engaged on like work or work of equal value with her comparator, Melanie's equal value claim is not affected by the fact that a man is employed on the same work as she. In *Pickstone* v *Freemans plc* [1988] ICR, 697, HL, the House of Lords held that a female warehouse operative could claim equal pay with a male checker warehouse operative, despite the fact that there was a male warehouse operative earning the same as she. Their Lordships held that this construction of s. 1(2)(c) was consistent with Art. 119 (new Art. 141), EC Treaty on the ground that a woman's equal value claim was not dependent on there being no man employed on the same work. There may, of course, be a GMF defence available to the employer (we are not given sufficient information to offer a view on this aspect of her claim).

The only remaining issue concerning Melanie's claim is whether she may claim a remedy (the difference in pay between herself and Rick) for the entire four-year period over which she wants to claim. The EqPA, s. 2(5) limited claims for arrears or pay or damages under the Act to the previous two years from the time proceedings were instituted. The ECJ held in *Levez* v *T H Jennings (Harlow Pools) Ltd* C–326/96 [1999] IRLR 36, that, while such a limitation was not, per se, contrary to EC law, the domestic court had to be satisfied that the provision did not transgress the principle of equivalence. This provides that domestic legal systems must not lay down procedural rules which are less favourable for EC actions than for equivalent domestic actions. When the case was remitted to the EAT, it was held that comparable domestic actions were those for breach of contract action or unlawful deduction from wages, where the normal six-year limitation applies, and that the provision in the EqPA was less favourable than comparable domestic actions (*Levez* [1999] IRLR 764, EAT).

In *Preston* v *Wolverhampton Healthcare NHS Trust* [2000] IRLR 506, ECJ, a case concerning indirect discrimination against part-time workers who were refused membership of their employer's pension scheme), the ECJ declared the two-year limitation period in s. 2(5) to be incompatible with Art. 141. Therefore, as the two-year period specified under s. 2(5) is incompatible with EC law it must be disapplied. The law has been changed in the light of the ECJ's ruling. A claimant may now seek arrears going back six years, so Melanie is able to claim under the EqPA for the four-year period in issue (EqPA, s. 2ZB).

Question 3

Mike and Nina work as Senior Housing Officers in Poppleton District Council, and Olivia works as a Housing Officer for the Workton District Council. The salary structure of all three employees was agreed between the Regional Housing Officers Association and the local authorities. The following events occur:

(a) Mike, who receives a salary of £31,000 per annum, has discovered that Nina receives £34,000 per annum for the same post, save for the fact that she works in Winkworth, a large city within Poppleton DC's area, whereas he is based in Mallerton, a smaller town with the Council's area. All employees in Winkworth receive a weighting allowance of £3,000.

(b) Nina has just returned to work after six months' maternity leave. She has discovered that last month all staff in her department received an end-of-year bonus which she did not receive. She has also discovered that Peter, another Senior Housing Officer, receives £1,500 more per annum than she. Peter carries out the same duties, except that he must attend Council meetings, make reports on various matters when requested to do so by the Councillors, and deliver these reports orally to the Councillors at the Council meetings.

(c) Olivia has discovered that Nick, a Housing Officer working for the Poppleton DC in the town of Lanbury, receives a salary of £24,000, whereas she receives only £21,000 (neither of them receives a weighting allowance).

Advise Mike, Nina, and Olivia, who all want to bring equal pay claims.

Commentary

The issues to be discussed in this equal pay question are:

(a) Mike

Whether Nina is an appropriate comparator and the basis of claim under the Equal Pay Act 1970 (EqPA), i.e. whether or not it is a like work claim. There must also be a discussion of whether the pay difference is justified.

(b) Nina

One of the issues here is whether Nina is entitled to the bonus paid to other employees. Another is whether Peter's higher pay is justified on the basis of the extra duties he is carrying out.

(c) Olivia

A key issue here is whether Nick is an appropriate comparator, since he works for a different district council. It should be noted that, although we are told that all Winkworth employees receive a weighting allowance, Nick works in Lanbury, so the fact that he does not receive one would not ground a claim under the Equal Pay Act 1970, unless she can identify an appropriate comparator working for Workton DC and the award of a weighting allowance to such employees cannot be justified.

Answer plan

- Mike
  - Discuss whether this is a 'like work' claim.
  - Consider whether Nina is an appropriate comparator.
  - Discuss whether the pay difference is justified (the GMF defence).
- Nina
  - Is the bonus a contractual benefit (and thus caught by the Equal Pay Act)? If not, Art. 141 may apply?
  - Is Peter engaged on like work?
  - Does the genuine material factor defence apply?
- Olivia
  - Consider the issue of whether it is permissible to select a comparator who works for a different employer, i.e. where the pay systems do not emanate from a 'single source'.
  - Does the collective agreement satisfy the 'single source' test?

Suggested answer

N.B. The parts of the following discussion concerning the genuine material factor defence follows the principle enunciated in the House of Lords in *Wallace* and *Marshall* (discussed in the previous question), i.e. that once a genuine material factor is identified that is not tainted by sex, there is no further requirement for objective justification.

(a) Mike

Since Nina and Mike both work for the same employer, Poppleton District Council, it would appear that Mike could use Nina as his comparator. Given that they are both Senior Housing Officers, Mike could bring a claim under the Equal Pay Act, s. 1(2)(a), EqPA, i.e. the 'like work' basis. This requires Mike to establish that his work and hers 'is of the same or a broadly similar nature, and the differences (if any) between the things [he] does and the things [she does] are not of practical importance in relation to terms and conditions of employment'.

In determining whether Nina is engaged on like work, the tribunal must make a broad judgment (*Capper Pass* v *Lawton* [1977] ICR 83). When judging whether Nina's work is like work, 'regard shall be had to the frequency or otherwise with which any such differences occur in practice as well as to the nature and extent of the differences': EqPA, s. 1(4).

Clearly, in this case Nina is carrying out like work, although the pay difference may be justified. In like work claims, the employer must prove that 'the variation is genuinely due to a material factor which is not the difference of sex'—the genuine material factor (GMF) defence: EqPA, s. 1(3). This material factor must be a 'significant and relevant factor' (*Rainey* v *Greater Glasgow Health Board* [1987] IRLR 26, HL). For example, in *Navy, Army and Air Force Institutes* v *Varley* [1977] ICR 11, EAT, the applicant worked in the NAAFI at Nottingham, on the same terms as the men there. All employees worked a 37-hour week but the male and female employees in the NAAFI in London worked only a 36-hour week. The EAT held that effectively this was a case of London 'weighting' accounting for the pay difference. Furthermore, this was a material factor untainted by sex. It established a genuine and material difference between Miss Varley's case and that of her male comparator in London. In Mike's case, it would appear that Poppleton could successfully argue the GMF defence. This would prevent the equality clause operating in Mike's contract.

(b) Nina

The end-of-year bonus which Nina did not receive may mean that she can claim under the EqPA if the bonus is contractual, as the Act only applies to contractual benefits (it applies to all contractual terms, not only pay (EqPA, s. 1(2)). However, if the bonus is not contractual, the EqPA cannot be used but it may be possible to claim under EC law, by virtue of Art. 141 of the Treaty. This is because a wider definition of 'pay' has been established under Art. 141, including, inter alia, non-contractual, voluntary bonuses (*Lewen* v *Denda* [2000] IRLR 67, ECJ).

In *Lewen*, the employer paid non-contractual Christmas bonuses to all employees in 'active' employment on 1 December which the complainant did not receive because she was on maternity leave on the relevant date. She claimed under Art. 141 and the ECJ held that the answer to whether the Article had been breached depended upon the nature of the payment. On the one hand, if the purpose of the bonus was to encourage loyalty and industriousness for the following year amongst those employees actually at work, it would not be discriminatory. If, on the other hand, the purpose of the bonus was to reward employees for their work over the previous year, it would be discriminatory to refuse such a payment to an employee absent on maternity leave. It was permissible to award a bonus on a pro rata basis to take account of her absence, but no account could be taken of any period during which she was prohibited from attending work by reason of her pregnancy.

Not enough is known in Nina's case about the nature of the bonus payment but, if the bonus is contractual, she has a claim under the EqPA. However, assuming that the bonus is non-contractual, she must rely upon Art. 141. In that case, on the authority of *Lewen*, one of the two situations identified by the ECJ would apply to her.

As Peter, being a Senior Housing Officer, is engaged upon like work, it would appear that Nina may have a claim under the EqPA. However, the employer might argue that under EqPA, s. 1(4), Nina and her comparator are not engaged on like work since the differences between their work, in terms of their nature and extent, and the frequency with which they occur in practice, are of practical importance. The differences in responsibilities between Nina's and Peter's jobs might mean that they were not engaged upon like work: see *Eaton Ltd* v *Nuttall* [1977] ICR 272, EAT.

Furthermore, if the different job duties did not prevent the comparator's work being like work, the employer would have the GMF defence available under s. 1(3), EqPA. The argument would be that the additional duties carried out by Peter supported an objective justification of the pay differential. However, the whole of the pay differential must be justified, so the council would have to establish that the whole £1,500 extra paid to Peter could be justified by the additional duties he carried out: see the speech therapists' case, *Enderby* v *Frenchay Health Authority* [1994] ICR 112, ECJ.

(c) Olivia

The problem with any equal pay claim launched by Olivia is that Nick may not be an appropriate comparator because he works for a different employer (Poppleton District Council). In the equal value case of *Lawrence* v *Regent Office Care Ltd* [2002] IRLR 822, ECJ, which was referred to the European Court of Justice, the court ruled that differences in the pay conditions of a claimant and a comparator must be 'attributed to a single source' which has the power to correct any pay disparity. In *Lawrence* the question was whether a pay comparison could be made between female workers employed by companies who had successfully tendered for catering and cleaning services for county council schools and male employees employed directly by the same council who were carrying out equivalent work. The female staff had, a few years earlier, been employed by the council to do the same work, but they were now employed by the private companies on lower rates of pay than they had received from the council. They claimed that, when they were council employees, an earlier job evaluation study had found that they were engaged upon work of equal value with their male comparators (who were still working for the council). The companies argued that as the identity of the claimants' employer had changed, they, as a completely different employer, could not explain the rates of pay paid by the council. Therefore, they would be unable to use the justification defence.

The ECJ ruled that Art. 141 could not be relied upon where the pay conditions cannot be attributed to a single source. However, in Scotland the Inner House of the Court of Session decided that a primary head teacher who claimed equal pay with a comparator who worked for a different local authority had selected an appropriate comparator since the source of their contractual terms was a national collective agreement applying to all teachers in Scotland. This meant that the collective agreement came within the interpretation of Art. 141 given in the ECJ's ruling in *Defrenne* v *Sabena* 43/75 [1976] ECR 455.

In conclusion, if Olivia and Nick are working under a collective agreement covering them both, the fact that they are working for different employers would not prevent an equal pay claim from proceeding, since there would be a single source of their contractual terms. However, if they are not covered by the same collective agreement. Olivia would not be able to use Nick as her comparator.

Question 4

Olivia, Stan, and Anne work for Brannen Industrial Karpets Ltd (BIK). Provide the advice sought by each employee:

(a) In June, Olivia, who has been working for BIK for 13 months, informs BIK that she wishes to take three weeks off this summer to look after her three-year-old son, Tommy. She is concerned that, if she applies for the leave, she will not be allowed to return to her old job. She is also concerned as to whether she will be able to support herself financially during the leave period (she knows that BIK has a policy of not paying employees who take such leave). Advise Olivia.

(b) Stan wishes to take three weeks' leave to care for his elderly parents. His mother has just suffered a serious stroke and will require constant care over the next week, and his elderly father is severely disabled, and Stan hopes to secure nursing-home accommodation for him with round-the-clock nursing (Stan's mother looked after him before her stroke). Stan estimates that it will take three weeks to make arrangements to relocate his father in a nursing home. In addition, Stan wishes to take a further four days of leave (in addition to the three weeks for his parents) to help Agatha, his frail, 94-year-old neighbour, whose health has deteriorated markedly recently, and for whom he has cared every evening for the last four years (she has no other relatives). Stan has promised Agatha that he will take a few days off work to drive her to a residential care home in Cornwall (300 miles away) and help her settle in. Advise Stan as to his entitlement to take the leave requested.

(c) Anne has worked for BIK for 15 months. She informed the company last week that she was pregnant and would be applying for maternity leave. She had been told that she was to be one of two employees shortlisted for promotion to Marketing Manager but, on receiving the news of her pregnancy and proposed maternity leave, the Personnel Director informed Anne that she would not be considered for the promotion.

Commentary

(a) Olivia

This part of the question concerns the Maternity and Parental Leave Regulations 1999 (SI 1999/3312). The issues raised concern parental leave, in particular: the period of qualifying employment required; entitlement based upon the date of birth of the child; the amount of time off (and when it may be taken); notice requirements; the entitlement to return to work after parental leave; and the fact that parental leave is unpaid.

(b) Stan

This part concerns the provisions relating to the right to time off for dependants under the Employment Rights Act 1996 (ERA), s. 57A. A detailed discussion of the provision, applied to Stan's circumstances, is required.

(c) Anne

A discussion of the provisions relating to additional maternity leave under the Maternity and Parental Leave Regulations 1999 (SI 1999/3312) (as amended by the Maternity and Parental Leave (Amendment) Regulations 2002 (SI 2002/2789) is required, with reference to the provisions giving protection from detriment for pregnant employees and those requesting such leave.

Answer plan

- Olivia
  - Consider the parental leave provisions in the Maternity and Parental Leave Regulations 1999: entitlement to claim unpaid leave; amount of time off allowed and when it may be taken.
  - Discuss notice requirements, and entitlement to return to work after leave.
  - Protection from detriment and the right to claim unfair dismissal.
- Stan
  - Consider the provisions on requesting time off for dependants (ERA, s. 57A).
  - Discuss who comes under the definition of a 'dependant'.
  - Consider the notice requirement.
  - Stan's remedy for unreasonable refusal to grant time off.
- Anne
  - Consider the maternity leave provisions, and the qualifying requirements.
  - Discuss the right to return to work—to the same job or, if that is not reasonably practicable, another suitable job.
  - Discuss the provisions on the notice to be given of the return to work.
  - Consider the provisions on protection from detriment, unfair dismissal, and sex discrimination.

Suggested answer

(a) Olivia

Under the Maternity and Parental Leave Regulations 1999 (SI 1999/3312) (MPLR 1999), as amended by the Maternity and Parental Leave (Amendment) Regulations 2001 (see also *R v Secretary of State for Trade and Industry ex parte Trades Union Congress* [2000] IRLR 565, HC, for the challenge made by the TUC on the implementation of the relevant Framework Directive by the 1999 Regulations), Olivia may exercise a right to unpaid parental leave of up to four weeks per year in respect of a child under the age of five, if she has continuous employment of one year or more, and parental responsibility for the child (originally, the MPLR 1999 provided that leave only applied for children born *after* 15 December 1999) (regs 13 and 14, as amended). Olivia is entitled to 13 weeks' unpaid leave in total (reg. 14). BIK may require evidence of all of these facts, i.e. parental responsibility; the child's date of birth/placement for adoption; his entitlement to disability allowance (where relevant) (Sch. 2, paras 1 and 2).

Olivia must comply with the notice requirements. These are: 21 days' notice, specifying the dates on which the period of leave is to begin and end, with a right for the employer to postpone the leave for up to six months where the business would be 'unduly disrupted' if the employee took the leave during the period stated in her notice: Sch. 2, paras 3 and 6.

Employees taking up to four weeks' leave may return to the job in which they were employed before the absence: reg. 18(1). As Olivia plans to take only three weeks' leave, she is entitled to return to the same job she left, unless it is not reasonably practicable for BIK to allow her to return to this job, in which case her right is to return to a 'suitable' and 'appropriate' job: reg. 18(2). In Olivia's case, it may not be reasonably practicable to allow her to return to her old job, because, for example, it may have disappeared under the reorganization.

Unless there is an agreement in place (individual, work force, or collective), the default provisions of Sch. 2 to the Regulations provide that leave must be taken in multiples of one week, up to a maximum of four weeks in any one year: Sch. 2, paras 7 and 8. The entitlement is to *unpaid* leave, so Olivia is not entitled to any financial support under the Regulations (and given BIK's policy, Olivia is unlikely to receive financial support from the company).

Finally, employees are protected against suffering any detriment by reason of taking or seeking parental leave (reg. 19(1), (2)(e)(ii)), and they may claim automatically unfair dismissal if parental leave is the reason for dismissal: ERA, s. 99.

(b) Stan

Under the Employment Rights Act 1996 (ERA), s. 57A, Stan has a right 'to take a reasonable amount of time off' during working hours in order to take action which is necessary to, inter alia, 'provide assistance on an occasion when a dependant falls ill', and to 'make arrangements for the provision of care for a dependant who is ill'. 'Dependants' include parents: ERA, s. 57A (3)(c).

Clearly, the illness of his mother falls within this provision, but the question is whether his father (who has not 'fallen ill' as such) comes within the section. His father would come under s. 57A(1)(b) and (d), in that his care has been disrupted by his wife's stroke and it is necessary for Stan to 'make arrangements for the provision of care for a dependant who is ill'. The time off allowed is 'a reasonable amount of time' (s. 57A(1)), and it would appear that Stan's request of three weeks' leave is reasonable in all the circumstances. Stan should give his employer notice of his absence so as to comply with the requirements of s. 57A(2) by informing his employer of the reason for his absence, and the expected period of absence.

Agatha, Stan's frail neighbour, would come under the definition of 'dependant' given in s. 57A(4), i.e. as someone who 'reasonably relies' on Stan 'to make arrangements for the provision of care in the event of illness': s. 57A(4)(b). Whether the four days' absence requested is reasonable is a question of fact, depending on all the circumstances.

Finally, if Stan's request for leave under s. 57A is unreasonably refused, he may complain to an Employment Tribunal within three months of the refusal. The Tribunal may make an award of such compensation as it considers to be just and equitable: s. 57B.

(c) Anne

Anne is entitled to statutory maternity leave of 52 weeks under the Maternity and Parental Leave Regulations 1999 (MPL Regs) (SI 1999/3312), regs 4, 5, and 7, as amended and the ERA, ss. 71, 73. Amendments were made to the 1999 Regulations by the Maternity and Parental Leave (Amendment) Regulations 2002 (SI 2002/2789), which applied to women whose expected week of childbirth began on or after 6 April 2003 and, more recently, by the Work and Families Act 2006 and amendment legislation in 2006. Since Anne qualifies for the period of Ordinary Maternity Leave (OML) of 26 weeks, she also qualifies for the period of Additional Maternity Leave (AML) of a further 26 weeks. Although Anne is not entitled to her remuneration during the statutory maternity leave (SML) period (reg. 9), she may claim statutory maternity pay for 39 weeks. Provided Anne complies with the statutory notice requirements (regs 11 and 12), she has a right to return to work. She is entitled to return to her job after OML without giving further notice (although she must give eight weeks' notice of her intention to return, if she wishes to return before the end of that period). She is entitled to return to her job after SML, normally on the same terms and conditions as if she had not been absent: ERA, s. 71(4)(c); MPL Regs, reg. 18(1). Anne's right to return to work after SML is a right to return to 'the job in which she was employed before her absence or, if it is not reasonably practicable for the employer to permit her to return to that job, to another job which is both suitable for her and appropriate for her to do in the circumstances': ERA, s. 73(4)(c); MPL Regs, reg. 18(2). She also has the right to return 'on terms and conditions not less favourable than those which would have applied if she had not been absent': MPL Regs, reg. 18A(1)(b)).

Anne could also claim that she has been subjected to a detriment in not being considered for promotion after being informed initially that she would be shortlisted for promotion (ERA, s. 47C; MPL Regs, reg. 19) but she would have to establish that her taking maternity leave was the reason for this treatment. Furthermore, if she is dismissed for any of the reasons or circumstances set out in, inter alia, the MPL Regs, the dismissal is automatically unfair. She could also claim under the Sex Discrimination Act 1975, s. 6(2)(b), which provides that it is unlawful to discriminate against a woman 'by dismissing her or subjecting her to any other detriment'.

Further, Anne has statutory protection from being subjected to a detriment (other than dismissal) by reason of the fact that she is pregnant or took, or sought to take, maternity leave: reg. 19(1), (2)(a), (d), (e); ERA, s. 47C. She must comply with the requirements of the MPL Regs, reg. 11 (relating to notifying her intention to return to work earlier than the end of her AML), by giving notice of her intention to return within eight weeks.

Anne may apply to the employment tribunal within three months of the relevant act: ERA, s. 48. The tribunal may order such compensation as it considers to be just and equitable: ERA, s. 49.

Further reading

Anderman, S. D., *Labour Law: Management Decisions & Workers' Rights,* 4th edn (London: Butterworths, 2000), chs 9 and 15.

Corbitt, T., 'Employees' family rights and the Data Protection Act 1998' (2001) 165 (42) *Justice of the Peace & Local Government Law* 824–5.

Deakin, S., and Morris, G. S., *Labour Law,* 4th edn (Oxford: Hart Publishing, 2005), ch. 6.

'ECJ rules on equal pay comparators' (2003) 348 *European Industrial Relations Review* 32–3.

'Employment law review 2002: maternity and parental rights' (2003) 724 *IDS Brief* 3–4.

'Equal pay: transferred workers cannot compare their pay with retained workers' (2003) *IRS Employment Law* 46–8.

'Flexible working regulations' (2003) 770 *IRS Employment Law* 48–9.

Godwin, K., 'Pressure builds for equal pay' (2002) 105 *Equal Opportunities Review* 7–17.

Honeyball, S., and Bowers, J., *Textbook on Labour Law,* 8th edn (Oxford: Oxford University Press, 2006), ch. 11.

Pitt, G., *Employment Law,* 6th edn (London: Sweet & Maxwell, 2007), chs 6 and 7.

10

Statutory rights regulating the employment relationship

Introduction

This chapter concerns some aspects of a number of important statutory rights affecting the employment relationship which are not covered in the other chapters of this book. These rights include those given under the following areas of employment law: rights under the Working Time Regulations 1998, as amended; the whistleblowers' provisions in the Employment Rights Act 1996 (ERA), derived from the Public Interest Disclosure Act 1998; the right to time off work; lay-offs and short-time working; rights to national minimum pay; statutory grievance and disciplinary/dismissal procedures in the Employment Act 2002; the right to an itemized pay statement, and unlawful deductions from pay.

The Working Time Regulations 1998 (SI 1998/1833) (WTR) implemented the Working Time Directive 93/104/EC and the Young Workers Directive 94/33/EC. The Regulations apply to 'workers' and not only employees ('workers' are defined as including an individual who 'undertakes to do or perform personally any work or services for another party to the contract whose status is not by virtue of the contract that of a client or customer of any profession or business undertaking carried on by the individual': reg. 2). Workers are those over 18, whereas 'young workers' are those between 15 and 18. Some categories of worker are currently excluded from the WTR, such as junior doctors. Some provisions (e.g. those relating to weekly working hours, night work, rest breaks) do not apply to those engaged in 'unmeasured working time, e.g. managing executives': reg. 20. A collective agreement of no more than five years' duration may be agreed which alters the basic provisions given below.

The main provisions of the WTR of which those studying for examinations in employment law should be aware are:

1. Average weekly working hours: the restrictions on average weekly working hours to 48. The Regulations state that 'a worker's working time, including overtime in any reference period ... shall not exceed 48 hours for each seven days': reg. 4(1).

This right is implied into every worker's contract of employment: see *Barber* v *RJB Mining (UK) Ltd* [1999] IRLR 308, HC. The default reference period is defined as 'a period of 17 weeks'. Workers may opt out of these provisions by stating in writing that they wish to do: reg. 5, although they have the right to terminate this agreement. The employer may ask for a maximum three-month notice period before the termination becomes effective.

2. Night worker: a night worker is defined in reg. 2 as an individual who either, (a) *as a normal course*, works at least three hours of his daily working time during night time, or (b) is 'likely, during night time, to work at least such proportion of his annual working time as may be specified . . . in a collective agreement or work force agreement (and see *R* v *Attorney General for Northern Ireland ex parte Burns* [1999] IRLR 315, NICA). A night worker's normal hours of work in any reference period must not exceed eight in any 24-hour period: reg. 6(1). Such workers are entitled to free health assessments before being put on to night work: reg. 7.

3. Night time: this is defined as a period of 'not less than seven hours, and which includes the period between midnight and 5 a.m.': reg. 2. In the absence of any relevant agreement, this period is between 11 p.m. and 6 a.m.: reg. 2.

4. Annual leave: from 1 October 2007, workers are entitled to 24 days' minimum annual paid leave (rising to 28 days' leave from 1 April 2009): reg. 13.

5. Rest breaks: an adult worker whose daily working time is more than six hours is entitled to a rest break of not less than 20 minutes. A young worker whose daily working time is more than four and a half hours is entitled to a rest break of at least 30 minutes: reg. 12.

The whistleblowers' provisions within the ERA derived from the Public Interest Disclosure Act 1998 (PIDA). These provisions are designed to protect individuals who make disclosures of information in circumstances where such disclosure is in the public interest. The provisions extend to workers, rather than just employees: ERA, s. 43K(1)(a). Key areas of which students preparing for an examination question in this topic would have to be aware are, inter alia, the definition of a 'qualifying disclosure'. A worker is only protected if he or she makes a qualifying disclosure (ERA, s. 43B), i.e. one tending to show one of six types of wrongdoing (ERA, s. 43B(1)). Further, the worker must have a reasonable belief that the information he or she holds tends to show one or more of them. The disclosure must be made in good faith: ERA, s. 43C(1). The dismissal of a worker making such disclosures is automatically unfair (ERA, s. 103), and any compensation awarded is not subject to the statutory maximum (ERA, s. 124).

The right to time off work arises in a number of situations. Some of the most important are the following. Trade union officials and trade union members are allowed time off to carry out their duties or take part in union activities: Trade Union and Labour Relations (Consolidation) Act 1992 (TULRCA), ss. 168–70. Union learning representatives are also allowed time off: TULRCA, s. 168A(1). Time off is allowed for public duties, such as the duties of a Justice of the Peace: ERA, s. 50. Employees under a redundancy notice have a right to reasonable time off during working hours to look for work: ERA, s. 52. Women are allowed time off for the purposes of receiving ante-natal care (ERA, s. 55), and reasonable time off is allowed to care for dependants during certain emergencies (s. 57A). Employee representatives are also allowed time off in order to perform their duties: ERA, s. 61.

A week of lay-off occurs when the employee works under a contract where remuneration depends upon work being provided and the employer provides no work for a particular week, so that the employee is therefore not entitled to any pay for that week: ERA, s. 147(1). Short time occurs when employees receive less than half of their week's pay as a result of the reduction in work: ERA, s. 147(2). Such employees are entitled to claim a redundancy payment if they are laid off or kept on short time for a period of four consecutive weeks or for a series of six or more weeks within a 13-week period. The employee must resign in order to claim the redundancy payment, and give notice of the intention to make such a claim: ERA, s. 150.

Under the National Minimum Wage Act 1998 (NMWA), and the National Minimum Wage Regulations 1999 (SI 1999/584) (NMWR) minimum wage rates, known as the National Minimum Wage (NMW), have been set. These apply to workers aged 18 and over, but there are three rates applicable: (i) the adult rate (£5.52 per hour from 1 October 2007), which is payable to those aged over 21; (ii) the 'youth rate' which is currently (from 1 October 2007) £4.60 per hour. This reduced rate is payable to two groups of workers: those between 18 and 21, and those aged 22 or over who are within the first six months of their employment and who have agreed to take part in accredited training on at least 26 days between the start of employment (or of the agreement) and the end of the six-month period: NMWR, reg. 13(2). The third rate is for 16–17 year olds, which is £3.40 from 1 October 2007.

The Employment Act 2002 introduced a new statutory grievance procedure, along with a statutory dismissal and disciplinary procedure. Dismissal of an employee without the completion of the statutory procedure, owing wholly or mainly to the employer's default, is automatically unfair: ERA, s. 98A(1). Section 30(1) of the Employment Act 2002 incorporates these procedures into the contract of employment. The standard procedure is set out in Sch. 2 to the 2002 Act, and consists, essentially, of three stages: first, the statement of the alleged conduct by the employer in the case of disciplinary/dismissal matters, or by the employee in the case of the grievance procedure; second, the meeting; third, the appeal.

Students should also be aware of the provisions concerning every employee's right to an itemized pay statement (ERA, s. 8), and the right not to suffer unlawful deductions from pay (Part II of the ERA), including the relevant case law in these areas.

Other provisions concerning pay with which students should be familiar are those relating to guarantee pay and medical suspension pay. Guarantee pay is payable to employees who have been employed for one month or more but for whom there is no work because of a diminution in the employer's need for the kind of work the employee carries out, or any other occurrence affecting the normal working of the business: ERA, ss. 28–35.

Medical suspension pay is payable to qualifying employees who have been suspended from work by their employer on medical grounds, e.g. for reasons relating to an unsafe working environment. Employees must be paid while suspended, up to a maximum period of 26 weeks. To qualify, an employee must have at least one month's continuous employment: ERA, s. 65(1). The statutory maximum for a week's pay applies, which is £310 from the 1 February 2007.

Question 1

Mal has been assigned by his employer, Chemical Advisory and Consultancy Services Ltd (CACS), to Winkton Industrial Processes Ltd (WIP), a company supplying chemicals to the metal finishing sector of industry, to act as an industrial chemical consultant to WIP. The agreement between CACS and WIP stipulates that Mal is to be engaged upon WIP's standard terms of employment, and that CACS is to ensure that Mal obeys all instructions issued to him by WIP concerning the work he is engaged upon. Mal has signed an agreement with WIP that he will obey all instructions issued to him by WIP. The agreement also states: 'All matters discussed at any management meetings, and all records of such meetings, are strictly confidential.' He has worked for WIP for 15 months.

At the last management meeting concerning operational activities, which Mal attended in his capacity as consultant. Bill, the Operations Manager, indicated that the Board had taken the decision to save the £100,000 it would cost to dispose safely of the company's highly toxic chemical waste over the coming year by discharging it directly into the river flowing past the company's chemical plant. Mal makes his concerns about this proposal known at the meeting, but is told by Bill that the decision has been taken at a higher level, and that he should not create any problems. He again raises the matter with Tom, the Managing Director, who says, 'Just forget about it. By the way, all matters discussed at management meetings are confidential. If you want to continue to work here, you'll remember that.' Mal informs Tom that he is very concerned that what is proposed is illegal, to which Tom replies, 'We may need to have a word with CACS if you create problems for us.'

Mal has informed the Environment Agency of WIP's proposed pollution of the river. Two weeks later, CACS withdraws Mal from the WIP work because of complaints about his poor timekeeping (Mal was ten minutes late for work on two occasions last month). CACS has encountered great difficulty in placing Mal with other clients. Mal was told by Brian, CACS's Managing Director, that this could be because of WIP's actions. Tom indicated to Brian, off the record, that WIP was going to 'make sure that Mal never works in the chemical industry again'.

Advise Mal of any protection afforded to him by employment law in this situation.

Commentary

This question concerns the so-called 'whistleblowing' provisions inserted into the Employment Rights Act 1996 (ERA) by the Public Interest Disclosure Act 1998 (PIDA). It should be noted that you are asked to advise Mal 'of any protection afforded to him by *employment law*' (emphasis added), i.e. you should not stray into a discussion of criminal law or environmental law. Since this is a relatively new area of employment law, there is little case law available to support your answer. Therefore, your discussion will be focused upon a detailed discussion of the relevant (rather detailed and complicated) statutory provisions.

The issues to be covered are: whether Mal, as a worker (rather than an employee), is covered by the provisions; whether the information about the proposed act of pollution is a 'qualifying disclosure' and, further, whether it is a 'protected disclosure'; whether it was reasonable for Mal to make the disclosure; whether the confidentiality provisions in the two agreements are valid; whether Mal has suffered a detriment; and, what are his rights to claim under the Employment Rights Act 1996 for being subjected to a detriment for a reason related to the disclosure.

Answer plan

- Consider the 'whistleblowing' provisions of the ERA.
- Discuss: whether Mal as a contract worker is covered; whether a 'qualifying disclosure' has been made, and whether it is a protected disclosure; whether Mal's disclosure was reasonable, and whether it was made to the appropriate persons.
- Whether the confidentiality agreements are valid.
- Has Mal suffered a detriment and was it causally linked to his disclosure?
- Consider what Mal's rights are under the ERA.

Suggested answer

Mal may have rights under the 'whistleblowing' provisions of the Employment Rights Act 1996 (ERA), as amended by the Public Interest Disclosure Act 1998 (PIDA): see the ERA, ss. 43A–43L, 47B–49. The protection afforded under PIDA extends to 'workers', a definition which is broader than 'employees' and covers contract workers (which Mal seems to be). The definition within ERA, s. 43K(1)(a), provides that a worker, for these purposes, is a person who:

works or worked for a person in circumstances in which—

(i) he is or was introduced or supplied to do that work by a third person, and

(ii) the terms on which he is or was engaged to do the work are or were in practice substantially determined not by him but by the person for whom he works or worked, by the third person or by both of them . . .

Mal is supplied to WIP by CACS (the third person): ERA, s. 43K(1)(a)(i). Mal works under WIP's terms of employment. There are express terms in the agreement between CACS and WIP, and in the agreement between Mal and WIP. In the former agreement, the terms are that CACS must ensure that Mal obeys all of WIP's instructions, and, in the latter agreement, a personal agreement by Mal to do so. Therefore, Mal works on terms which are 'in practice substantially determined ... by the person for whom he works', i.e. WIP: ERA, s. 43K(1)(a)(ii).

Mal is only protected if he has made a 'protected disclosure'. A disclosure will attract protection if it is a 'qualifying disclosure', as defined under s. 43B of the ERA, and the disclosure must be made in accordance with any of ss. 43C to 43H of the Act. A qualifying disclosure is one that is information that, in the reasonable belief of the disclosing worker, 'tends to show' one or more of six categories of wrongdoing: ERA, s. 43B(1). These categories include situations where, in the reasonable belief of the worker, (i) 'a criminal offence has been committed, or is being committed or is likely to be committed': s. 43B(1)(a); (ii) 'that a person has failed, is failing or is likely to fail to comply with any legal obligation to which he is subject': s. 43B(1)(b); (iii) 'that the health or safety of any individual has been, is being or is likely to be endangered': s. 43B(1)(d); (iv) 'that the environment has been, is being or is likely to be damaged' s. 43B(1)(e); or, (v) 'that information tending to show any matter falling within any one of the preceding paragraphs has been, or is likely to be deliberately concealed': s. 43B(1)(f).

It should be noted that Mal must establish that he holds a 'reasonable belief' that the information 'tends to show' the situations described in (i)–(v) above. The courts and tribunals must decide what constitutes a 'reasonable belief'. In *Babula* v *Waltham Forest College* [2007] IRLR 346, the Court of Appeal held that provided the belief (objectively considered) is reasonable, it is irrelevant if it turns out to be wrong. The situations need not actually have occurred, or be about to occur, only that the information disclosed 'tends to show' one or more of them. It seems that Mal does indeed hold such a reasonable belief, and it is likely that the information tends to show that (i) above is satisfied in that it is likely that a criminal offence will be committed if the chemicals are discharged into the river, as proposed; under (ii) above, WIP is a person likely to fail to comply with its legal obligations concerning the discharge; under (iii) above, if discharged, the chemicals are likely to endanger the health and safety of individuals; under (iv), the environment is likely to be damaged in that the river will be polluted; and under (v), given the behaviour of WIP's senior employees, it seems that information relating to these matters is likely to be deliberately concealed.

Mal has made the disclosure in good faith to WIP (a third party), rather than to his employer, in accordance with EPA, s. 43C(1)(b), as the matter is the responsibility of WIP, rather than CACS (this is an internal, third party disclosure to a prescribed person, for these purposes). 'Good faith' in this context means that Mal must honestly hold the belief, even if he was promoting it for reasons of personal antagonism (see *Street* v *Derbyshire Unemployed Workers' Centre* [2005] ICR 97, CA). Further, Mal has gone on to make a disclosure to a second prescribed person, i.e. the Environment Agency, in accordance with EPA, s. 43F(1)(a): the Agency is a prescribed person under the Public Interest Disclosure (Prescribed Persons) Order 1999 (SI 1999/1549). Mal must make the disclosure in good faith and reasonably believe that the failure falls within the description of matters in respect of which the Agency is prescribed, and reasonably believe that the information is substantially true: EPA, s. 43F(1)(a), (b). These provisions would appear to be satisfied in Mal's case.

It is possible that Mal's disclosure would fall within the 'exceptionally serious failures' category under EPA, s. 43H. No definition is given of what might come under this category, but similar provisions apply in terms of good faith, substantial truth of the allegation, that it was reasonable to make the disclosure, that the failure is of an exceptionally serious nature, and that it is not made for personal gain.

The contractual confidentiality provisions prohibiting disclosure of matters discussed at or a record kept of management meetings are void, 'in so far as it purports to preclude [Mal] from making the protected disclosure': ERA, s. 43J.

Mal has the right not to suffer a detriment for making the protected disclosure: ERA, s. 47B. He clearly has suffered a detriment, first, in being withdrawn from the assignment with WIP, and, second, the inference is that WIP has used its influence to prevent other persons in the industry from engaging Mal (which seems to have been successful). It must be established that the detriment is suffered because he made the disclosure, rather than because of his lateness. This is a question of fact, but the little case law on the issue suggests that the courts and tribunals will take a fairly robust view of the matter: see *Eleady-Cole* v *Brothers of Charity Services*, Liverpool Employment Tribunal, Case No. 2103410/99, where the purported reason for dismissal was poor performance; *Fernandes* v *Netcom Consultancy (UK) Ltd*, London (North) Employment Tribunal, Case No. 2200060/00, where the reason for dismissal given by the employer was financial misdeeds by the employee—Mr Fernandes was awarded £293,441 in compensation. Mal may bring a claim to the employment tribunal within three months of the act or the failure to act: ERA, s. 48(1A), (3).

Question 2

Jim has worked for Randall's Independent Traders Ltd (RIT) for three months as a clerical assistant. He has worked a 52-hour week for the last three months. Gary and Tina work as customer service assistants. Gary and Tina are part-time workers working on Saturdays. They have worked for RIT for one month. Gary, who is 17, works for seven hours on Saturdays, with one rest break of 20 minutes. Tina, who is 24, works for six hours with one 15-minute break. Gary and Tina have complained to RIT that their breaks are too short to allow them time for lunch, but RIT says that they can allow only the breaks allocated.

Mark, who is 26, works as a shelf-stacker on the late shift, working a five-day week: on three days a week he works from 6 p.m. to 2 a.m., and on two days a week he works from 7 p.m. to 2 a.m. He has started to suffer from lapses of concentration which, his doctor says, are related to his night shifts. The doctor has advised him to change to day shifts, if possible.

Oliver, a maintenance technician, works a 48-hour week, although he is also required to be on-call at home for four hours, from 6 p.m. to 10 p.m. every fortnight. Advise all of the above employees of their rights under the Working Time legislation.

Commentary

This question concerns various rights under the Working Time Regulations 1998 (SI 1998/1833), which implement the Working Time Directive 93/104/EC. The issues arising are: eligibility to claim under the Regulations; maximum hours permitted in the working week; rest breaks; the provisions relating to night work; and whether on-call time is included in the calculation of working time.

You should take each employee in turn and discuss their rights and entitlements under the Regulations, supported by reference to relevant case law. Your discussion on each employee should conclude with a consideration of the remedies available, and an indication of who is the appropriate person to enforce (or make claims under) the relevant rights or entitlements contained within the Regulations. For certain rights, e.g. those relating to daily/weekly rest periods, rest breaks, and annual leave, the individual may apply to the employment tribunal for a remedy: reg. 30. For other provisions, e.g. those concerning weekly working hours, length of night work, and health assessments, the enforcement responsibility rests with the Health and Safety Executive: reg. 28.

Answer plan

- Consider the following aspects of the Working Time Regulations: eligibility to claim; maximum working hours permitted (calculated by reference to the reference period).
- Discuss the provisions on night work, free health checks, and possible transfer to other work outside night working hours.
- Whether on-call time is part of working time.
- Consider the provisions on rest breaks for both adult workers and young workers.
- Discuss the relevant remedies, and the appropriate person or body entitled either to make claims under the Regulations or to enforce them.

Suggested answer

The employees working for RIT may have rights under the Working Time Regulations 1998 (SI 1998/1833) (WTR), which implement the Working Time Directive 93/104/EC. None of the employees falls within the scope of the excepted sectors of activity, e.g. transport; sea fishing; and doctors in training: reg. 18. The Regulations cover not only employees but also those who personally perform work or provide services: reg. 2(1). It would appear that none of the workers has signed an opt-out from the 48-hour working week provisions: reg. 4(1). No qualifying periods of employment are required to claim rights under the WTR (the original requirement in the WTR that workers must work for at least 13 weeks before accruing any entitlement to paid annual leave was successfully challenged in *R* v *Secretary of State for Trade and Industry ex parte BECTU* [2001] IRLR 559, ECJ; the Working Time (Amendment) Regulations 2001 (SI 2001/3256) subsequently amended the WTR by removing this qualifying period).

It does not appear from the question that there are any collective, work force, or relevant agreements modifying the application of the Regulations in respect of RIT and its employees, as defined in reg. 2.

Jim's weekly working hours exceed the default position of an average 48-hour week: regs 4(1), (2), (5), 23(b). However, the WTR require that the average is calculated over a reference period of 17 weeks (this is extended to 26 weeks for 'special cases', none of which is applicable here: regs 4(5), 21). As he has already completed 12 weeks of service, he (and RIT) should ensure that he has an average of a 48-hour week over the reference period (it seems to be a rolling 17-week period in Jim's case, since no period is specified by a relevant agreement: reg. 4(3), (4), by adjusting his hours over the remaining five weeks of the period). An employer must take all reasonable steps to ensure that this limit is complied with: reg. 4(2). The Health and Safety Executive (HSE) has enforcement rights against RIT: reg. 28. However, in *Barber* v *RJB Mining (UK) Ltd* [1999] IRLR 308, the High Court held that reg. 4(1) imposed a mandatory contractual obligation on the employer, and gave rise to a free-standing contractual right enforceable by employees. This could give rise to the possibility of a claim in the civil courts for a declaration of rights and an injunction preventing the employer from requiring the employee to work more than a 48-hour week.

Gary is classed as a young worker, since he is 15 or over but under 18: reg. 2(1). As such, and given that his working hours exceed four and a half hours, he is entitled to a rest break of at least 30 minutes (to be taken consecutively if possible: reg. 12(4)). It would appear that the *force majeure* provision relating to young workers is not applicable here: reg. 27. Gary would be able to bring a complaint in the employment tribunal (reg. 30), for which no qualifying period of continuous employment is required. Such a claim must be brought within three months of the act or omission which is the subject of the complaint.

Tina's daily working time is six hours and, as an adult worker, she cannot complain about her 15-minute break as she does not come within reg. 12(1), which requires a 20-minute break only where daily working time is *more* than six hours.

Mark may come within the definition of 'night worker' under the WTR. A night worker is defined in reg. 2 as someone who either, (a) *as a normal course*, works at least three hours of his daily working time during night time, or (b) 'who is likely, during night time, to work at least such proportion of his annual working time as may be specified ... in a collective agreement or work force agreement'. Under (a) above, a person works hours 'as a normal course ... if he works such hours on the majority of days on which he works': reg. 2. In *R v Attorney General for Northern Ireland ex parte Burns* [1999] IRLR 315, the Northern Ireland High Court held that a worker who worked for at least three hours during the night on one week in each three-week cycle was a night worker. It further held that 'as a normal course' meant 'as a regular feature'. Night time is defined as a period of 'not less than seven hours, and which includes the period between midnight and 5 a.m.': reg. 2. In default of any relevant agreement, this period is between 11 p.m. and 6 a.m.: reg. 2.

Clearly, Mark works for three hours of his daily working time during night time, so he satisfies the definition of a night worker under the WTR. Regulation 6 of the WTR provides that a night worker's normal hours of work in any reference period is limited to an average of eight hours for each 24 hours. In the absence of any agreement, the reference period is 17 weeks. Mark's hours comply with this requirement.

As he is a night worker, RIT should have provided him with the opportunity to have a free health assessment before assigning him to such work: reg. 7(1)(a)(i). It should also ensure that he has the opportunity of a free health assessment 'at regular intervals of whatever duration are appropriate in his case': reg. 7(1)(b). Under reg. 7, any health assessment must be done 'for the purposes of this regulation'. It seems that Mark's doctor has not carried out such an assessment for these purposes. Therefore, Mark should request such an assessment, and RIT has a legal duty to provide one. Assuming that his health problems are connected with his night work, and a registered medical practitioner so advises RIT, it should transfer him to suitable work, to be carried out during periods outside night time, where it is possible to do so: reg. 7(6).

Assuming that there are no agreements or an opt-out in place modifying RIT's statutory obligations under the WTR. Oliver appears to be working the maximum number of hours permitted under the WTR, i.e. an average of 48 hours for each seven days during the reference period, which is 17 weeks: reg. 4(3)(b). Therefore, RIT seems to be complying with the WTR. However, his on-call time would take him over this maximum, if it is included as part of his working time. Under reg. 2, 'working time' is any period when a worker is 'working, at his employer's disposal and carrying out his activity or duties'. Whether on-call time constitutes 'working time' came before the context of a reference from a Spanish court concerning the correct interpretation of Art. 2(1) of the Working Time Directive 93/104/EC. In *Sindicato Medicos Publica v Valenciana* Case C-303/98 [2000] ICR 116, the ECJ held that time on-call at the place of work counts as 'working time', but time on-call but not at the place of work does not. This meant that doctors working in primary health care teams, whose contracts stipulated that their working time was 40 hours per week plus any other time on-call, were only engaged in 'working time' when they were on-call *and physically present* at their place of employment. Time on-call when they were not at their place of employment but only contactable, was not working time. On the basis of this ECJ decision, it would appear that there is no infringement of the WTR in terms of the maximum weekly working hours of Oliver, as he is not required to be physically present at work during his on-call time.

Finally, in certain circumstances where dismissal of an employee is for a reason (or, where there is more than one, the principal reason) relating to rights conferred by the WTR, it will be automatically unfair: ERA, s. 101A. These circumstances include, (a) the refusal (or proposed refusal) of the employee to comply with a requirement which the employer imposed (or proposed to impose) in contravention of the WTR: or (b) the refusal (or proposed refusal) of the employee to forgo a right conferred on him or her by the Regulations: ERA, s. 101A(a), (b). Similarly, where the reason or principal reason for dismissal was that the employee brought proceedings to enforce a right given, inter alia, by the WTR (or where the employee alleged, in good faith, that his/her employer had infringed such a right), this will amount to the assertion of a statutory right, and it will be automatically unfair: ERA, s. 104. Furthermore, where a claim is made under the ERA, ss. 101A or 104, no qualifying period of continuous employment is required: ERA, s. 108(3)(dd).

In addition to these rights, where a *worker* has suffered a detriment for, inter alia, (i) refusing (or proposing to refuse) to comply with a requirement which the employer imposed (or proposed to impose) in contravention of the WTR or (ii) refusing (or proposing to refuse) to forgo a right conferred on him/her by the Regulations, he/she may bring a claim for breach of the WTR.

Question 3

Joe has worked for Lattima's Chemicals Ltd (LCL) for five years. He has been given notice of termination of his employment by reason of redundancy. While working out his notice, he requested time off to look for other work, but his request was refused by Tom, the Managing Director, who informed Joe that the company required all employees to be present at work until the expiry of their notice period. Roger, who has worked for LCL for eight months, and who is not under notice of redundancy, was informed last week that, owing to the interruption of certain chemical supplies to LCL, he would have to be laid off without pay for a short period (under an express term of his contract allowing LCL to do this), as there was no other work for him to carry out. He has not worked for the last seven working days. LCL told him to check whether any work was available on a daily basis, by telephoning LCL every working morning at 9 a.m. Roger did this on what would have been the first two working days after lay-off but he has not done so since then. Mike, who has worked for LCL for five weeks, was told yesterday that he would have to be taken off the chemical process he was engaged upon because there was a risk of exposure to a hazardous substance, in order to ensure that LCL complied with the Control of Lead at Work Regulations 1998 (SI 1998/543). There is no other suitable work available, and LCL has indicated that it may be four weeks before the problem is sorted out. In the meantime, it has stated that it will pay him £225 per week, although his normal weekly wage is £245.

Advise the employees of any rights they may have.

Commentary

This question concerns the following employment rights: time off to look for work while under notice of redundancy; guarantee payments when laid off for a short period; and medical suspension pay.

Issues arousing concern: the requirements to be satisfied in order to qualify for the respective rights; whether the employer has complied with its obligations under the legislation; and any remedies available to the employees. Each employee should be discussed in turn, and your analysis should be supported by reference to the relevant statutory provisions, and any supporting case law.

Answer plan

- Consider the provisions relating to time off to look for work while under a redundancy notice; employees' eligibility requirements; whether the employer has complied with its obligations; whether the employees have complied with requirements under the relevant provisions.
- Consider the legislation on guarantee payments after lay-offs, and medical suspension pay.
- Discuss the remedies available following complaint to an employment tribunal.

Suggested answer

As an employee with the qualifying period of continuous employment (two years) who is under notice of redundancy, Joe has the statutory right to take 'reasonable time off' to look for work, or to make arrangements for training for future employment: ERA, ss. 52–4. There is no burden on the employee to prove that time off has been taken for proper purposes, but failure to do so would be taken into account by the tribunal in determining whether the time off was 'reasonable': see *Dutton v Hawker Siddely Aviation Ltd* [1978] IRLR 390, EAT. The employer may ask for such proof.

He also has the right to be paid his normal hourly remuneration during the time taken off work for this purpose (ERA, s. 53), subject to the statutory maximum (£280 per week from 1 October 2005), calculated by reference to a week's pay as specified in ERA, ss. 221–9 and 234. However, the remuneration to be paid cannot exceed 40 per cent of a week's pay for that employee: ERA, s. 53(5). In practice, this means that most employees will not take off more than two days from work while under redundancy notice, unless they are happy to forgo their pay for any days taken off over that number. There may be contractual provisions concerning pay for time off in these circumstances, and where these mean that contractual pay is equal to or in excess of the statutory pay, the contractual pay goes to discharge the employer's liability: ERA, s. 53(7).

Unreasonable refusal by the employer to give an employee time off, or payment for time off, allows the employee to bring a complaint to the Employment Tribunal under ERA, s. 54, which may make a declaration, and award any sum due (up to 40 per cent of the weekly wage).

Despite the express contractual term allowing LCL to lay Roger off without pay, he is entitled to a guarantee payment under ERA, ss. 28–35. Employees who have been continuously employed for one month or more are entitled to this payment for working days when there is no work because of 'a diminution in the requirements of the employer's business for work of the kind which the employee is employed to do, or any other occurrence affecting the normal working of the employer's business' in relation to that kind of work: ERA, ss. 29, 28(1)(a), (b). This seems to apply to Roger's case. Roger may lose his right to guarantee payments where, inter alia, he fails to comply with 'reasonable requirements imposed by his employer with a view to ensuring that his services are available': ERA, s. 29(5). Whether the requirement to telephone LCL every morning at 9 a.m. is a reasonable one would be a matter of fact for the tribunal to decide: it is submitted that this would be a reasonable requirement. Whether Roger's failure to do so amounts to a failure to comply is more difficult. Strict compliance with this provision may be required, and his failure to do so for five out of the previous seven working days may disqualify him from claiming. In *Meadows v Faithful Overalls Ltd* [1977] IRLR 330, it was held that the employer's request to employees to remain on the premises and wait for less than one hour, to await the arrival of emergency supplies of oil for the central heating (which meant that the workplace temperature was below the statutory minimum) was reasonable. The refusal of the employees to wait after 9.45 a.m., when the employer had reason to believe that the supplies would arrive by 10 a.m., constituted a failure to comply with that reasonable requirement. The employees were not entitled to guarantee payments.

Roger may present a complaint to the employment tribunal within three months of the relevant working day for which a guarantee payment is claimed, and the tribunal may award the amount of the guarantee payment which it finds due to him.

Mike's claim concerns medical suspension pay. He has clearly been suspended on medical grounds (the Control of Lead at Work Regulations 1998 come within the legislation requiring suspension in the event of certain dangers arising from specified chemicals, including lead). He qualifies to make such a claim because he needs only one month's continuous employment (he has five weeks): ERA, s. 65(1). He has the right to be paid up to 26 weeks, if capable of work: s. 64(2). He is entitled to a week's pay (up to a maximum of 26) for every week of suspension, calculated according to ERA, ss. 220–29, subject to the statutory maximum (£310 from 1 February 2007).

Further reading

Barnard, C., 'The Working Time Regulations 1999' (2000) 29(2) ILJ 167–71.

Collins, H., Ewing, K. D., and McColgan, A., *Labour Law: Text and Materials* (Oxford: Hart Publishing, 2002), chs 4 and 6.

Edwards, A., '*Barber v RJB Mining* in the wider context of health and safety legislation' 2000 29(3) ILJ 280–7.

'Employment law review 2002: working time' (2003) 724 *IDS Brief 24–5.*

Hepple, B., and Morris, G. S., 'The Employment Act 2002 and the crisis of individual employment rights' (2002) 31(3) ILJ 245–69.

Honeyball, S., and Bowers, J., *Textbook on Labour Law,* 8th edn (Oxford: Oxford University Press, 2006), ch. 12.

'Lay-offs and short-time working' (1998) 589 IRLB 2–10.

Lewis, D., 'Whistleblowing at work: on what principles should legislation be based?' (2001) 30(2) ILJ 169–93.

'Public interest disclosure: date of dismissal determines applicability of whistleblowing provisions' (2002) 694 IRLB 13–14.

Sargeant, M., *Employment Law,* 3rd edn (Harlow: Pearson, 2005), ch 8.

Smith, I. T., and Thomas, G., *Industrial Law,* 8th edn (Oxford: Oxford University Press, 2003), ch. 4.

'Work-life balance in the UK' (2000) 468 *IDS Employment Europe* 22–3.

11

Trade unions and industrial action

Introduction

In recent times the trade union movement has declined in size and, perhaps, in influence. In 1979 it reached its peak membership of over 13.2 million members. By 2006, this had declined to some 7.6 million, although this represents a levelling out of the decline. There is perhaps not enough evidence to prove a causal relationship between this decline and the rules on strike ballots and other measures, including the ability to take strike action, introduced by the Conservative governments between 1979 and 1997 and continued subsequently, but it is safe to assume that they contributed towards that decline.

The right to associate has been a concern of international organizations and is seen by many as a basic right of workers in a democratic society, e.g. Art. 11 of the European Convention of Human Rights states that everyone has the right of peaceful association and freedom of association. This Article was incorporated into national law, from October 2000, by the Human Rights Act 1998.

The freedom to join a trade union is linked with the freedom not to join. Whether the 'negative right' not to join can be equated with the 'positive right' to join one is an issue of debate. *Young, James and Webster* v *United Kingdom* [1981] IRLR 408 concerned three employees of British Rail who lost their jobs for refusing to join one of the trade unions with which British Rail had concluded a closed shop agreement. It appears that, in total, some 54 individuals were dismissed for refusing to join one of the trade unions, out of a total work force of some 250,000. The European Court of Human Rights held that Art. 11 of the Convention had been breached.

Trade unions and independence

A list of trade unions is maintained by the Certification Officer (CO). Being on the list is evidence that an organization is a trade union. An organization of workers can apply to be included in the list and will need to supply the CO with various materials, including a copy of its rules and a list of its officers. If the CO is satisfied with the information, then the organization will be added. Conversely the CO may remove an organization if the CO decides that it is not a trade union or if the organization so requests it or if the organization has ceased to exist (for example where two trade unions merge).

An advantage of being on the list maintained by the CO is that any trade union on that list may apply to the CO for a certificate that it is independent: s. 6(1) of the Trade Union and Labour Relations (Consolidation) Act 1992 (TULRCA). The statutory benefits accruing to trade unions usually go to those that are independent, e.g. the duty of employers to disclose information under s. 181, TULRCA. The CO may withdraw the certificate if the CO is of the opinion that the trade union is no longer independent. The certificate, while it is in force, is conclusive proof of independence. Section 5, TULRCA provides a definition of an independent trade union.

Industrial action

The common law has traditionally regarded a strike as a breach of the contract of employment and the calling or organizing of a strike as an inducement to another to breach the contract of employment. The courts have developed a number of torts to limit the actions of workers, both individually and collectively. One perspective is to regard the history of the law regarding industrial action as a series of steps by the courts to introduce new torts to make individuals and unions liable, with the state stepping in from time to time to limit the worst excesses of the courts and providing some statutory immunity to individuals and unions for actions in contemplation or furtherance of a trade dispute. These liabilities in tort include inducing a breach of contract, interference with a contract or business, intimidation, and conspiracy.

Inducing a breach of contract

An inducement to breach a contract of employment is when a trade union, for example, instructs its members to take strike action against their employer. Without further intervention the employer may have a case against the trade union for inducing its employees to breach their contracts of employment. *DC Thomson & Co v Deakin* [1952] 2 All ER 361 concerned the delivery of bulk paper from a supplier to a printing firm. The employees of the supplier refused to deliver paper to the printer and an injunction was sought to stop the trade unions concerned from inducing the supplier to breach its contract with the printer.

Interference with a contract or business

This tort is closely connected with the tort of inducing a breach of contract. *Torquay Hotel Co Ltd v Cousins* [1969] 2 Ch 106 concerned an attempt by a trade union to stop the supply of heating oil to a hotel with which there was not a trade dispute. Lord Denning MR extended the principle expounded in *Quinn v Leathem* [1901] AC 495 that 'it is a violation of legal right to interfere with contractual relations recognised by law if there be no sufficient justification for the interference'. Lord Denning stated that there were three aspects to the principle. These were, first, that there needed to be interference in the execution of a contract; second, that interference must be deliberate, meaning that the person interfering must know of the contract; and, third, that the interference must be direct.

Intimidation

In its direct form this is committed where an unlawful threat is made directly to the plaintiff with the intention of causing loss to the plaintiff. In its indirect form it is where C suffers as a result of action taken by B as a result of an unlawful threat by A. An example of this can be seen in *News Group Newspapers Ltd* v *SOGAT '82* [1986] IRLR 337. This concerned the breakdown of negotiations between the plaintiff and the union over the employment of union members at its new plant in Wapping. The unions called their members out on strike, and they were then dismissed. This was followed by picketing, large-scale rallies, and demonstrations outside the Wapping plant. Although, according to the High Court, the tort of intimidation is not complete unless the person threatened succumbs to the threat and damage results, in this case there were sufficient threats of violence and molestation, which were taken seriously, to justify the granting of injunctive relief.

Conspiracy

There are two types of conspiracy. One is the conspiracy to injure and the other is the conspiracy to commit an unlawful act.

A conspiracy to injure occurs when a combination of two or more combine together to injure a person in their trade by inducing customers or employees to break their contracts or not to deal with that person, which results in damage to that person: *Huntley* v *Thornton* [1957] 1 WLR 321. Of importance is the real purpose of the combination. If the predominant purpose was an intention to injure the plaintiff, then the tort is committed, even if the means used to inflict the damage were lawful and not actionable: *Crofter Hand Woven Harris Tweed Co Ltd* v *Veitch* [1942] 1 All ER 142.

A conspiracy to commit an unlawful act is when a combination of persons conspires to intentionally inflict damage on another person by an unlawful act. Even if the primary purpose was to further or protect some legitimate interest, it is enough that this was achieved by the use of unlawful means: see *Lonhro plc* v *Fayed* [1991] 3 All ER 303.

Protection from tort liabilities

Protection is given against certain potential liabilities in tort by s. 219, TULRCA. The immunity from liability is on the grounds that the act, first, induces another to break a contract or interferes, or induces another to interfere, with the performance of the contract and, second, that it consists in threatening these actions. There are three requirements in respect of this protection. First, the act done should be in 'contemplation or furtherance of a trade dispute'; second, it must be a trade dispute between workers and their employer; and, third, it must relate, wholly or mainly, to a number of specific issues, including terms and conditions of employment, engagement or non-engagement, allocation of work or the duties of employment between workers, and matters of discipline.

Trade unions and industrial conflict is a big subject and may require a student to focus on those areas directed by the course of study in which they are participating. The questions here cover a considerable area, but are not intended to be comprehensive.

Question 1

A trade union's ability to exclude, expel, or discipline any of its members has been severely curtailed by statutory and judicial intervention.
Critically consider this statement.

Commentary

This is a straightforward question asking you to display your knowledge of some aspects of the relationship between trade unions and their members. You are invited to critically consider the statutory rules on exclusion, expulsion, and discipline and consider the extent to which these rules inhibit trade unions from taking action.

It is sometimes difficult to resist, in a question like this, the use of detailed analysis of relevant statute. Remember that you are unlikely to be awarded many marks for repeating great chunks of statute.

Answer plan

- Introduction and reference to relevant statute
- Issues related to exclusion or not being admitted to membership
- Issues related to expulsion and the Bridlington Principles
- Issues related to discipline including suspension and unjustifiable discipline
- Conclusions about curtailment

Suggested answer

Until the 1971 Industrial Relations Act there was little statutory regulation limiting a trade union's powers to admit, discipline, or expel a member. Section 65 of this Act introduced rules against arbitrary exclusions or expulsions and unfair or unreasonable disciplinary action. Although this section was repealed in 1976, it was re-introduced in the 1980 Employment Act as part of the new government's attack on the closed shop. The rules on exclusion, expulsion, and discipline are now contained in the Trade Union and Labour Relations (Consolidation) Act 1992 (TULRCA).

An individual may not be excluded or expelled from a trade union, except for four specific reasons, s. 174, TULRCA. Exclusion in this case means not being admitted to membership: see *NACODS* v *Gluchowski* [1996] IRLR 252. These include when an individual does not satisfy an enforceable membership requirement. This means a restriction on membership as a result of employment being in one specific trade, industry, or profession; or of an occupational description such as a particular grade or level; or of the need for specific trade, industrial, or professional qualifications or work experience. It also includes when the exclusion or expulsion is attributable to the individual's conduct. Conduct related to membership of another union, being employed by a particular employer, or being a member of a particular political party are not included.

These restrictions on the ability of unions to exclude or expel necessitated a revision of the original 'Bridlington Principles'. These were a set of recommendations agreed at the 1939 Trades Union Congress (held at Bridlington). They were designed to minimize disputes over membership questions. They laid down the procedures by which the TUC dealt with complaints by one trade union against another and were designed to stop inter-union disputes over membership and representation.

The courts have not always shared this hostility to allowing trade unions to decide these matters on their own. *Cheall* v *APEX* [1983] IRLR 215 concerned an individual whom a trade union was ordered, by the disputes committee of the TUC, to exclude from membership. This was permitted by the union's rules at the time. The House of Lords rejected the view that this was contrary to public policy. Lord Diplock stated that there can be no right of an individual to associate with other individuals who are not willing to associate with him. This was clearly not the view of the government, as shown by their subsequent legislation.

An individual may present a complaint to an employment tribunal if he or she has been excluded or expelled in contravention of s. 174, TULRCA. Compensation can be reduced if the union member is partly at fault. In *Saunders* v *The Bakers, Food and Allied Workers Union* [1986] IRLR 16 an applicant resigned from the union over a disagreement about an unofficial strike. The individual later re-applied for membership and the application was refused. An appeal was made to the national executive committee in writing, but the individual failed to attend in person. The EAT agreed with the employment tribunal when it stated that the individual could have done more to help himself by attending the meeting of the national executive committee. Compensation was reduced as a result of this. It is the trade union's duty to put the member back into the position that he or she was in before the wrongful expulsion: see *NALGO* v *Courtney-Dunn* [1992] IRLR 114.

The courts have the role of interpreting the application of union disciplinary rules, often in favour of the individual, especially where the offences are of a broad nature such as being 'detrimental to the interests of the union'. Rules which appear to conflict with public policy can also be struck out, see *Lee* v *Showmans Guild* [1952] QB 329, as can rules requiring action in breach of the rules of natural justice. In *Losinska* v *CPSA* [1976] ICR 473, a union president was able to stop the union's executive committee and its annual conference from discussing matters critical of themselves on the grounds that both played a part in the union's disciplinary process. They could not therefore be allowed to condemn the individual until that process had taken place.

Section 64(1), TULRCA states that an individual who is, or has been, a member of a trade union has the right not to be 'unjustifiably disciplined' by that trade union. A person is disciplined by a trade union if the action takes place under the rules of the union or is conducted by an official of the union or by a number of persons who include an official. Section 64(2), TULRCA provides a list of six meanings of 'disciplined'. These include expulsion from the union, payment of a sum to the union, depriving the individual of access to any services or facilities that he or she would be entitled to by virtue of belonging to the union, encouraging another union or branch not to accept the individual into membership, and subjecting the individual to some other detriment.

Suspension of membership can mean depriving someone of access to the benefits of membership. In *NALGO* v *Killorn and Simm* [1990] IRLR 464 an individual was suspended from membership for refusing to cross a picket line. The trade union also sent out a circular naming her, and others, as being suspended for strike breaking. Both the suspension and the circular were held to be forms of unjustifiable discipline.

'Unjustifiably disciplined' is in accordance with s. 65 TULRCA. This provides a further list, this time of ten different items of conduct, for which any resulting discipline will be 'unjustified'. This conduct includes failing to participate in or support a strike or other industrial action, or indicating a lack of support for, or opposition to, such action. In the case of *Knowles* v *Fire Brigades Union* [1996] IRLR 617, the complainants failed in showing unjustifiable discipline because the pressure exerted on employers by the union did not amount to industrial action.

An individual who claims to have been unjustifiably disciplined may present a complaint to an employment tribunal within three months of the infringement, unless it was not reasonably practicable for the complaint to be presented in that time. Additionally, if there is a delay resulting from an attempt to appeal against the discipline or have it reviewed or reconsidered, the three-month limit may be extended: s. 66(2)(b), TULRCA. This happened, for example, in *Killorn* where a letter to the union branch chair, in which the complaint raised a series of questions about the suspension, was held to be a 'reasonable attempt' to appeal in accordance with this section. The EAT held that the statute did not lay down any specific method of appealing, so an employment tribunal should consider the reality of the events, rather than look for formal appeal proceedings.

Question 2

Consider the protection provided in s. 219, TULRCA from 'certain tort liabilities'. Specifically consider this protection in relation to picketing.

Commentary

This is actually a simple question. It asks you first to consider the protection from certain tort liabilities offered by s. 219, TULRCA. It is, of course, a conditional protection and you will need to examine the qualifications outlined in statute. The question then requires some critical discussion of this protection in relation to picketing and, perhaps, secondary action. Resist the temptation to go down the path of considering all the other torts for which s. 219 offers some protection, as the question has limited the scope to picketing.

Answer plan

- Reference to statute providing immunities from potential liabilities in tort
- Consider example of tort of inducing a breach of contract
- Qualified protection offered
- Meaning of 'in contemplation or furtherance of a trade dispute'
- Discussion of s. 220, TULRCA in relation to picketing
- Secondary action

Suggested answer

Protection is given against certain potential liabilities in tort by s. 219, Trade Union and Labour Relations (Consolidation) Act 1992 (TULRCA). Examples of tortious acts for which trade unions and individuals may be liable, without statutory immunity, include the common law torts of inducing a breach of contract and interference with a contract or with business.

The immunity from liability is on the grounds that the act, first, induces another to break a contract or interferes, or induces another to interfere, with the contract's performance and, second, that it consists in threatening these actions. Any agreement or combination of two or more persons to do, or procure, the doing of an act in contemplation or furtherance of a trade dispute will not be actionable in tort if the act is one that would not have been actionable if done without any agreement or combination.

There are three requirements in respect of this protection. First, the act done should be in 'contemplation or furtherance of a trade dispute' (sometimes called the 'golden formula'), second, it must be a trade dispute between workers and their employer and, third, it must relate, wholly or mainly, to a number of specific issues. These include terms and conditions of employment, allocation of work or the duties of employment between workers, and matters of discipline.

The phrase about relating 'wholly or mainly to' is intended to direct attention to what the dispute is about, or what it is mainly about: see *Mercury Communications*

Ltd v *(1) Scott-Garner* [1983] IRLR 494. This means a consideration of more than the event that caused the dispute, but includes the reasons why there is a dispute. This, in turn, perhaps, means investigating the motives of a trade union and whether there are other reasons which might be perceived as the real ones, such as possible political motivations, as in *University College London Hospital* v *Unison* [1999] IRLR 31.

The term 'in contemplation or furtherance of a trade dispute' requires a subjective judgment as to how widely it should be interpreted. In *Bent's Brewery Co Ltd* v *Luke Hogan* [1945] 2 All ER 570 a union did attempt to collect such information. The court held that the union was inducing employees to breach their contracts of employment by revealing confidential information. The union was not entitled to statutory protection, because there was no imminent or existing dispute. There was a possibility of a future dispute, but no certainty that such a dispute would arise. A trade dispute also needs to be related to the contractual or other relationship between workers and the employer: see *British Broadcasting Corporation* v *DA Hearn* [1977] IRLR 273.

The dispute must be between existing workers and their current employer. Thus it is not possible to conduct a dispute, within the protection of s. 219, TULRCA, about the contracts of employment of future workers: see *University College London Hospital* v *Unison* [1999] IRLR 31, CA.

There are a number of actions which will not qualify for the immunity provided by s. 219, TULRCA, including some picketing. As well as the economic torts, pickets are potentially liable for other torts, such as trespass to the highway, the tort of private nuisance, and the tort of public nuisance which consists of an act or omission which causes inconvenience to the public in the exercise of their common rights, such as the unreasonable obstruction of the highway: see *News Group Newspapers* v *SOGAT '82* [1986] IRLR 337.

There is no immunity from actions in tort for acts done in the course of picketing unless they are done in accordance with s. 220, TULRCA. This provides that it is lawful for a person, in contemplation or furtherance of a trade dispute, to attend at or near their own place of work for the purpose of either peacefully obtaining or communicating information, or peacefully persuading any person to either work or abstain from working. The same provision allows an official of a trade union to accompany, for the same purposes, a member of the union, whom the official represents, at or near their workplace. There is no precise definition of what is meant by 'at' or 'near' the place of work. May LJ declined to provide one as the number of circumstances that one might have to provide for were so variable as to make it impossible to lay down a test: see *Rayware Ltd* v *TGWU* [1989] IRLR 134, CA. The court suggested the use of a common-sense approach. The issue had been whether a group of workers picketing at the entrance to a private trading estate, some seven-tenths of a mile from the workplace were 'at' or 'near' the place of work. The word 'near' was to be an expanding word, not a restraining one.

The meaning of the word was to be expanded to give effect to the purpose of the legislation. This purpose was to give a right to picket.

The legislation does not prescribe the number of pickets that are to be allowed at or near the place of work. The requirement is for the picketing to be peaceful. It may be that picketing by large numbers of individuals may be intimidating enough for it no longer to be seen as peaceful. *Thomas v NUM (South Wales Area)* [1985] IRLR 137 concerned mass picketing at the gates of a number of collieries in South Wales during the 1984 miners' strike. It was held to be tortious because of its nature and the way that it was carried out. It represented an unreasonable harassment of those miners who were working. Mass picketing by trying to block the entry to the workplace may be a common law nuisance.

Secondary action is not lawful picketing: s. 224, TULRCA. It is defined as an inducement to, or a threat to, break or interfere with a contract of employment where the employer in that contract is not party to the dispute. An employer shall not be regarded as party to a dispute between another employer and the workers of that employer, and where more than one employer is in dispute with its workers, the dispute between each employer and its workers is to be treated as a separate dispute. Finally, a primary action in one dispute, which is protected if in contemplation or furtherance of a trade dispute, cannot be relied upon as secondary action in another dispute.

Question 3

Critically consider the approach of the courts to the torts of

(a) inducing a breach of contract,

(b) interference with a contract or business,

(c) intimidation,

(d) conspiracy

in relation to industrial action.

 Commentary

These are just four of the torts developed by the courts in restraining trade unions and others from interfering in the contractual relations between employer and worker and between business. They are important ones, however, and indicate the importance of the statutory immunities offered by s. 219, TULRCA in protecting acts done in contemplation or furtherance of a trade dispute.

Answer plan

- Derivation and development of liability for inducing a breach of contract
- Direct and indirect inducement
- Meaning of tort of interfering with a contract or business
- Derivation and issues around the tort of intimidation
- Meaning and issues concerning a conspiracy to injure

Suggested answer

The common law has traditionally regarded a strike as a breach of the contract of employment and the calling or organizing of a strike as an inducement to another to breach the contract of employment. The courts have developed a number of torts to limit the actions of workers, both individually and collectively.

The tort of inducing a breach of contract derives from the case of *Lumley* v *Gye* (1853) 2 E & B 216. This concerned an opera singer who was induced by a theatre manager to breach her contract with one theatre in order to appear at the defendant's own theatre. The court held that each party had a right to the performance of the contract and that it was wrong for another to procure one of the parties to break it or not perform it.

An inducement to breach an employment contract is when a trade union, for example, instructs its members to take strike action against their employer. Without further intervention the employer may have a case against the trade union for inducing its employees to breach their contracts of employment. A direct inducement to the breach of a commercial contract is when A puts pressure on B not to fulfil a contract with C.

Thus if trade union A were, for example, to apply pressure on employer B, in order to stop employer B making a delivery to employer C, then C, without further intervention, may be able to take action against B for breach of contract to supply. It is also possible for A to indirectly induce B to breach its contract with C. If the trade union instructed its members to take strike action against employer B in order to stop them supplying employer C, then they might be liable for indirectly inducing that breach.

DC Thomson & Co v *Deakin* [1952] 2 All ER 361 concerned the delivery of bulk paper from a supplier to a printing firm. The employees of the supplier refused to deliver paper to the printer and an injunction was sought to stop the trade unions concerned from inducing the supplier to breach its contract with the printer. The conditions necessary to show that there had been an actionable interference with one of the parties to the contract were, according to the court, that the person charged with the actionable interference knew of the existence of the contract and intended to procure its breach; that the person so charged did persuade or induce the employees to break their contracts of employment; that the persuaded or induced employees did break their contract of employment; that the breach of contract was a natural consequence of the employees' breaches of their contracts of employment. For this last point it needs to be shown that, because of the employees' actions, their employer was unable to fulfil the contract: see *Falconer* v *ASLEF and NUR* [1986] IRLR 331.

The difference between direct and indirect inducement to breach a contract is one of causation. For direct inducement to take place, as in *Lumley* v *Gye,* the persuasion had to be directed at the parties to the contract. *Middlebrook Mushrooms Ltd* v *TGWU* [1993] IRLR 232 concerned the distribution of leaflets, by dismissed employees, outside a supermarket aimed at persuading customers not to buy their ex-employer's produce. This was, at best, indirect inducement on the parties to the contract, namely the supplier and the shop. The court held that there was no evidence that contracts existed between the shop and the supplier. It may be possible to infer knowledge, but not in this case.

The knowledge needed, however, may be minimal: see *JT Stratford & Sons Ltd* v *Lindley* [1965] AC 269. In *Falconer* v *ASLEF* [1986] IRLR 331, a railway passenger claimed damages from two rail unions for costs incurred as a result of industrial action. The action had been called without a ballot, resulting in the union being unable to rely on any statutory immunities. The claim was successful because not only did the unions know of the existence of contracts between the railway company and passengers, their intention was to affect the plaintiff and other passengers in order to put pressure on the employer. The county court judge decided that the unions were reckless in their intent, as they knew the effect of the action on the plaintiff, but nevertheless pursued it.

Interference with contract or with business is a tort closely connected with the tort of inducing a breach of contract. *Torquay Hotel Co Ltd* v *Cousins* [1969] 2 Ch 106 concerned an attempt by a trade union to stop the supply of heating oil to a hotel with which there was not a trade dispute. Lord Denning MR extended the principle in *Quinn* v *Leathem* [1901] AC 495 that it is a violation of legal right to interfere with contractual relations if there is not sufficient justification for the interference. Indirect interference would not be enough and might, according to Lord Denning, take away the right to strike. The conditions were satisfied in this case, where there was direct and deliberate interference in the contractual relations between the customer and supplier.

A further example can be found in *Timeplan Education Group Ltd* v *National Union of Teachers* [1997] IRLR 457. This concerned a teachers' union attempting to interfere with the advertising for recruits by a teachers' supply agency. The Court of Appeal held that, in order to establish the tort of wrongful interference with contractual rights, five conditions need to be fulfilled. It must be shown, first, that the defendant persuaded or procured or induced a third party to break a contract; second, knowledge of the contract; third, intention to procure a breach; fourth, that the complainant suffered more than nominal damages; fifth, that the complainant can rebut a defence of justification. In this case no tort was committed because there was a failure to show knowledge of contracts or intention to procure a breach of them.

In its direct form the tort of intimidation is committed where an unlawful threat is made directly to the plaintiff with the intention of causing loss to the plaintiff.

In its indirect form it is where C suffers as a result of action taken by B as a result of an unlawful threat by A. An example of this can be seen in *News Group Newspapers Ltd* v *SOGAT '82* [1986] IRLR 337. The unions called their members out on strike, and they were then dismissed. This was followed by picketing, large-scale rallies, and demonstrations outside the Wapping plant. According to the High Court, the tort of intimidation is not complete unless the person threatened succumbs to the threat and damage results; in this case there were sufficient threats of violence and molestation, which were taken seriously, to justify the granting of interim relief. See also *Thomas* v *National Union of Mineworkers (South Wales Area)* [1985] IRLR 136.

In *Rookes* v *Barnard* [1964] AC 1129 it was held that a threat to breach a contract of employment, by threatening to go on strike, was an unlawful threat for the purposes of a tort of intimidation. In this case an airline company had a closed shop agreement for a part of its operation. The union threatened the airline that it would call its members out on strike if they did not remove an individual employee who had resigned from the union. The House of Lords reacted by making it almost impossible to threaten a strike without being subject to the tort of intimidation. The court stated that there was nothing to differentiate a threat of a breach of contract from a threat of physical violence or any other illegal threat. This decision undermined the immunities enjoyed by trade unions in certain circumstances since the 1906 Trade Disputes Act. Strikes are often preceded by threats of industrial action which would have fallen foul of this decision if the immunity had not been restored by the Trade Disputes Act 1965.

A conspiracy to injure occurs when a combination of two or more combine together to injure a person in their trade by inducing customers or employees to break their contracts or not to deal with that person, which results in damage to that person: see *Quinn* v *Leathem* [1901] AC 495. In *Huntley* v *Thornton* [1957] 1 WLR 321 an individual member of a trade union failed to support a strike. Thereafter there were various successful attempts made to prevent the individual finding other work. The individual then successfully brought an action for damages and conspiracy against a number of members of the trade union, who were held to have combined to injure the plaintiff in his trade and the acts were not done to further the legitimate trade interests of the defendants. Those acts were held to be done without justification. Of importance is the real purpose of the combination. If the predominant purpose was an intention to injure the plaintiff, then the tort is committed, even if the means used to inflict the damage were lawful and not actionable. In *Crofter Hand Woven Harris Tweed Co Ltd* v *Veitch* [1942] 1 All ER 142 the courts recognized that no liability should be attached to a trade union in a genuine trade dispute. It was held that the real purpose of an embargo on Harris Tweed exported by certain crofters was to benefit the members of the trade union. This contrasts with *Huntley* v *Thornton* where the motives were deemed to be personal, rather than in furthering a trade dispute.

Question 4

The Unloading Co Ltd employed 500 people unloading ships at Seaside docks. During a recession they decided to dismiss as redundant 150 of their employees. This was announced to the work force on a Monday, with the dismissals to take effect on the following Friday.

All the employees belonged to the Dockworkers Union. The branch committee of the union called a mass meeting of the employees on the Wednesday and obtained a vote in favour of strike action. This was done by a show of hands. After the meeting the branch committee informed the company that, unless the dismissal notices were withdrawn immediately, the employees would go on strike from the Friday. The employers refused to withdraw the notices and a strike commenced, forcing the closure of the docks.

The employers have informed the general secretary of the union that they are to take legal action and seek compensation for damages. Advise the national executive committee of the union on its legal position.

Commentary

Note that you are being asked to comment on the actions of the branch committee and the trade union, not on the legal implications of the employer's actions.

Detailed rules on the need for trade unions to conduct ballots before taking industrial action were introduced by successive Conservative governments during the 1980s and early 1990s. After the legislation, if industrial action took place without a ballot complying with the rules then there would be no immunity from actions in tort, as per s. 219, TULRCA.

An underlying assumption on the need for such ballots was that many strikes were organized and led against the wishes of the majority of members of a particular trade union. Compulsory balloting of the membership would stop this happening. It would also reduce or eliminate 'wildcat' strikes. It was intended to stop public voting at mass meetings where individuals might feel, it was suggested, coerced into showing solidarity and voting for industrial action.

Answer plan

- Need to follow statutory procedures in order to receive protection from liability
- Notification to the employer
- Sample of ballot paper
- Methods of voting
- Need for repudiation of action by Dockworkers Union or executive

Suggested answer

A trade union will lose its protection under s. 219 of the Trade Union and Labour Relations (Consolidation) Act 1992 (TULRCA) if it induces a person to take part or to continue to take part in industrial action that is not supported by a ballot and the rules concerning notifying the employer about the ballot, contained in s. 226A, TULRCA. This is so even if the inducement is unsuccessful, whether because the individual is not interested or for some other reason. The vote organized by the branch committee of the Dockworkers Union does not meet the requirements of the legislation.

The first stage is that the trade union must take steps as are reasonably necessary to notify the employer of persons entitled to vote in the ballot, that the union intends to hold a ballot, and the date which the union reasonably believes will be the opening day of the ballot: s. 226A, TULRCA. The notice, which is to be in writing, must also contain information, which is in the union's possession, about whom it believes is entitled to vote in the ballot, such as would help the employer make plans and bring information to the attention of the employees. This notice must be given not later than the seventh day before the opening day of the ballot. Prior to amendment by the Employment Relations Act 1999, there was a requirement for the union to be much more specific in describing who would be entitled to vote. It is still unlikely, however, that the statement of an intention to hold a ballot amongst 'all our members in your institution' would fulfil the requirements of the legislation: see *Blackpool and Fylde College* v *NATFHE* [1994] IRLR 227. The rule is that if the trade union possesses information as to the number, category or workplace of the employees concerned, that is the minimum information that must be supplied: *BT* v *Communications Workers Union* [2004] IRLR 58.

The second stage is that, not later than the third day before the opening day of the ballot, the trade union must also submit a sample of the ballot paper to the employer of the persons likely to be entitled to vote. If, for some reason, not all the ballot papers are the same, then a sample of all of the different versions must be given to the employer. Before the ballot takes place, the trade union needs to appoint a suitably qualified person as a scrutineer.

The entitlement to vote is to be given only to those members of the trade union whom it is reasonable at the time of the ballot for the union to believe will be induced to take part in, or to continue to take part in, the industrial action. No one else has any entitlement to vote: see *University of Central England* v *NALGO* [1993] IRLR 81. Small accidental failures in the process are to be ignored if the failure was both accidental and unlikely to have an effect on the result of the ballot: s. 232B, TULRCA. There are problems for trade unions in organizing ballots that meet the statutory requirements: see *London Underground* v *NURMTW* [1995] IRLR 636 concerning an influx of new members.

Voting at mass meetings by raising a hand, to support industrial action or not, was perhaps commonplace once. It is not permissible now. Every member entitled to vote must be given a voting paper which must state the name of the independent scrutineer, and clearly specify the address to which it is to be sent and the date by which it must be sent: s. 229, TULRCA.

The voting paper must also contain at least one of two questions, depending upon the industrial action envisaged. The first question is whether the voter is prepared to take part in, or to continue, a strike. The second is whether the voter is prepared to take part in, or to continue, industrial action short of a strike. If the union wishes to pursue both options, then it must ask both questions. The questions need to be in such a form that the members can vote either yes or no.

There are also strict rules applied to the ballot itself. As far as is reasonably practicable, voting must be done in secret, s. 230, TULRCA, which would exclude the sort of vote that was taken in this case. Every person who is entitled to vote in the ballot must be allowed to do so without interference from the trade union or its officials. They need to have a voting paper sent to them by post to their home address, or any other address to which the individual has requested the union to send it.

An act done by a trade union to induce a person to take part in, or to continue, industrial action will not be regarded as protected unless the trade union gives a relevant notice to the affected employer or employers, within seven days of having notified the employer of the result as required by s. 231A, TULRCA.

The Dockworkers Union has failed to follow any of these procedures, so it is unlikely that the action would be protected from liability in tort, unless it repudiates the action of the branch committee and the members on strike. Trade unions are to be taken as having endorsed or authorized an act if it was authorized or endorsed, by, first, any person who is empowered by the rules of the union to authorize or endorse such action; or, second, by the executive committee or the president or general secretary of the union; or, third, by any other committee or official of the union: s. 20(2), TULRCA; see *Express & Star Ltd* v *NGA* [1985] IRLR 455. For the purpose of this last category a committee of the union is any group of persons constituted in accordance with the union's rules and an act is to be taken as authorized or endorsed by an official if it was authorized or endorsed by a committee of which the official was a member and the committee had as one of its purposes the organizing or coordinating of industrial action: see *Heatons Transport (St Helens) Ltd* v *TGWU* [1972] IRLR 25. There is no need to look for specific authority in a particular case if the authority to act has been expressly or impliedly delegated to different levels of the organization. As a result of proceedings the court may grant an injunction requiring the union to ensure that there is no further inducement to take part in industrial action, and that no person continues to act as if they had been induced to take part.

It is possible for a trade union to avoid this liability for the actions of members, in this respect, by the executive, president, or general secretary repudiating the act as soon as is reasonably practicable after it came to their knowledge. For such a repudiation to be effective, the union must give, without delay, a written notice to the committee or official in question and do its best, without delay, to give the notice to every member that the union believes might be involved with the action and to the employer of every such member: s. 21, TULRCA.

It is only by following this procedure that the union can avoid liability for the act and its consequences. There is a requirement for strict compliance with a repudiation, for the union not to be held liable for further breaches. Section 21(5), TULRCA provides that an act will not be treated as being repudiated if, subsequently, the executive, president, or general secretary of the union acts in such a way that is inconsistent with a repudiation. Thus it is not enough to issue a written repudiation and then continue as before: see *Richard Read (Transport) Ltd* v *NUM (South Wales Area)* [1985] IRLR 67.

The union will be specifically held not to have repudiated if, within three months of the repudiation, there is a request from a party to a commercial contract (i.e. not an employment contract) whose performance has been, or is being, interfered with and who has not been given the necessary written notification, for a written confirmation that the act has been repudiated.

Thus, if the Dockworkers Union wishes to avoid liability for the payment of damages it will need to take the necessary action to repudiate the actions of its branch committee and members.

Further reading

Barrow, C., *Industrial Relations Law*, 2nd edn (London: Cavendish, 2002).

Elias, P., and Ewing, K., *Trade Union Democracy, Members Rights and the Law* (London: Mansell Publishing, 1987).

Hendy, J., QC, Union rights and wrongs: the reform of Britain's anti-union laws (London: Institute of Employment Rights, 2001).

Morris, G. S., and Archer, T. J., *Collective Labour Law* (Oxford: Hart Publishing, 2005).

Sargeant, M. and Lewis, D., *Employment Law*, 4th edn (Harlow: Pearson, 2008).

Simpson, B., 'Trade unions and industrial action ballots in the twenty first century' (2002) 31(3) ILJ.

12

Collective bargaining and consultation

Introduction

Any discussion about the relevance, historical or otherwise, of trade unions will include an analysis of the inequalities of the relationship between employer and employee. While the law of contract regards the parties to the contract (in this case a contract of employment) as being equal parties who have willingly entered into a contractual arrangement, the reality is somewhat different. It is only a privileged few that are able to negotiate and agree their terms and conditions of employment. For most the choice is represented by being offered a position, with associated terms and conditions of employment, by an employer, and deciding whether to take it or leave it. For some, perhaps, even this choice may be absent. If there is little alternative employment to be had, then the economic realities for individuals may mean that they have no choice but to accept the contract offered to them.

The inequalities in the employment relationship are, to some extent, levelled out by workers joining together into trade unions which can then negotiate with employers on more equal terms. Perhaps because of the traditional influence of trade unions and the perceived importance of wage levels by governments in their attempts to regulate the economy, collective bargaining and the agreements that are reached are subject to statutory definition.

Collective agreements

Collective bargaining is a means of achieving a collective agreement. In statutory terms it means any agreement or arrangement made between trade unions and employers relating to a number of specific issues: s. 178 of the Trade Union and Labour Relations (Consolidation) Act 1992 (TULRCA). Of importance in deciding that there is a collective agreement, is whether or not there has been an agreement between a trade union and an employer. This may be as a result of negotiations in a formal setting or it might be the result of deliberations of a joint consultative committee or other committee which makes recommendations: see *Edinburgh Council* v *Brown* [1999] IRLR 208, which concerned a local authority joint consultative committee.

Collective agreements are binding in honour and are subject to social sanctions, rather than legal sanctions. It is possible, however, for the terms of collective agreements to become legally binding through the route of incorporation into the individual contract of employment. This can be as a result of express or implied incorporation. Express incorporation is most effectively achieved by including a term of the contract of employment which refers to the incorporation of a collective agreement: see *Robertson and Jackson* v *British* Gas Co Ltd [1983] IRLR 302. If a collective agreement is not expressly incorporated in this way or by some other form of agreement, then the courts may be prepared to impliedly incorporate an agreement, thus giving it legal effect. It is possible that this may be done on the basis of custom and practice, but the collective agreement would need to be well known and established practice and need to be 'clear, certain and notorious': *Duke* v *Reliance Systems Ltd* [1982] IRLR 347, CA.

Once the collective agreement has become incorporated into the contract it is not open to the employer to unilaterally alter it: see *Gibbons* v *Associated British Ports* [1985] IRLR 376. It is only when terms are varied collectively by agreement that the individual contracts of employment could be varied. If the collective agreement is unilaterally varied or the employer withdraws from it, the contracts of employment containing the provisions are likely to remain intact.

Disclosure of information

For effective collective bargaining to take place, both parties are likely to require sufficient information about the undertaking and other relevant matters. For one side to be kept in the dark on important matters is to encourage that side to negotiate on insufficient information.

Section 181(1), TULRCA provides a general duty for an employer, who recognizes an independent trade union, to disclose certain information for the purposes of all stages of collective bargaining. The duty relates to the categories of workers for whom the trade union is recognized as representing them for collective bargaining purposes.

The information to be disclosed is information that, first, relates to the employer's undertaking and, second, is in the possession of the employer. There is a twofold test to decide the relevance of the information. It must be information without which the trade unions would be 'to a material extent impeded in carrying out collective bargaining' and information the disclosure of which 'would be in accordance with good industrial relations practice'.

There is an ACAS Code of Practice on the disclosure of information to trade unions for collective bargaining purposes. This was updated in 2003 and can be found on the ACAS website.

An employer is not required to disclose information if the disclosure is affected by one of the reasons given in s. 182, TULRCA. All these exceptions place important limitations on the right of trade unions to make employers disclose information. It is, perhaps, of significance that during the period of the 1980s and early 1990s, when

Conservative governments were introducing legislation to limit the power of trade unions, this particular piece of legislation remained untouched.

The ineffectiveness of this legislation is illustrated by the fact that between 1976 and 1997 the Central Arbitration Committee (CAC) received 463 disclosure of information complaints, which was an average of 22 per annum and, in 2006/07, for example, there were only 11 complaints received.

Information and consultation

One of the occasions when a worker is perhaps at his or her most vulnerable, in relation to work, is when the business is reorganized in some way. The reorganization may be the result of a takeover by another employer, or because the worker's own employer has become insolvent or there is a perceived need to reduce the number of employees. In such situations a worker's security of employment and terms and conditions are often at risk.

Consultation with employees or their representatives is required in a number of situations. These include collective redundancy situations, transfers of undertakings, and health and safety matters.

The employer must consult with the *appropriate representatives* of any of the employees who may be affected by the proposed dismissals or transfers. The appropriate representatives are the employees' trade union representatives if an independent trade union is recognized by the employer. If there is no such trade union then either they may be employee representatives appointed or elected by the affected employees for some other purpose, but who have authority to receive information and be consulted about the proposed dismissals, or they may be employee representatives elected by the employees for the purpose of such consultation. The choice of which of these two alternatives should be consulted is left to the employer.

Directive 2002/14/EC, the Information and Consultation Directive, was the first EU Directive to introduce a generalized requirement to provide information and to consult with employees or their representatives. The Directive will eventually (by April 2008) apply to all undertakings with 50 or more employees.

The Directive was implemented in the United Kingdom by the Information and Consultation with Employees Regulations 2004. These Regulations are complex and the process has a similar approach to that which is used in the statutory recognition of trade unions. The process can begin in one of two ways. Either the employer can initiate the process or it starts with a request from the employees. At least 10 per cent of the employees, either together or separately, need to make the request to the employer to open negotiations to reach an Information and Consultation Agreement in order for it to be a valid request. This 10 per cent is subject to a minimum of 15 employees and a maximum of 2500. The employer may also initiate negotiations without waiting for the employees to request action.

As soon as is reasonably practicable the employer must make arrangements for the appointment or election of 'negotiating representatives' and then invite the negotiating representatives to enter into negotiations to reach a negotiated agreement. It must set out the circumstances in which the employer must inform and consult the employees.

If the employer fails to initiate negotiations then there are standard provisions which will apply. The standard provisions first itemize what information must be provided to the representatives. These are:

1. The recent and probable development of the undertaking's activities and economic situation.

2. The situation, structure, and probable development of employment within the undertaking and on any anticipatory measures envisaged, in particular, where there is a threat to employment.

3. Decisions likely to lead to substantial changes in work organization or in contractual relations.

Where there is a failure to comply with any of the terms of a negotiated agreement or a standard provision, a complaint may be made to the CAC within three months beginning with the date of the failure. The CAC may then issue an order for compliance. Failure to carry this out within three months may lead to a further complaint, this time to the EAT which has the power to issue a penalty of up to £75,000.

Some of the issues related to collective bargaining and consultation are concerned with such questions as between whom should it take place, what should be the subject matter and when should the bargaining or consulting commence. There is an established statutory framework around collective bargaining involving trade unions and employers and a growing framework around information and consultation that should take place with employees or their representatives.

Question 1

The provisions contained in TULRCA 1992 which compel an employer to disclose information to trade unions are totally inadequate.
 Critically consider this statement.

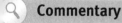 **Commentary**

A perhaps natural consequence of the recognition of a trade union by an employer is the need for both parties to have sufficient information about the undertaking and other relevant matters, in order for them to be able to bargain effectively. That there needs to be a statutory requirement, albeit a weak one, to ensure that information is disclosed to the trade union by the employer is an indication that not all employers have regarded it as important that the trade union, with which they negotiate, should be kept informed. One may equally surmise that there have been trade union negotiators who, at times, have not wished to know about the employer's financial position, in order to press their claims for a pay rise, regardless of the consequences for the employer.

Answer plan

- Statutory duty of the employer to provide information
- Test for relevance of information
- ACAS Code of Practice
- Exceptions to duty to disclose
- Impact of Information and Consultation Regulations

Suggested answer

Section 181(1) of the Trade Union and Labour Relations (Consolidation) Act 1992 (TULRCA) provides a general duty for an employer, who recognizes an independent trade union, to disclose certain information for the purposes of all stages of collective bargaining. The duty relates to the categories of workers for whom the trade union is recognized as representing them for collective bargaining purposes. The information must be disclosed to representatives of the union, who are defined as officials or other persons authorized by the union to carry on such bargaining. According to *R v Central Arbitration Committee ex parte BTP Oxide Ltd* [1992] IRLR 60 these provisions contemplate that there may be alternative types of relationship between employers and unions, rather than just collective bargaining, that entitle a union to information. The information to be disclosed is information that, first, relates to the employer's undertaking and, second, is in the possession of the employer.

There is a twofold test to decide the relevance of the information. It must be information without which the trade unions would be 'to a material extent impeded in carrying out collective bargaining', and, second, information the disclosure of which 'would be in accordance with good industrial relations practice'.

There is an ACAS Code of Practice on the disclosure of information to trade unions for collective bargaining purposes. Paragraph 11 of this Code provides examples of information which might be relevant in certain collective bargaining situations. These examples are information, relating to the undertaking, about pay and benefits, conditions of service, manpower, performance, and financials. Although the ACAS Code is an important guide, it is not intended to exclude other evidence that might be in accord with good industrial relations practice. The request for information by the trade union must be in writing, if the employer so requests, as must the employer's reply, if requested by the trade union.

There are a number of situations in which an employer is not required to disclose information, e.g. if the disclosure would be against the interests of national security or could not be disclosed without contravening a statutory prohibition.

This list of exceptions contributes to making the legislation ineffective. The need for confidentiality, for example, could result in important and relevant information not being disclosed to a trade union. In *Sun Printers Ltd* v *Westminster Press Ltd* [1982]

IRLR 292, CA a widely circulated document about the future of a company was held not to be confidential, but it was suggested, *obiter*, that the stamping of the word 'confidential' on the document would have been enough to allow wide circulation, while retaining confidentiality. Perhaps of more concern to trade unions is the difficulty shown in obtaining pay information concerning parts of a business that are put out to competitive tender. In *Civil Service Union* v *CAC* [1980] IRLR 253 a trade union was stopped from obtaining information about a tenderer's proposed wage rates on the basis that they were given in confidence and that it was information the lack of which could not be held to impede, to a material extent, the union's ability to carry out collective bargaining.

There are further limitations, on the obligations of employers to disclose information, contained in s. 182(2), TULRCA. An employer is not required to produce any documents or extracts from documents, unless the document has been prepared for the purposes of conveying or confirming the information, and the employer is not required to compile or assemble any information which would involve an amount of work or expenditure out of proportion to the value of the information used in the conduct of collective bargaining.

All these exceptions place important limitations on the right of trade unions to make employers disclose information. It is, perhaps, of significance that during the period of the 1980s and early 1990s, when Conservative governments were introducing legislation to limit the power of trade unions, this particular piece of legislation remained untouched. The remedy for trade unions, for failure to disclose, is to make a complaint to the CAC. The CAC will refer the matter to ACAS if it thinks that there is a reasonable chance of a conciliated settlement. If this fails the CAC will hear the cases of all sides and make a decision on whether the complaint is well founded. If it does so, then the employer is given a period, of not less than a week, to disclose the information. If the employer still fails to disclose, then the trade union may present a further complaint to the CAC, which will hear all sides and decide if the complaint is well founded and specify the information in respect of which it made that decision. The CAC may then make an award in respect of the employees specified in the claim. This award will consist of the terms and conditions being negotiated and specified in the claim, or any other terms and conditions which the CAC considers appropriate. These terms and conditions can only be for matters in which the trade union is recognized for collective bargaining purposes.

It is possible that some of the weaknesses of this particular legislation may be mitigated by the introduction of the Information and Consultation with Employees Regulations 2004. These require the employer to consult representatives of employees about decisions which are likely to affect future employment developments within organizations as well as about the development of the employer's business and economic situation. There is no obligation under the Regulations for the employer to negotiate about these matters, but it is possible that the information obtained may be useful, subject to confidentiality requirements in collective bargaining on other matters.

Question 2

Collective agreements are not, normally, legally enforceable. Consider ways in which the terms can become part of the contractual relationship between employer and employee.

Commentary

Perhaps for mostly historical reasons, trade unions have been suspicious of the intervention of the law in industrial relations and although there is the opportunity for trade unions to enter into legally binding agreements with employers, few actually do so. Collective agreements are presumed not to be legally enforceable contracts, unless the agreement is in writing and contains a provision which states that the parties intend the agreement to be a legally enforceable contract. Any agreement which does satisfy these provisions will be 'conclusively presumed to have been intended by the parties to be a legally enforceable contract'. It is also possible to enter into agreements of which only part are designated as being legally enforceable contracts. In such circumstances that part which is not legally enforceable may be used in interpreting that part which is: s. 179, TULRCA.

Answer plan

- Intentions of the parties crucial
- Express and implied incorporation
- Changing the terms unilaterally or by agreement
- Remedies

Suggested answer

The intention of the parties appears to be crucial and unless that intention to enter into a legally enforceable agreement is clear, then there is likely not to be such an agreement. The collective agreement needs to show that, at the very least, the parties have directed their minds to the issue of legal enforceability and have decided in favour of such an approach. *National Coal Board* v *National Union of Mineworkers* [1986] IRLR 439, concerned whether a 1946 agreement on consultation was legally binding or not. The court held that there would need to be evidence that the parties had at least directed their minds to the question and decided on legal enforceability.

Without this there will be an insufficient statement of intent for the purposes of the statute. The court may take into account the surrounding circumstances and even the general climate of opinion about this issue when the agreement is made. In *Ford Motor*

Co Ltd v *Amalgamated Union of Engineering and Foundry Workers* [1969] 2 QB 303 the court found the generally unanimous climate of opinion as relevant. This view was that collective agreements were binding in honour and were subject to social sanctions, rather than legal sanctions.

It is possible for the terms of collective agreements to become legally binding through the route of incorporation into the individual contract of employment. This can be as a result of express or implied incorporation. Express incorporation is most effectively achieved by including a term of the contract of employment which refers to the incorporation of a collective agreement. Examples of such incorporation can be seen in *Robertson and Jackson* v *British Gas Co Ltd* [1983] IRLR 302 and *Whent* v *T Cartledge* [1997] IRLR 153, in which the issue was whether the national agreement had transferred to a new employer as a result of the Transfer of Undertakings (Protection of Employment) Regulations 1981 (SI 1981/1794) (the TUPE Regulations). If a collective agreement is not expressly incorporated in this way or by some other form of agreement, then the courts may be prepared to impliedly incorporate an agreement, thus giving it legal effect. It is possible that this may be done on the basis of custom and practice, but the collective agreement would need to be well known and established practice and need to be 'clear, certain and notorious': see *Duke* v *Reliance Systems Ltd* [1982] IRLR 347.

Alexander v *Standard Telephones & Cables Ltd* [1991] IRLR 286 concerned a claim that a redundancy procedure had become incorporated into individuals' contracts of employment. The High Court summarized the principles to be applied in deciding whether there had been incorporation of a part of the collective agreement.

The fact that another document such as the collective agreement is not legally enforceable does not prevent it becoming incorporated if it can be shown that this was the intentions of the parties: see *Marley* v *Forward Trust Group Ltd* [1986] IRLR 369. Where there is express incorporation, it is still necessary to consider whether it is a term of the contract or not. Where there is no express incorporation contractual intent can still be inferred. In this case the character of the document and the relevant part of it is central to the decision.

Once the collective agreement has become incorporated into the contract it is not open to the employer to unilaterally alter it: see *Gibbons* v *Associated British Ports* [1985] IRLR 376. It is only when terms are varied collectively by agreement that the individual contracts of employment could be varied. If the collective agreement is unilaterally varied or the employer withdraws from it, the contracts of employment containing the provisions are likely to remain intact. The possible exception to this is when there are provisions which allow the employer to vary the terms. If there is a collective agreement which allows an employer to vary part of the contents unilaterally, then the fact that it has become part of the contract of employment will not inhibit this option. See *Airlie* v *City of Edinburgh District Council* [1996] IRLR 516.

In certain situations the courts are willing to be assertive in their remedies. *Anderson* v *Pringle of Scotland Ltd* [1998] IRLR 64 concerned a decision about whether an agreed redundancy procedure should be followed as a result of incorporation or whether the employer could introduce a more selective method. In order to stop the employees being made redundant under the new procedure the court was willing to grant an interdict (injunction) restraining the employers from changing the selection procedure, even though this might amount to an order for specific performance, which would not normally be granted by the courts when intervening in the employment relationship. In this case the court felt that there was still no lack of trust and confidence in the employee by the employer. There may also be some judicial reluctance to imply terms into collective agreements when they are found wanting in relation to particular issues. Where a collective agreement leaves a topic uncovered the inference is not that there has been an omission so obvious as to require judicial intervention. The assumption should be that it was omitted deliberately for reasons such as the item being too controversial or too complicated: see *Ali* v *Christian Salvesen Food Services Ltd* [1997] IRLR 17 CA.

Question 3

Critically examine the requirements for consultation in situations of collective redundancies and transfers of undertakings.

Commentary

There are now a number of occasions when an employer is required by law to consult and inform employees. These include situations concerning collective redundancies, transfers of undertakings, transnational employers of a certain size, and health and safety.

Council Directive 98/59/EC on the approximation of the laws of the Member States relating to collective redundancies is a consolidation directive. It consolidates Directive 75/129/EEC as amended by Directive 92/56/EEC on the same subject. The original Directive was adopted in 1975 and transposed into British law very quickly. It was incorporated into the Employment Protection Act 1975 and has been part of national law, subject to various amendments, ever since. The provisions are now contained in Part IV, Chapter II of the Trade Union and Labour Relations (Consolidation) Act 1992 (TULRCA), which outlines the procedure for handling collective redundancies.

The purpose of the Acquired Rights Directive and the TUPE Regulations is contained in Art. 3(1) of Directive 2001/23/EC. Article 3(1) states that the transferor's rights and obligations arising from a contract of employment or from an employment relationship existing on the date of the transfer shall be transferred to the transferee employer. It is as if the contract of employment was originally made between the transferee and the employee. The obligation to consult is contained in regs 13 to 16 of the TUPE Regulations 2006.

Answer plan

- Consultation and collective redundancies
- When is the employer 'proposing to dismiss'?
- Purpose of consultation
- Consultation and transfers
- When employers need not consult

Suggested answer

The duty to consult rests upon an employer who is proposing to dismiss 20 or more employees at one establishment within a period of 90 days or less for reasons of redundancy: s. 188, TULRCA. This may include situations where the employer is proposing to dismiss a work force and then immediately re-employ them as part of a reorganization: *GMB* v *MAN Truck & Bus UK Ltd* [2000] IRLR 636. This consultation shall begin 'in good time' and in any event at least 30 days before the first dismissal takes effect, or at least 90 days before the first dismissal takes effect if the employer is proposing to dismiss 100 or more employees at one establishment within a period of 90 days.

An important issue here, of course, is exactly when the employer is 'proposing to dismiss'. It is likely that, except perhaps in a disaster situation, there is a period of time over which the decision to dismiss employees by reason of redundancy is reached. There is, perhaps, first, the decision in principle to dismiss employees. There may be a second stage where the parts of the organization in which the redundancies are to take place are identified, followed by a further stage when particular employees are identified.

In *R* v *British Coal Corporation and Secretary of State for Trade and Industry ex parte Price* [1994] IRLR 72 the court approved an approach to fair consultation which meant that it began when the proposals were still at a formative stage, adequate information was given on which to respond, there was adequate time in which to respond and to give conscientious consideration in response to the consultation.

This issue was considered in *Hough* v *Leyland DAF Ltd* [1991] IRLR 194. The EAT held that matters should have reached a stage where a specific proposal had been formulated and that this is a later stage than the diagnosis of a problem and the appreciation that at least one way of dealing with it would be by declaring redundancies. The EAT then went on to state that it would not be more helpful to seek a more precise definition because of the large variety of situations that might arise.

Article 2(1) of the Collective Redundancies Directive states that consultation should begin when the employer is 'contemplating' collective redundancies. This was considered in *Re Hartlebury Printers Ltd* [1992] ICR 174. The court held that proposing redundancies could include merely thinking about the possibility of redundancies. Contemplating redundancies in the sense of proposing them meant 'having in view or expecting' them. It is, therefore, likely to be at an early stage, but not so early that it is merely an idea that the company is thinking about. If, however, the employer's decision making has progressed to the stage of contemplating two options for the future, one of which is closing down the business and the other is selling it as a going concern, then the employer has reached the stage of 'proposing to dismiss as redundant': see *Scotch Premier Meat Ltd* v *Burns* [2000] IRLR 639. This consultation needs to take place before the decision to terminate the contracts of employment. There needs to be substantive consultation before the employees are given the notice period required by the Directive; *Junk* v *Kühnel* [2005] IRLR 310.

The consultation itself is to include consultation about ways of avoiding the dismissals, reducing the number of employees to be dismissed, and mitigating the consequences of the dismissals. There is an obligation for the employer to undertake such consultations with a view to reaching agreement with the appropriate representatives: s. 182, TULRCA.

Regulations 13 and 14 of the TUPE Regulations are concerned with the duty to inform and consult employee representatives and regs 15 and 16 with the consequences of failing to do so. Information should be provided 'long enough before a relevant transfer to enable the employer of any affected employees to consult all the persons who are appropriate representatives of any of those affected employees'. The High Court, in *Institution of Professional and Civil Servants* v *Secretary of State for Defence* [1987] IRLR 373 decided that the words 'long enough before' a transfer to enable consultation to take place meant as soon as measures are envisaged and *if possible* long enough before the transfer. The court held that the words did not mean as soon as measures are envisaged and *in any event* long enough before the transfer.

The information to be provided should consist of the fact that a relevant transfer is to take place, approximately when it is to take place and the reasons for it, the legal, economic, and social implications for the affected employees, and the measures which are envisaged to take place in connection with the transfer, in relation to the affected employees or the fact that there are no such measures envisaged.

It is, of course, both the transferor and the transferee that need to consult and there is an obligation upon the transferee to provide the transferor with information about their plans, so that the transferor can carry out their duty to consult. Where the employer actually envisages taking measures in relation to any of the affected employees, then the employer must consult the appropriate representatives 'with a view to seeking their agreement to the measures to be taken'. In the course of these consultations the employer will consider the representations made by the appropriate representatives and, if any of those representations are rejected, the employer must state the reasons for so doing.

There are two 'escape' clauses for employers unable to comply with their obligations under s. 188, TULRCA. First, where there are special circumstances which make it not reasonably practicable for an employer to comply with the consultation and information requirements, they are to take all steps towards compliance that are reasonably practicable in the circumstances. Second, where they have invited affected employees to elect representatives and the employees have failed to do so within a reasonable time, then the employer must give all the affected employees the information set out above. In *The Bakers' Union* v *Clarks of Hove Ltd* [1978] IRLR 366 the court held that there were three stages to deciding whether there was a defence in any particular case. These were, first, were there special circumstances, second, did they render compliance with the statute not reasonably practicable, and, third, did the employer take all the reasonable steps towards compliance as were reasonably practicable in the circumstances? In this case even an insolvency was not a special enough circumstance in itself to provide a defence against the lack of consultation.

The shedding of employees in an attempt by a receiver to sell the business was not a sufficient justification in *GMB* v *Rankin and Harrison* [1992] IRLR 514. The fact that the business could not be sold and that there were no orders were common to insolvency situations and not enough in themselves to justify being special. Special circumstances means something out of the ordinary or something that is not common. In any complaint to an employment tribunal, the onus is upon the employer to show that there were special circumstances or that they took all reasonably practical steps towards compliance.

Question 4

European Community requirements for consultation at the transnational level cannot succeed without similar requirements at the national level.
  Critically consider this statement.

Commentary

The European Works Council Directive was transposed into national law by the Transnational Information and Consultation of Employees Regulations 1999 (TICE Regulations) (SI 1999/3323), which came into effect on 15 January 2000. By this time many British employees were already represented in European Works Councils (EWCs) set up by multinational companies influenced by the law of other Member States which had already transposed the Directive. The TICE Regulations did not have effect if there was already in existence an Art. 6 or an Art. 13 agreement, unless the parties have decided otherwise. An Art. 6 agreement is one that establishes an EWC in accordance with the Directive. An Art. 13 agreement is one that established their own information and consultation procedures before the Directive was transposed into national law.

Consultation is defined in the TICE Regulations as meaning the exchange of views and the establishment of a dialogue in the context of an EWC or in the context of an information and consultation procedure.

The question for consideration here is whether this can be successful without there being statutory requirements to consult at a national level also. The angle from which you can answer this question will depend upon the content of your course, but set out below is one approach.

Answer plan

- Transnational levels and national levels of consultation
- Effectiveness of European Works Council
- European Company Statute
- Measures at the national level
- Conclusions

Suggested answer

The European Commission has two levels on which it aims to harmonize the approach of Member States to the issues of consultation of employees. These are, first, the transnational level, as exemplified by the introduction of European Works Councils (EWCs), and, second, by the Information and Consultation Directive introducing mandatory consultation at the national level.

The European Works Council Directive (EWC Directive) was finally adopted in 1994 after some 14 years of debate. The purpose of the Directive was to improve the right to information and to consultation of employees in Community-scale undertakings and Community-scale groups of undertakings. The Directive's lack of effectiveness was shown in the 'Vilvoorde' crisis in 1997. This was where the French car maker, Renault, announced the closure of its Belgian plant without any consultation whatsoever with its Belgian workers or its EWC. The Renault EWC met once a year, but was not called together until after the company had announced the closure. Although Renault subsequently agreed amendments to its EWC agreement to consult on future transnational structural changes, the whole process perhaps reflects the weakness of the requirements and of any potential sanctions. A similar lack of consultation appeared to take place when BMW of Germany sold its Rover car-making subsidiary in the United Kingdom in 1999. Consultation appeared to take place with German workers represented on the company's supervisory board, but not with British workers' representatives on its EWC.

There are other EU initiatives concerning transnational companies and transnational takeovers and mergers. In 2000 the Council of Ministers adopted a regulation establishing a European Company Statute. In addition the Council adopted a Directive, 2001/86, establishing rules for worker involvement in the European Company. When the European Company is created there will generally need to be negotiations with representatives of all the workers affected. In the absence of any agreement there are standards established by the Directive which will need to be followed. These require management to provide regular reports to the workers' representatives and to consult those representatives on the information provided. These reports will contain details of business plans; production and sales levels; the implications for the work force; management changes; mergers, potential closures, and lay-offs.

The European Commission is also active at the national level and has adopted a Directive on establishing a general framework for informing and consulting employees. The objectives of this Directive are to ensure the existence of the right to regular information and consultation of employees. Such consultation will include the anticipated development of employment for the employees concerned and ensure that workers are consulted prior to decisions which are likely to lead to substantial changes in work organization.

The European Community has long recognized that a problem for workers employed by multinational organizations is the ability of the employer to move work between countries. Taking work from one country and relocating it to another is a way of making workers more compliant. The EWC Directive was designed to ensure that such employers consult their employees on a multinational basis. There have been some well-publicized failures, such as those at Renault in Belgium in 1997 and BMW and Ford in the United Kingdom in 2000. The Renault case led to one of the first Europe-wide strikes and an amendment to their EWC agreeing to consult their workers in similar situations in the future.

A common feature of these and other closures was the lack of prior consultation with, and, usually, provision of information to, the affected workers or their representatives. It is not possible to say whether such information and consultation would have made any difference to the final outcome, but it is possible to say that different outcomes might have resulted. The reason for the closures was not a lack of consultation. It had to do with overcapacity in particular industries when looked at from a global scale as multinational companies made decisions to reduce their capacity. It is arguable, however, that the apparently reduced consultation requirements and the lower redundancy penalties in the United Kingdom make this country more likely to be selected in the event of such decisions to reduce productive capacity.

What is clear is that the transnational consultation requirements were inadequate. The EWC Directive appeared to have little impact in these events and, in some cases, the obligation for consultation on collective redundancies was also ignored. This may be a strong argument for a comprehensive obligation to consult and perhaps an acceptance that the EWCs cannot work in isolation. There also needs to be some consultation at national level.

Consultation, in the Information and Consultation Directive, is defined as an exchange of views and the establishment of a dialogue. It will cover, importantly, information and consultation about an employer's economic and financial situation, as well as any potential changes which might pose a threat to employment. It is suggested here that only with the requirement to consult on these matters at a national level as contained in the Information and Consultation with Employees Regulations 2004 can the transnational consultation be successful. There will then be no opportunity for an employer to disregard the views of the employees in one Member State in favour of those in another.

Further reading

Barrow, C., *Industrial Relations Law,* 2nd edn (London: Cavendish, 2002).

Elias, P., and Ewing, K., *Trade Union Democracy, Members Rights and the Law* (London: Mansell Publishing, 1987).

Gospel, H., and Lockwood, G., 'Disclosure of information for collective bargaining' 1999 28(3) ILJ.

Hendy, J., QC, *Every worker shall have the right to be represented at work by a trade union* (London: Institute of Employment Rights, 1998).

Morris, G. S., and Archer, T. J., *Collective Labour Law* (Oxford: Hart Publishing, 2005).

Sargeant, M., *Consultation with Employees* (London: Work Foundation, 2002).

Sargeant, M., and Lewis, D., *Employment Law,* 4th edn (Harlow: Pearson, 2008).

Simpson, B., 'Code of Practice on Industrial Action Ballots and Notice to Employers 2000' (2001) 30(2) ILJ.

Simpson, B., 'Trade union recognition and the law' (2000) 29(3) ILJ.

Wedderburn, Lord, 'Collective bargaining and legal enactment: the 1999 Act and union recognition' (2000) 29(1) ILJ.

13

Data protection and human rights

Introduction

The European Convention on Human Rights listed a series of civil and political rights and freedoms. The objective of the authors was to contribute towards the enforcement of certain of the rights stated in the United Nations Universal Declaration of Human Rights. Importantly, it also set up a structure for enforcement with the establishment of the European Court of Human Rights (ECHR). Any contracting State or individual claiming to be a victim of a violation of the Convention may make an application directly to the Court.

The United Kingdom has not always been enthusiastic about accepting these statements of fundamental rights. They imply that individuals have rights which are somehow not reliant upon national governments passing laws to grant them. Other Member States of the European Community have written constitutions, some of which guarantee certain individual and collective rights. The United Kingdom has relied upon an unwritten constitution which has had the idea of the sovereignty of Parliament at its centre. This sovereignty was limited by the entry of the United Kingdom into the European Community and further limited by the incorporation of the European Convention into national law.

Human rights

The United Kingdom finally incorporated the European Convention into its national law through the Human Rights Act 1998, most of the provisions of which came into effect in October 2000. The Act, of course, has an effect that is much wider than just employment law issues, but it is only those aspects that are important here.

The primary focus of the Convention is the public relationship between the individual and the State. It is not focused on the private relationship between employer and employee. Nevertheless it is likely that it will have an effect on many aspects of the employment relationship.

The Articles of the Convention that are of most relevance to students of employment law are Art. 8 concerned with respect for private and family life; Art. 9 on the right to freedom of thought, conscience, and religion; Art. 10 concerned with the right to freedom of expression; Art. 11 on the right to freedom of peaceful assembly and to freedom of association with others, including the right to form and join trade unions; and Art. 14 on the enjoyment of the rights and freedoms set out in the Convention without discrimination on any ground such as sex, race, colour, language, religion, political or other opinion, national or social origin, association with a national minority, property, birth, or other status.

Data protection

Employers, as with many other organizations, are able to discover and keep large amounts of information about their employees. Some of this information may not be directly relevant to work and some may be out of date. Employers collect information at recruitment, through application forms, selection interviews, and references. During an individual's career they may continue to collect data on such matters as an employee's health, criminal convictions, trade union activities, and so on. They may also be concerned with the transmission of this information either internally, to associated companies (some of which may be in a different country), or externally, in the giving of references to other bodies or employers.

One of the early concerns with the collection and storage of information about individuals was the need to create common standards between countries so that data could successfully be transmitted across national borders without the integrity of that information being affected. On 28 January 1981 the Council of Europe adopted a Convention for the Protection of Individuals with regard to Automatic Processing of Personal Data. Countries which adopted the Convention agreed to adopt common standards which would allow the transmission of such information between them. The United Kingdom ratified the Convention in 1987. This was after the passing of the Data Protection Act 1984. This Act introduced a number of data protection principles and an obligation to register as a data user. It also established the office of the Information Commissioner.

In 1995 the European Community adopted the Data Protection Directive 95/46/EC. There was concern that the failure of some Member States to adopt domestic legislation might hinder the development of the single market. The Directive's requirements are reflected in the Data Protection Act 1998, which came into effect in March 2000. The Act regulates the activities of data controllers and, through them, of data processors in the processing of personal data. A data controller is any person who, either alone or jointly with others, determines the purpose for which personal data are to be processed (and the manner in which the process is conducted). The data processor is any person who processes the data on behalf of the data controller.

The 'personal data' that are affected by the Act's provisions are data that relate to a living individual who can be identified from the data. The data include any expressions of opinion about the individual and any indication of the intentions of the data controller or any other person in respect of the individual. Thus an employer's appraisal of an individual or expressions of intent about the future employment prospects of an individual may constitute personal data. The Data Protection Act 1984 only had a very limited application to manual records. The Data Protection Act 1998 (DPA 1998) has a wider definition that includes, apart from data which are processed by automatic means, data that are part of 'a relevant filing system'. Thus manual filing systems are included, provided the data are structured either by reference to individuals or by reference to criteria relating to individuals, in such a way that specific information about an individual is readily accessible. The important issue is not, however, whether data are held on computerized systems or in manual records. The key subject matter of the DPA 1998 is not what type of storage system is used, but the personal data that are stored. Unless a data controller can comply with the data protection principles they will be unable to process personal data at all.

The data protection principles

Part 1 of Sch. 1 to the Data Protection Act 1998 lists a number of data protection principles. The data controller has an obligation to comply with these principles in relation to all personal data for which the person is the data controller.

Question 1

Do employees have a legal right to privacy at work?

 ## Commentary

It is not possible to predict how the right to privacy in an individual's private life will affect the employment relationship. There might be a special issue related to 'lifestyle' dismissals, which concern the dismissal of an employee for activities, or views expressed, outside working hours. The European Court of Human Rights has considered this issue in relation to sexual orientation and gender reassignment. There are other rights and restrictions that need to be considered such as those in the Regulation of Investigatory Powers Act 2000 and the Telecommunications (Lawful Business Practice) (Interception of Communications) Regulations 2000 (SI 2000/2699).

 ## Answer plan

- Art. 8(1) of the European Convention on Human Rights
- Art. 8(2) of the European Convention on Human Rights
- Privacy and telephones and email
- The 2000 Act and the Telecommunications Regulations 2000
- Potential conflict with Data Protection Act 1998

Suggested answer

Article 8(1) of the European Convention on Human Rights, incorporated into UK law by the Human Rights Act 1998, provides that everyone has a right to respect for his or her private and family life. This right has certainly assisted some individuals in resisting discrimination on the grounds of their sexuality.

Smith and Grady v *United Kingdom* [1999] IRLR 734, ECHR concerned an application by two individuals who had been discharged by the Royal Air Force on the grounds that they were homosexuals. At the same time the European Court of Human Rights (ECHR) considered the case of *Lustig-Praen and Beckett* v *United Kingdom* which concerned two individuals discharged from the Royal Navy on the same grounds. The complaint was that the investigation into their homosexuality and their discharge from the armed forces was a breach of Art. 8 alone and also in conjunction with Art. 14 on non-discrimination. Mr Lustig-Praen, for example, was interviewed on a number of occasions and asked about his sexuality. He was ultimately discharged for that reason, despite a good evaluation by his commander. The British government accepted that there had been interference with the applicants' right to respect for their private lives, but made clear that its policy on homosexuals was well known at the time. The court decided that the investigations by the military police and the detailed interviews to which the applicants were subjected were a direct interference in contravention of Art. 8 of the European Convention, as were the subsequent administrative discharges on the grounds of their sexual orientation.

Article 8(2) of the Convention contains grounds for a possible justification for the interference. Such interference must be 'in accordance with the law', have an aim which must be legitimate and must be 'necessary in a democratic society'. Legitimate aims might be in the interests of national security, public safety or the economic well-being of the country, the prevention of disorder or crime, the protection of health or morals, or the protection of the rights and freedoms of others. The policy on excluding homosexuals from the armed forces was certainly lawful in the United Kingdom. The ECHR also accepted that it had legitimate aims of national security and the prevention of disorder. The conclusion was, however, that the government's reasons were not 'weighty or convincing' enough to justify the interference, especially as the investigations had continued after the applicants had admitted their homosexuality.

The right to privacy extends, of course, beyond the interference with an individual's private sexual life. It will include other activities and may also include those that take place when the individual is working in the employer's premises. In *Halford* v *United Kingdom* [1997] IRLR 471, ECHR the applicant complained to the ECHR that, amongst other matters, the interception of telephone calls made from her office and home amounted to unjustifiable interference with her right to respect for her private life and violated Art. 8 of the Convention. Ms Halford was Assistant Chief Constable of the Merseyside police force. After a number of unsuccessful applications for promotion she complained to an employment tribunal that she had been discriminated against on the grounds of her sex. This case was settled, but it was suggested that her telephone calls had been intercepted during the period after her complaint.

The UK government argued that telephone calls made from the office fell outside the scope of Art. 8 as she could have had no reasonable expectation of privacy in relation to them. The government argued that employers should in principle be able to monitor calls made by employees on telephones owned by the employer. This, they argued, could be done without the employee's prior knowledge. The court did not accept this and stated that Ms Halford should have had a reasonable expectation of privacy, especially as she had been given permission to use her phone for the purposes of the sex discrimination case.

Apart from telephones there is also the issue of emails and access to the use of the Internet. The issue is to what extent the employer is able to monitor employees' mail and Internet usage. Section 1 of the Regulation of Investigatory Powers Act 2000 (RIP Act) provides that it is unlawful for a person, without lawful authority, to intentionally intercept a communication in the course of its transmission by way of a public or private telecommunications system. Section 3 provides that such an interception will not be unlawful if the interceptor believes that both parties had agreed to the interception.

The Telecommunications (Lawful Business Practice) (Interception of Communications) Regulations 2000 (SI 2000/2699) (the LBPIC Regulations) came into force in October 2000. These Regulations give the systems controller the right to monitor certain communications. A communication is either one that relates to the business or one that takes place in the course of carrying on that business. The LBPIC Regulations authorize conduct which involves the monitoring or recording of communications, on the employer's telecommunications systems, without consent, for certain purposes including establishing the existence of facts, in the interests of national security and preventing or detecting crime.

There is an apparent contradiction between these rules and the right to privacy contained in the Human Rights Act 1998, although the ability to monitor or record communications can only be authorized in certain circumstances, including the requirement that the interception is solely for the purpose of monitoring and recording communications relevant to the business. It is difficult to see, however, how an employer could distinguish between emails relevant to the business and those not relevant without examining them all.

There have been a number of situations where the downloading of 'obscene' material using employers' equipment have led to problems for employees. For example, the downloading and viewing by male employees of obscene material in the presence of female colleagues can amount to sex discrimination or sexual harassment: see *Morse* v *Future Reality Ltd* Case no. 54571/95, ET. There is a real difficulty for employers in monitoring and then processing any data collected with regard to infringing the right to privacy of individuals.

Question 2

The GCHQ case showed that Article 11 of the European Convention on Human Rights has an important role in protecting freedom of assembly.

Comment on the accuracy of this statement and the relationship between Art. 11 and Art. 14.

Commentary

This question is primarily about Art. 11, which provides that everyone has the right to freedom of peaceful assembly and to freedom of association with others, including the right to form and to join trade unions for the protection of his interests. In answering any questions about the Convention you will need to be able to cite cases illustrating how the particular Article has been interpreted by the Courts. This question, of course, asks about a specific case in relation to Art. 11. The relationship between Art. 11 and Art. 14 is the same as the relationship between any Article of the Convention and Art. 14. Article 14 is not a free-standing Article in its own right. It serves to enforce a principle of non-discrimination in applying the rest of the Convention. However, once it has been raised, it can be considered on its own merits.

Answer plan

- Right to peaceful assembly and the right to freedom of association
- Article 11(2) allows restrictions
- Analysis of GCHQ case
- Article 14 on non-discrimination

Suggested answer

There are two distinct and interrelated rights contained in Art. 11 of the European Convention on Human Rights: first, the right to peaceful assembly and, second, the right to freedom of association and, in particular, the right to form or join a trade union. Whether this positive right to join a trade union also implied a negative right not to join one was considered in *Young James and Webster* v *United Kingdom* [1981] IRLR 408, ECHR. The court was clearly divided on the issue, although there was a majority that held that there had been a breach of Art. 11. The matter concerned the introduction of a closed shop agreement between British Rail and a number of trade unions. The applicants all objected to complying with the trade union membership requirement and were subsequently dismissed. The court held that the applicants' rights under Art. 11 had been breached because the effect of the compulsion to join a specific trade union or unions, or lose their jobs, was to remove the applicants' choice about which trade union they should belong to. The court held that not all compulsion might be outside the Convention, but that the freedom to join implied some measure of the freedom to choose.

There is a distinction between protecting the right to join or form a trade union and enforcing any right to recognition of that union. The European Court of Human Rights (ECHR) stated, in *National Union of Belgian Police* v *Belgium* [1980] EHRR 578, that Art. 11(1) does not guarantee any particular treatment of trade unions or their members by the State, such as the right to be consulted by it.

Article 11(2) allows restrictions to be placed on the Art. 11 rights as are prescribed by law and are 'necessary in a democratic society' in the interests of national security or public safety, the prevention of disorder or crime, the protection of health or morals, or for the protection of the rights and freedoms of others. The court held, in *Young, James and Webster*, that 'necessary' does not mean the same as 'useful' or 'desirable'. The fact, therefore, that the closed shop agreement between British Rail and the trade unions had produced positive benefits in terms of industrial relations was not sufficient to justify the 'necessity' of the interference complained of.

The government's ability to restrict trade union membership was tested when trade union membership was banned at the Government Communications Headquarters (GCHQ) at Cheltenham in 1984, and staff were offered membership of an in-house staff association. This action followed a number of different industrial disputes at GCHQ over the previous three years. The government justified its action by the need to maintain the security work done at GCHQ. The last sentence of Art. 11(2) of the Convention states that the Article shall not prevent the imposition of lawful restrictions on members of the armed forces or the police or of members of the administration of the State. The European Commission of Human Rights, in *Council of Civil Service Unions* v *United Kingdom* [1987] 10 EHRR 269, considered these words and concluded that the civil servants at GCHQ fell within this exception, as they were concerned with national security. The term 'lawful' in this exception suggested a lack of arbitrariness and the Commission concluded that the actions of the UK government also met this test. The government was concerned that trade unions outside GCHQ could call their members in GCHQ out on industrial action at any time and this appeared to justify the action against trade union membership. The same issue of security was crucial for the House of Lords also: *Council of Civil Service Unions* v *Minister for the Civil Service* [1985] ICR 374, HL. The court held that the applicants would have normally had a legitimate expectation to be consulted before and the failure to consult would have made the process unfair. Fairness, however, was outweighed by the requirements of national security. It was for the executive to decide whether there were such requirements, not the courts. It was enough for the Minister to show that the decisions had been based upon considerations of national security.

Article 14 states that the enjoyment of the rights and freedoms set out in the Convention shall be secured without discrimination on any ground such as sex, race, colour, language, religion, political or other opinion, national or social origin, association with a national minority, property, birth, or other status.

This right to non-discrimination re-enforces the other rights in the Convention. It can only be relied upon in so far as it relates to the rights set out elsewhere. The Article is potentially wide in its effect. It mentions specifically a number of grounds upon which discrimination is not permitted, but uses the phrase 'on any grounds such as' which suggests that its effect could be much broader. According to the ECHR, in *Sheffield and Horsham* v *United Kingdom*, Art. 14 affords protection against discrimination in respect of benefiting from the rights and freedoms contained in the other provisions of the Convention.

Although this right depends upon alleged infringement of other rights, it does not depend upon the successful prosecution of those other rights. In *Inze* v *Austria* [1987] 10 EHRR 394, for example, the allegation that Art. 1 of the first protocol was infringed failed, but a breach of Art. 14 was still held to have taken place (Austrian law gave precedence to legitimate heirs over illegitimate heirs and this was held to be an infringement of Art. 14).

Because of the secondary nature of Art. 14, it appears to have had a limited impact. The ECHR has shown a reluctance to consider it when the substantive claim has been upheld. In *Smith and Grady* v *United Kingdom,* the Court of Human Rights failed to consider Art. 14 separately after it upheld the applicants' complaints under Art. 8.

Question 3

There is an important need for the regulation of employers concerning their right to know about and keep records of the personal lives of their employees.
   Critically discuss.

Commentary

Clearly the way that such a question is answered will depend upon the material that is covered in the course. Here it is taken to mean issues raised by the Access to Medical Reports Act 1988, the processing of sensitive data, and the monitoring of employees' telephone and email usage as in the Regulation of Investigatory Powers Act 2000 (RIP Act).

Answer plan

- Access to Medical Reports Act 1988
- To whom does a doctor owe a duty of care?

- Processing of sensitive personal data
- Extent to which an employer can monitor an employee's activities
- RIP Act 2000 and Regulations

Suggested answer

It is not uncommon for employers to request a medical report from an applicant's doctor prior to confirming an offer of appointment or work. These reports may play a crucial part in the appointment process and their accuracy is therefore of importance. The Access to Medical Reports Act 1988 (AMRA 1988) provides a right of access by individuals to reports about themselves made by medical practitioners for employment or insurance purposes. A prospective employer may not apply to a medical practitioner for a medical report for employment or insurance purposes, unless the employer has notified the individual of their intention to do so and that individual has notified the employer of their agreement.

It is open to the individual, when giving agreement, to ask for access to the report before it is supplied by the medical practitioner. Once a medical practitioner has been notified of this request, that practitioner must not supply the report until the inspection has taken place or a period of 21 days has elapsed since the request without any arrangements being made for access. It is open to the individual, who has been given access to the report, to request that the report be amended to correct errors. If the practitioner refuses to do so, then a statement to this effect must be added to the report before it is sent to the employer.

The medical report must be kept by the practitioner for at least six months, and the individual allowed access to it, although there are important exceptions. A medical practitioner may refuse to allow access to a report if the disclosure is likely to cause serious harm to the physical or mental health of the individual, or if the disclosure might reveal information about another person unless that person has consented or is a health professional acting in that capacity. In such a situation the medical practitioner will not supply the report to the applicant unless the individual consents.

The AMRA 1988 relates to reports prepared by a medical practitioner who is, or has been, responsible for the physical or mental care of the individual. In such cases it is likely that the doctor will have a duty of care towards the individual. Some employers will ask for reports from medical practitioners, usually doctors, who have no relationship at all with the applicant. In such cases the doctor is likely to have an employment or business relationship with the employer, but there seems less than clear guidance as to the relationship between the applicant and that doctor. It may rest upon the particular circumstances of each case. *Baker* v *Kaye* [1997] IRLR 219 concerned a medical report given by a doctor at the request of a potential employer. The applicant had completed a medical questionnaire and was examined by the doctor, who carried out various tests. The outcome was that the doctor recommended that the candidate should not be employed by the employer concerned. The High Court held that the doctor did owe the applicant a duty of care and that all the tests required in *Caparo Industries plc* v *Dickman* [1990] 2 AC 605, namely the foreseeability of economic loss and the degree of proximity between the parties, had been met and that it was just and reasonable for such a duty to be imposed. In *Kapfunde* v *Abbey National plc* [1999] ICR 1 the Court of Appeal took a different approach. This case concerned a part-time employee who applied for a full-time position with the same employer. She was asked to complete a medical questionnaire and disclosed that she suffered from sickle cell anaemia. The questionnaire was referred to a general practitioner to whom the employer paid an annual retainer. The GP stated that the medical evidence showed a likelihood of higher than average levels of absenteeism and the employer declined to give the employee a full-time post. The court held that the GP was under a contract of service with the employer when assessing medical questionnaires and that there was no special relationship from which a duty of care to the applicant could be shown. This approach was also followed in *London Borough of Hammersmith & Fulham* v *Farnsworth* [2000] IRLR 691, CA, where an occupational health physician was held to be an agent of the employer when preparing a report on a potential employee.

There are also rules in relation to the processing of 'sensitive personal data' by employers. These are data relating to the racial or ethnic origin of the data subject; the subject's political opinions; the subject's religious or similar beliefs; whether the subject is a member of a trade union; the subject's physical or mental health or condition; the subject's sexual life; the subject's commission, or alleged commission, of any offence and other matters listed in Sch. 2, DPA 1998. The processing of these sensitive personal data can only take place if the data subject has given consent or there is a necessity as defined in Sch. 3, DPA 1998. This includes any processing that is necessary to protect the vital interests of the data subject or any processing that consists of racial or ethnic monitoring for the purposes of an equal opportunities policy.

A major issue is to what extent the employer is able to monitor an employee's activities and thereby gain access to personal information. This includes those that take place when the individual is working in the employer's premises. In *Halford* v *United Kingdom* [1997] IRLR 471, ECHR the applicant complained to the ECHR that, amongst other matters, the interception of telephone calls made from her office and home amounted to unjustifiable interference with her right to respect for her private life and violated Art. 8 of the European Convention on Human Rights. The UK government argued that telephone calls made from the office fell outside the scope of Art. 8 as she could have had no reasonable expectation of privacy in relation to them. The government argued that employers should in principle be able to monitor calls made by employees on telephones owned by the employer. This, they argued, could be done without the employee's prior knowledge. The court did not accept this and stated that Ms Halford should have had a reasonable expectation of privacy.

Apart from telephones there is also the issue of emails and access to the use of the Internet. Section 1 of the Regulation of Investigatory Powers Act 2000 (RIP Act) provides that it is unlawful for a person, without lawful authority, to intentionally intercept a communication in the course of its transmission by way of a public or private telecommunications system.

The Telecommunications (Lawful Business Practice) (Interception of Communications) Regulations 2000 (LBPIC Regulations), however, give the systems controller the right to monitor certain communications. The LBPIC Regulations authorize conduct which involves the monitoring or recording of communications, on the employer's telecommunications systems, without consent in certain circumstances for the purposes of, amongst other matters, establishing the existence of facts; this may concern the recording of messages and telephone conversations in order to establish the facts of an event.

Systems controllers are authorized to monitor, first, communications for the purpose of determining whether they are communications relevant to the system controller's business; this will clearly permit employers to examine individual employees' email accounts. Second, communications made to confidential telephone counselling or support services or helplines may be monitored; this may be done to support counselling staff, but the potential implication in interfering with confidential calls is significant.

The LBPIC Regulations 1998 provide some limitations. The ability to monitor or record communications can only be authorized if the interception is solely for the purpose of monitoring and recording communications relevant to the business and the telecommunications system in question is provided for use wholly or partly in connection with the business.

There is also a potential conflict with the requirements of the DPA 1998 which imposes important restrictions on the processing of such data once they have been recorded. The Information Commissioner's guidance is that such monitoring should only take place after it has been established that there is a problem which needs to be examined and that the methods used should not be too intrusive into an individual's privacy.

Further reading

Allen, R., and Crasnow, R., *Employment Law and Human Rights* (London: Blackstone Press, 2002).

Carey, P., *Data Protection in the UK* (London: Blackstone Press, 2000).

Craig, J. D. R., and Oliver, H. D., 'The right to privacy in the public workplace' (1998) 27(1) ILJ.

Ewing, K. D., 'The Human Rights Act and Labour Law' (1998) 27(4) ILJ.

Ford, M., 'The Data Protection Act 1998' (1999) 28(1) ILJ.

Ford, M., 'Two conceptions of worker privacy' (2002) 31(2) ILJ.

Sargeant, M., and Lewis, D., *Employment Law*, 4th edn (Harlow: Pearson, 2008).

Spencer, J., and Spencer, M., *Human Rights and Employment Law* (London: Work Foundation, 2002).

14

Coursework

Introduction

Methods of assessment vary and examinations are only one form of assessment. They are a requirement for core modules, of course, but there are other and, arguably, better methods of assessment. The setting of a piece of coursework requiring the student to submit a piece of written work by a certain date is one obvious alternative.

When a student is set a piece of coursework, they are being asked to:

- write a certain number of words;
- usually answer only one question;
- submit it by a certain date.

There is, of course, more to it than just that. The requirements for coursework will vary from institution to institution and the first and important step is to ensure that you are familiar with, and understand, the requirements of your examiner. It can be a source of amazement to examiners sometimes that students do not read simple instructions and, as a result, are penalized for not following rules concerning presentation and content. Given that these rules will vary and that you should be aware of yours, there are still enough common factors worth considering.

What the examiners are looking for

You need to know what the examiners are looking for before you start, but it is unlikely that they will only be looking for a straightforward descriptive and factual answer to a set question. One of the purposes of setting a piece of work over a period of time is to enable the student to show evidence of at least the following:

- *reading*;
- *research*;
- *reflection*.

All these, of course, are intertwined and not really separate from each other, but they are worth considering separately, because to do so will enable you to plan the work you intend to carry out in completing the assignment. Remember that it is not enough just to do the reading, research, and reflection, you need to show evidence, in your coursework, of having done it.

Reading

Reading means more than just reading the core textbook for the module and reproducing the material in the written coursework. It may be self-evident that this is insufficient, but it happens. You should be aware that the examiners have read the core textbook and probably most of the other relevant textbooks. They are, therefore, likely to recognize the work if it is reproduced in the coursework. There are two issues here. One is related to the extent of reading. One or two books is unlikely to be enough. There is likely to be a range of articles available, or waiting to be discovered, on the subject matter. These may examine aspects of the question in more detail or present an alternative view or perspective on the assignment question. The second issue is one of plagiarism. Plagiarism is the use of other people's ideas and/or materials without acknowledging the source. Thus to copy material from a book or article into your coursework and give the impression that it is your own work is plagiarism. It is perfectly acceptable to use other people's ideas and material as long as you acknowledge that it does originate with someone else. Plagiarism will, at best, lose you marks. At worst it may lead to no marks and disciplinary action.

Research

Research obviously includes reading, but it is not just recommended reading. It is about searching out relevant material and using primary sources wherever possible. Here are some examples of research:

- Where a textbook refers to the ideas of someone else or quotes from someone else's work or writing, then research means not just using the textbook information, but using the references given to search out the original work or writing quoted.

- Using the Internet. There is a huge amount of material on employment law issues available on the Internet. Government departments, Parliament, and various bodies such as the Equal Opportunities Commission and the Council for Racial Equality have their own websites. Any good employment law textbook should have a list of such sites and it is worth investigating those that are relevant to the assignment.

- Using primary sources, rather than secondary ones. A good researcher will follow up a lead in a newspaper or an article by going to look at the original document, rather than just relying upon the report in the newspaper or the article. Often these documents, especially if official ones, can be found on the Internet.

Evidence of such relevant research contained in a piece of coursework will undoubtedly add value to the work.

Reflection

Reflection is a characteristic that should distinguish coursework submissions from examination answers. In the hurly-burly of an exam it is not easy to sit back and reflect upon a question. There is usually so little time and so much to be written in that time. This should not be the position when writing coursework. There is the opportunity to sit back and reflect upon the issues raised in the assignment. A good piece of written law coursework is likely therefore to consider arguments in favour and against a particular viewpoint. The display of a considered reflection of both sides of an argument is important, so long as that consideration can be supported by citing cases or other material. It is not enough to express a point of view on its own. It needs to be a point of view supported by the evidence presented in the assignment, this evidence, of course, having been gathered through a process of reading and research!

The process

Here is an example of a piece of coursework given to students taking an employment law option as part of their undergraduate studies:

> *The contract of employment conceals the reality of the unequal relationship between workers and employers.*
> *Critically consider the extent to which the law has intervened to correct the imbalance in this relationship and to provide greater protection for workers.*
> *Your answer should consider both the individual and collective aspects of the relationship.*

Here is the guidance given to the students:

> This module is assessed by the submission of a piece of coursework to be handed in to the student office by the University coursework deadline. This coursework should be approximately 5,000 words in length and consist of the following parts:
>
> - the methodology: you are asked to describe the process you undertook to write the assignment; this will include what resources you used, what difficulties you encountered and what conclusions you reached on how to tackle the assignment;
> - the substantial answer: this part will be assessed on your ability to show an understanding of the relevant issues, an application of the law (statute and cases) and evidence of your own work and research;
> - conclusion: this will contain a summary of your arguments and some reflection on any related matters and the wider context in which the employment law issues can be placed.
>
> You should note the following:
>
> - credit will be given for papers showing a logical and clear presentation;
> - the 5,000 word limit does not include footnotes, endnotes, or bibliography; failure to use the number of available words will lead to papers being penalized; any parts over the 5,000 word limit will not be marked;
> - evidence of plagiarism or of material that is not the student's own work will lead to disciplinary action; do not quote at length from statutory materials or books, articles, etc.;
> - all papers should be word processed, double spaced and contain a word count.

The question was designed to cover all or any of the material on the course, so that the student should not be able to take just one aspect and concentrate on that at the expense of the other parts. The length of the coursework was 5,000 words, excluding footnotes, endnotes, and bibliography. The course demanded that students spent a lot of time in self-learning, rather than being 'taught' in a formal manner. Part of the credit in marking was for evidence of this self-learning process.

The students were also told that the question required them to *critically consider,* so a straightforward recitation of facts would be insufficient. The written assignment was in three parts. The methodology section required the student to describe how they approached the question, what research sources and methods they used, and what problems they encountered in the writing of the assignment. Second was the substantial part, in which they were required to provide the substance of the answer to the question. Direct quotations from statute were discouraged; a critical use of cases was important. Students were encouraged to refer to all parts of the lecture programme, but it was permissible for them to illustrate their answer by concentrating on one part of the course; e.g. an examination of anti-discrimination laws would be a good way of considering the question about the extent to which the law has intervened. Third, the conclusions section was expected to include a summing up of the arguments and the issues. The nature of the conclusion was irrelevant as long as it was supported by argument and logic.

The purpose of this structure was to encourage reflection by students. It was not possible to obtain a good mark without the critical element. If any of these three elements were missing, students were penalized.

As a result, of course, there was no such thing as a right or wrong answer; but the contents of the substantial part of such an answer might have been a consideration of:

- the distinction between those working under a contract of service and a contract for personal services;
- some comparison, perhaps, between contracts of employment and other contracts;
- perhaps some discussion of different types of employment contracts;
- express and implied terms;
- ways in which the contract can be brought to an end; common law and statute;
- the role of trade unions in balancing the unequal relationship;
- rules on consultation and the protection of workers in transfers, collective redundancies, and insolvencies;
- some reference to the employment protection issues covered in the course, such as those concerned with discrimination, maternity and parental leave, working time, a national minimum wage, etc.

There was a large amount of material available and one of the challenges for the student was in assessing its relative importance in the answer.

Issues for consideration

A number of issues arise out of planning and writing such a piece of coursework. These issues are relevant to all forms of coursework questions.

1. Planning—like any piece of written work it needs planning, particularly so in a question which allows the writer the scope to decide what material to cover and what not to cover. Although this assignment asked specifically for an introductory part, a substantive part, and a conclusion, this is likely to be an implicit requirement in any piece of written work and each section needs to be planned. It may be that work is required before a coherent plan can be adopted, but the plan itself should direct the writer to the reading and research that may be necessary to answer the question.

2. Endnotes/footnotes—you should have clear guidance about what is required and whether these will count towards a word total. Resist the temptation to put large amounts of material into endnotes or footnotes as a way round the word limit. You will not be the first person who has attempted this and it is unlikely that such writing will be taken into account. This is not the place to describe the format of endnotes/footnotes, but, as a minimum, they should include enough information for the reader to find the source of information easily (as in a case citation). Remember that adequate referencing is essential to avoid any charges of plagiarism.

3. The word total—different examiners will have different approaches to this and you should ensure that you know yours. Generally, though, word limits are there for a reason, partly to make the examination process manageable. Going substantially over the word limit or not using the words available are both to a writer's disadvantage. It is likely that words over the limit will not be taken into account and under-usage will be seen as, at the very least, a waste of an opportunity. Avoid the use of extensive quotations or quoting from statute as these use up valuable word numbers with, usually, little effect.

4. Other information—read the requirements carefully. If you are asked to produce a word count, then do so. If the work must be double spaced and/or word processed, then it must be done. Failure to do so is likely to carry penalties.

After the assignment quoted above was completed and assessed, the examiner provided the following feedback:

> The outcome was a considerable breadth in the quality of the coursework submitted. The best pieces contained a high degree of reflection backed up with evidence of research and reading. The poorer pieces tended to be very reliant upon one or two textbooks and showed little originality. Those students who copied from textbooks without attributing their sources were severely penalized.

Particular comments are:

1. A number of students failed to include any sort of methodology and their mark suffered as a result. Sometimes the methodology was inadequate and was merely treated as an introduction.

2. There were also a number of inadequate conclusions, which failed to summarize the evidence and argument put forward in the substantive part.

3. Some students used excessive quotations. Those that quoted at length from statute were penalized. In contrast some students used them effectively when presenting evidence from cases. Judges are often very good at summing up issues and principles of law, so they can be effectively used.

4. Clearly many students agonized over what subjects to include and what to leave out. The markers took a pretty generous line in not requiring specific subjects, but rather looked at the overall shape of the material and the argument that it supported. On the whole students chose well, although one or two tried to cover everything, which impacted on the overall quality.

5. Some students did not take notice of the instructions in the module handbook—typed, double spaced, and a word count. Some of the pieces given in had so many appendices that they amounted to a document of book-like length. The mark was given for the 5,000 words of the main text. Similarly some students had footnotes which were, to say the least, excessive in length. In such cases the mark was again given for the 5,000 words in the main text. Many pieces failed to include a word count, which always makes a marker suspicious. Those that undershot the word limit by a significant amount suffered from not using sufficient material.

6. The real difference between the higher marks and the lower ones was the evidence of research and reflection. It was clear that some students had used a variety of sources and materials. These were reflected in their work, as well as their bibliography. This was in stark contrast to students who used little material apart from the module handbook and a textbook.

Worked example of a coursework question

There follows a worked coursework question as an example of the approach to be taken.

Question 1

Cherry, 35, and Tony have worked for Megabucks plc for some time. Cherry is a receptionist, Tony an engineer. The company has recently updated its Staff Handbook. One section now reads:
   Dismissal for gross misconduct
   [there follows a lengthy list of misbehaviour for which the penalty is instant dismissal]
   use of emails for private purposes
   use of telephones for private communication.
The last two items are new.
   One evening Cherry is seen by her supervisor, Alistair, to use the phone to ring her husband, Leo, to ask him to pick her up by car after work. It has been snowing and all buses and trains to her home village have been cancelled. She is dismissed immediately by Alistair. On the same

evening Tony is discovered using emails for private purposes (communicating with his girlfriend, Mo) by his foreman, Gordon, who gives him an oral warning.

Cherry comes to you for advice. You find out from her:

(a) that she has been working for Megabucks for ten years;

(b) that her record is unblemished, whereas Tony, who has been employed by the company for four years, has had two warnings for misconduct in the last year;

(c) that her contract provides for an annual salary of £16,000 and a notice period of four weeks;

(d) that she has been revealing details of clients to her husband who works for Smallco Ltd, a firm which competes with Megabucks; and

(e) that she did appeal internally but that appeal was rejected.

Advise Cherry as to any liability Megabucks may have for wrongful and unfair dismissal, if any.

Commentary

The answer to this question encompasses a lot of material but not sex discrimination: the answer is expressly restricted to wrongful and unfair dismissal. The basic material, however, is quite straightforward and may be used in any question involving these topics. It is worth noting that it will be a rare question paper which does not have something on these claims. Differences between wrongful and unfair dismissal are favourites of examiners. Note too that the wording of the question points to the relevant areas of law: e.g. what is the effect of a reason for dismissal discovered *after* dismissal? Students often spend too much time on the qualifications for unfair dismissal at the expense of the main body of the question. On the present facts all that is needed is a quick statement that Cherry is an employee (there is nothing in the facts to indicate otherwise): there is no need to outline and apply all the tests for employment status. The same can be said about whether Cherry has been dismissed. The question states that she has been: a discussion of dismissal would be a waste of time, would not be scoring marks, and may well lead to the deduction of marks for irrelevancy. Finally, the authors recommend the use of a framework for answering questions on unfair dismissal. Several are possible. Here is one:

- qualifications

- dismissal

- reason

- reasonableness, including the 2004 Discipline and Dismissal Procedure

- remedy

(Undergraduate courses do not normally require calculations of damages or compensation but it is worth showing how awards are calculated. Not every student gains 'easy' marks for remedies: you should!)

Answer plan

- Variation of contract
- Wrongful dismissal: dismissal, no or insufficient notice, no cause
- Unfair dismissal: qualifications, dismissal, reason, reasonableness, remedy (QDRRR); procedural unfairness and the 2004 changes

Suggested answer

This problem involves discussion of variation of contract, and wrongful and unfair dismissal. In respect of the last, of particular importance is procedural fairness.

Adding to the list of gross misconduct

Potentially Cherry (C) has a claim for breach of contract. A contract of employment is a contract and like other contracts it cannot be varied without agreement on both sides (though there can be a dismissal followed by re-engagement on different terms: this is really a termination followed by a new contract). A unilateral variation by her employers will entitle C to terminate the contract and claim damages for breach provided that the breach is of a fundamental term, whether express or implied; if the breach is of a lesser term, in contractual language a warranty, she has only a right to damages. In relation to the former scenario, there is a potential repudiatory breach and no notice has been given.

Possible claims lie for wrongful dismissal (WD) and unfair dismissal (UD). See below for a discussion of these claims. A case illustrating a breach of contract is *Burdett-Coutts* v *Hertfordshire CC* [1984] IRLR 91. A unilateral reduction in the employees' rate of pay resulted in a successful claim for back pay. The fact that the complainants had continued to work was irrelevant: they protested throughout. This authority can be applied to the present facts. C continued to work and perhaps there was a protest from her; however, even if there was no protest, it is not necessarily the case that the employee has accepted the variation. In *Aparau* v *Iceland Frozen Foods Lid* [1996] IRLR 119, EAT, the new term was a mobility clause. It was irrelevant that the employee did not protest until she was asked to transfer because only then did the clause affect her. A similar case is the more famous one of *Jones* v *Associated Tunnelling Co Ltd* [1991] IRLR 477, EAT, which also involved the imposition of a mobility clause. The employee worked for four years under the revised contract. The tribunal held that he had not consented to the variation by failing to protest. His failure was attributable to his desire to avoid a clash with his employers. There was more than a hint in the judgment that if the clause had immediate effect (as occurred in *Burdett-Coutts*, the reduction in pay), failure to protest would mean that the employee would be taken to have accepted the variation. The facts look like those in *Jones* and *Aparau*.

An alternative possibility is that the contract permits the employers to vary it, another one is that the clause is non-contractual. In the former circumstances there is no unilateral variation entitling the employee to resign or claim damages or both (depending on the importance of the term). In the latter there is no change affecting the contract and therefore no breach of contract. Modern contracts often have a flexibility clause, permitting the employers to do various things and perhaps on the facts—depending on the wording—one of those permitted changes would be to the list of 'gross misconduct'. In relation to the possibility that the clause is not binding *Dryden* v *Greater Glasgow HB* [1992] IRLR 469, EAT is to the point. The introduction of the employers' ban on smoking was not a breach of contract. Employers can make rules governing conduct at the place of work. This right is part of their right to give reasonable orders. It is suggested that rules in staff handbooks, as here, may well not be contractually binding.

Wrongful dismissal

There may be a WD in respect of the possible unilateral variation discussed above. There may also be one in relation to dismissal by the supervisor. The facts state that C has been dismissed, which is one element in a claim for WD. She has not been given the correct length of notice. Her contract provides for four weeks' notice: under statute, the Employment Rights Act 1996 (ERA), s. 86, because she has worked for ten years she is entitled to ten weeks' notice. Where the statutory period is longer than the contractual one the former applies. C has been dismissed summarily ('immediately'). Accordingly, the first two requirements of a WD action are present. The third one is that the employers cannot justify the summary dismissal. If the employee has committed gross misconduct as defined at common law or by the contract, Megabucks has a defence. This is the situation here. If, however, the dismissal had been wrongful, the discovery after the dismissal that C had been divulging confidential information to her husband would have retrospectively justified the previously wrongful dismissal: *Boston Deep Sea Fishing & Ice Co Ltd* v *Ansell* (1888) 39 Ch D 339, CA. Compare the UD position, which is noted below.

If C had succeeded in her action for WD, she would in the normal run of cases have been awarded damages. Since WD is an action for breach of contract, damages are calculated in the contractual way: to put the employee in the position she would have been in, had the contract been performed. Since these employers could have lawfully dismissed C by giving ten weeks' notice, she is entitled only to damages for that period. As is well known, no damages are awarded for injured feelings or for the manner of dismissal: *Addis* v *Gramophone Co* [1909] AC 488, HL; but they are now available for the financial loss occasioned by the dismissal in breach of the express or (more usually) implied term of mutual trust and confidence when the breach seriously reduces the possibility of obtaining a similar job: *Malik* v *BCCI* [1998] AC 20, HL. See also *BCCI* v *Ali* [2000] ICR 1154, Lightman J. The other common law rules such as mitigation apply too, and in the event of C's succeeding, the likelihood is that the quantum of damages will be small.

Both employment tribunals and the ordinary courts have jurisdiction over claims for breach of contract up to £25,000 on termination of the contract: Employment Tribunals Extension of Jurisdiction (England and Wales) Order 1994 (SI 1994/1623). The limitation period in the ordinary courts is six years, the normal contractual period. This duration is vastly different from that for UD (three months from the effective date of termination subject to extension on the 'not reasonably practicable' ground). Legal aid is available for WD in the courts but not at the employment tribunal level for UD.

Unfair dismissal

The first issue is whether C is qualified to apply. She has to prove that she is on the balance of probabilities. Assuming that she brought her claim within the limitation period (see above), on the facts she seems to qualify. She has worked for her employers for over one year, which has been the qualifying period since 1 June 1999: Unfair Dismissal and Statement of Reasons for Dismissal (Variation of Qualifying Period) Order 1999 (SI 1999/1436). There is little doubt that C is an employee and not a member of an excluded class such as share fishermen. She does not work for the electrical contracting industry (see s. 110, ERA), she is not being retired (she is 35), she seems to have no national security links. She is, therefore, qualified.

The next hurdle is that of dismissal (ERA, s. 95). She has to prove on the civil law standard of proof that she has been dismissed. The facts state that she has been; so there is no problem. The effective date of dismissal from which the limitation period is calculated runs from the day of dismissal when there is an 'actual' dismissal.

The third issue is to find out the reason or if more than one the principal reason for dismissal. On the facts, the sole reason is the use of the phone in contravention of the rule in the staff handbook. As the heading to the list ('gross misconduct') states, she is dismissed within s. 98, ERA for misconduct, a prima facie valid or a potentially fair reason for dismissal. There is again no difficulty. The burden of proof at this stage lies on the employers. If they fail on the balance of probabilities to prove that the dismissal was for misconduct, C wins her case: see *Smith* v *City of Glasgow DC* [1987] ICR 796, HL.

She has another string to her bow in that she should within s. 92, ERA ask her employers to provide her with written reasons for dismissal. If the employers refuse or persistently fail to respond, an employment tribunal may order the award of two weeks' pay. Should the employers seek to change the reason they state in their reply, the tribunal may take a strong line against them in the UD claim. The qualifying period was reduced to one year by the Unfair Dismissal Order noted above.

The difficulty lies at the next stage, reasonableness. The employers must act reasonably in treating the reason, misconduct, as a sufficient reason for dismissal: s. 98(4), ERA. That subsection directs the tribunal to have regard to the circumstances, including the size and administrative resources of the employers' undertaking; also important in determining the fairness of the dismissal are equity and the substantial merits of the case, as s. 98(4) makes clear too. At this juncture there has since 1980 been no formal burden of proof: it is 'neutral'. The tribunal must consider whether a reasonable employer might have dismissed. The law was subjected to upheaval in the 1999/2000 period (see especially *Haddon* v *Van den Bergh Foods* [1999] ICR 1150) but the Appeal Court firmly reasserted orthodoxy in *HSBC* v *Madden* [2000] ICR 1283.

The leading statement of the law remains that of Browne-Wilkinson J in *Iceland Frozen Foods* v *Jones* [1983] ICR 17:

- start with the words of s. 98(4);
- look at the employers' treatment of the employee, not at whether the tribunal thought that the dismissal was unfair: the tribunal must not substitute its judgment for that of the employers;
- usually 'there is a band of reasonable responses... within which one employer might reasonably take one view, another quite reasonably take another';
- the tribunal, acting as 'an industrial jury', must determine whether the dismissal was fair by using this range.

The 'range of reasonable responses' test is pro-employers, but the Appeal Court in *Madden* did not deal with this criticism.

The tribunal must take into consideration the 2004 *Code of Practice on Disciplinary and Grievance Procedures* (ACAS), which deals inter alia with the new right to be accompanied, which is laid down by s. 10 of the Employment Relations Act 1999. ACAS's handbook, *Discipline at Work,* 1987, is influential. The Code recommends that rules ought to be in writing, as here, and given to every employee (here via the staff handbook), and stipulate that the sanction (here dismissal for gross misconduct) should be spelt out. The employers must believe on reasonable grounds that the employee was guilty of gross misconduct: *BHS* v *Burchell* [1980] ICR 303. There is no problem here: C was seen to use the phone. Procedural fairness remains important even after the 2004 amendments discussed in the unfair dismissal chapter (note in particular the use of the 'modified' dismissal procedure for gross misconduct) and can render unfair an otherwise fair dismissal. Except for gross misconduct the Code recommends a series of warnings. If the conduct is gross, there is no need for warnings. C had been granted the right to appeal, another aspect of procedural fairness, at least when the firm is a large one, as seems to be the case here. However, Megabucks did not investigate the facts lying behind the dismissal (the transport situation caused by the snow), or listen to any explanation before dismissing. Both are demanded by the Employment Act 2002 as implemented in 2004. It is suggested that for these reasons, which are aspects of natural justice, the dismissal was unfair. It would not have been futile to have conducted an investigation: see *Polkey*. Moreover, the employers should have taken her record of good behaviour into account, particularly in the light of the contrast with that of Tony.

In relation to the after-discovered reason, disclosure of confidential information, *W Devis & Sons* v *Atkins* [1977] AC 931, HL ruled that the employers cannot use it to render fair an otherwise unfair dismissal, but it may go to reduce compensation.

If the dismissal is unfair, the tribunal considers remedies in the order of reinstatement (same job), re-engagement (similar job) (both together often called re-employment), and compensation. In brief the rules are these. When re-employment is under consideration, the tribunal must consider C's wishes and whether it is practicable for Megabucks to take her back, and whether, when as here the employee contributed to her dismissal, it is 'just' so to order. In the last event the tribunal could for example prefer re-engagement over reinstatement, and it may award less than the full amount of back pay. It may be impracticable to order re-employment when the employee has divulged confidential information. If there is re-employment, continuity is preserved.

If, however, compensation is ordered, there is both a basic and a compensatory award. The former is calculated according to a set formula dependent on the employee's age, here 35, the duration of her employment (to a maximum of 20 years), here ten, and her gross pay, subject to a maximum, currently £9,300, which is increased in line with the Retail Prices Index. There is a deduction for pre-dismissal misconduct, whether discovered pre or post-dismissal. The call was before and the disclosure was after dismissal. Some percentage would be deducted on these facts: there is no limit to that percentage. The compensatory award, which must be assessed on the 'just and equitable' basis (s. 123(1), ERA), is organized under heads of compensation laid down in *Norton Tool Co Ltd* v *Tewson* [1973] 1 WLR 45 by Donaldson MR and is restricted to financial loss (therefore, for example, compensation for injured feelings is not available): immediate loss, future loss (often hard to assess), loss of pension, loss of statutory rights: from this sum various deductions are made, e.g. for contributory fault (s. 123(6)), as here, and for mitigation. A sum is also deducted as in WD for accelerated receipt. Where there was a chance that C would have been dismissed anyway, another deduction is made (the '*Polkey*' deduction). Mitigation and the *Polkey* deduction do not apply to the basic award. After-discovered reasons are taken into account at the s. 123(1) stage, not at the s. 123(6) one. The order of deductions is now relatively fixed. There is a maximum, which was increased by the Employment Relations Act 1999, and which is now increased annually by way of a statutory instrument. The current maximum applying to the compensatory award is £60,600. This sum too is index-linked.

In conclusion C would be best advised to claim a remedy for UD and, if relevant, for the failure of the employers to provide written reasons for dismissal.

Glossary

Additional award—if the employers fail to reinstate or re-engage an employee whose unfair dismissal claim is successful, the employment tribunal may make an additional award of between 26 and 52 weeks' pay (at the time of writing capped at £310 per week).

Automatically unfair reasons—usually in an unfair dismissal claim the employment tribunal has to determine whether the dismissal is fair or unfair having regard, for example, to the size and administrative resources of the employers and equity and the substantial merits of the claim: s. 98(4), Employment Rights Act 1996. However, there is a growing list of reasons for dismissal where Parliament deems the dismissal to be unfair without recourse to s. 98(4). Examples include dismissal for being pregnant and for whistleblowing. Dismissals on these grounds are said to be for automatically unfair reasons.

Basic award—compensation for unfair dismissal comprises two elements, the basic award and the compensatory award (q.v.). The former consists of a sum of money (maximum from 1 February 2007 is £9,300, an amount that since 1999 has been increased annually in line with the Retail Prices Index) calculated according to a formula dependent on the age of the claimant, the number of years in continuous employment (to a maximum of 20) and the statutory maximum pay (currently £310) per week. From this quantum are deducted various sums.

'Break' clause—this is an express term in the contract of employment that permits the employers to terminate the contract without the employee having a legal remedy. For example, if the employee is employed under a fixed-term contract for five years, the contract cannot be lawfully terminated until the five years have elapsed (plus the notice period) and damages for wrongful dismissal (q.v.) would be based on that period; if, however, there is a break clause the

employers may lawfully terminate the contract before the five years have elapsed.

Closed shop—for many years trade unions sought to reach agreement with managements that the latter would not employ workers who were not union members either before being taken on (a pre-entry closed shop) or shortly after being engaged (a post-entry closed shop). Unions saw such arrangements as protecting their membership base and many employers were sympathetic to the institution because disciplining of their work force could often be left to the recognized union. However, the Conservative governments of the 1980s and 1990s saw the closed shop as antithetical to the employers' right to manage, including their rights to hire and fire, and by 1990 they had made closed shops more or less impossible to maintain, though the institution has never been made illegal.

Collective agreement—this is a non-legally binding agreement between management and unions. Clauses from it e.g. on pay may be incorporated into the legally binding contract of employment.

Compensation in discrimination claims—unlike unfair dismissal's compensatory award (q.v.) compensation in discrimination cases covers both economic and non-economic loss (e.g. injury to feelings). Unlike in unfair dismissal there is no financial cap to compensation for claims involving discrimination but the Court of Appeal in *Vento* v *Chief Constable of West Yorkshire* [2003] ICR 318 laid down that compensation for injured feelings should normally fall within one of three bands: £15,000–£25,000 for the worst cases e.g. of harassment; £500–£5,000 for the least worst isolated acts of discrimination; and £5,000–£15,000 for the middle band. Sums of under £500 should not normally be awarded in order to mark the seriousness of even minor discrimination. Other remedies for discrimination are declarations and recommendations. Any one or more of these remedies may be awarded.

Compensatory award—in addition to the basic award (q.v.) of compensation employment tribunals also grant a compensatory award when compensation is the remedy to be awarded. The maximum amount from 1 February 2007 is £60,600. The quantum is derived by adding together sums due under various headings such as loss to the date of the hearing, future loss, loss of pension rights, loss of statutory rights, and loss of benefits such as a company car (see *Norton Tool Co Ltd v Tewson* [1973] 1 WLR 45 (NIRC)); only economic loss is recompensed: *Dunnachie v Kingston upon Hull City Council* [2005] 1 AC 226 (HL) (so, for example, no compensation is awarded for injured feelings; cf. discrimination law). From this quantum are deducted various sums including an amount representing the percentage likelihood that the claimant would have been dismissed in any case (the so-called '*Polkey*' deduction named after the House of Lords' case in which the principle was enshrined: *Polkey v AE Dayton Services Ltd* [1988] AC 344) and an amount representing the percentage to which the claimant caused or contributed to his or her dismissal. Once the quantum is calculated in this way, then the statutory cap is applied.

Constructive dismissal—for the purposes of statute when the employers act in such a way that they breach a fundamental express or implied term of the contract of employment, the employee may elect to treat the contract as at an end. If he or she does so within a reasonable time, the employers are said to have constructively dismissed the employee. The same applied when there is an anticipatory breach of contract. The principal authority is *Western Excavating (ECC) Ltd v Sharp* [1978] QB 761 (CA). At common law the same concept is expressed by the term 'repudiation' but over time the common law term is being replaced by 'constructive dismissal'.

Continuous employment—for the purposes of some statutory claims the claimant must have been continuously employed for a certain length of time. For example, there is a qualifying period of two years' continuous employment for redundancy payments. There are laws found in the Employment Rights Act 1996 that tell the tribunal how to calculate continuous employment, and do so even in certain circumstances whether or not there is a contract in existence, e.g. when a woman is absent from work because of pregnancy. When continuity is broken, the employee has to start building up the weeks of continuous employment. Time spent on industrial action does not break continuity but the time does not count towards the calculation of whether the employee has or has not satisfied the qualifying period. The concept of continuity of employment is also important when calculating redundancy payments (q.v.) and the basic award (q.v.) for unfair dismissal.

Discrimination—since 2006 England and Wales have had six so-called strands of discrimination: sex (from 1975) (including gender reassignment (1999)), race (1976), disability (1995), religion or belief including lack of belief (2003), sexual orientation (2003), and age (2006). These strands share several characteristics but there are differences among them. Generally speaking there are four types of discrimination—

- *direct discrimination*: this is where the employers treat the worker (e.g. on the grounds of sex) less favourably than they do treat or would treat another similarly situated worker. This type of discrimination cannot be justified by the employers except in relation to discrimination on the ground of age. In respect of disability there is both direct discrimination and disability-related discrimination;

- *indirect discrimination*: there are currently two different varieties of this form of discrimination but either type may be justified by the employers. There is no form of indirect disability discrimination but the functional equivalent is the failure by the employers to make reasonable adjustments;

- *harassment*: most forms of this type of discrimination bear a common definition, the violation of the worker's dignity at work; and

- *victimisation*, which occurs when the employers treat the worker less favourably than they do treat or would treat an otherwise similarly situated worker on the grounds that she has brought a discrimination claim against them. For the purposes of racial discrimination only segregation is a fifth form of discrimination.

Economic torts—these torts if committed in contemplation or furtherance of a trade dispute (q.v.) do not give rise to trade union liability: s. 219, Trade Union and Labour Relations (Consolidation) Act 1992. These torts are: inducing breach of contract, interference with contract by unlawful means, intimidation, and conspiracy. Other torts, economic or otherwise, do not fall within s. 219.

Employment tribunals—these are the fora in which most employment law claims, e.g. discrimination, unfair dismissal, and redundancy payments, are heard. Since 1994 tribunals have also been entitled to hear claims relating to termination of contract, e.g. actions for wrongful dismissal when the claim is for under £25,000 (a sum which has not been increased in line with inflation) and any counterclaims by the ex-employers. The ordinary courts retain concurrent jurisdiction for claims under £25,000 and have exclusive jurisdiction above that amount. Claims for breach of contract during the running of the contract remain excluded for the jurisdiction of the employment tribunals, as are any claims involving restraint of trade covenants, confidentiality clauses, personal injury and accommodation. Appeal lies to the Employment Appeal Tribunal and thence to the Court of Appeal and the House of Lords.

Equal pay—workers of one gender may bring claims for pay equal to that of their comparators of the opposite gender under the provisions of the Equal Pay Act 1970. They must do so on one of three bases: 'like work' (i.e. the work is the same or is broadly similar), work rated as equivalent, and equal value. If the workers are successful at this point, the employers may have a defence of genuine material difference or genuine material factor. If the workers are successful, their contracts are deemed to include an equality clause that gives them the benefit of what their comparators have. It should be noted that while the statute is called the Equal Pay Act, it is not restricted to matters of pay but covers all contractual matters. If the issue is related to non-contractual matters such as promotion, the relevant statute is the Sex Discrimination Act 1975. In relation to differences in both contractual and non-contractual matters involving racial discrimination, the relevant statute is the Race Relations Act 1976.

Express terms—these are contractual obligations that the parties have agreed either in writing or orally.

Flexibility clause—this is a term in the contract of employment that permits the employers to move the employee to work other than that which he normally does.

Freedom of association—workers have, subject to various constraints, the freedom to join unions according to various international instruments including Art. 11 of the European Convention on Human Rights. English law is as may be expected more complicated: briefly, dismissal for belonging to an independent trade union is one of the automatically unfair reasons for unfair dismissal (q.v.). At least where not joining a trade union would result in dismissal (as in a closed shop, q.v.), workers have a right not to be members of trade unions.

Implied terms—these are contractual obligations that the parties have not expressly agreed. In employment law these clauses may arise on the facts of each individual contract (sometimes known as 'terms implied in fact') or from the fact that the contract is one of employment ('terms implied in law'). Examples of the latter include the employee's duty of faithful service and the employers' duty to pay wages.

Industrial action—this term comprises strikes and other forms of behaviour involved in conflicts at work. For the law relating to dismissal in connection with industrial action see ss. 237, 238, and 238A of the Trade Union and Labour Relations (Consolidation) Act 1992. Industrial action in response to a trade dispute (q.v.) may result in immunity from suit for trade unions.

Mobility clause—this is a term in the contract of employment that permits the employers to move the employee from her normal workplace to another. The clause may be express but may be implied.

Notice—at common law where there is an express term that stipulates that the employers may lawfully dismiss the employee by giving a period of notice of dismissal, that clause applies; if there is no express term, an implied notice clause of a reasonable length applies. How long is 'reasonable' depends on the facts. In addition statute (originally the Contracts of Employment Act 1963, now the Employment Rights Act 1996, s. 86) provides that employers must give employees a minimum period of notice. This minimum is one week when the employee has been employed for less than two years; it is one week for each year of employment between two and 12 years; and it is 12 weeks when the employee has been employed for more than 12 years. For example, the statutory minimum is seven weeks for an employee who has been employed for seven years and 12 weeks when the employee has been employed for 20 years. Where the contractual period is less than the statutory period, the latter applies; where it is less, the statutory minimum applies. This is part of the 'floor of rights' provided to employees by Parliament. It should be noted that (i) no notice need be provided by employers when the employee is summarily dismissed for 'cause'; and (ii) by statute the period of notice to be provided by an employee is one week but the contract may provide for a longer period.

Pregnancy—dismissal for being pregnant is one of the automatically unfair reasons (q.v.) for dismissal and constitutes sexual discrimination without the need to compare the woman against a similarly situated male.

Recognition—trade unions may seek to influence employers over many areas of working life such as pay. In order to reach collective agreements with management the union must be recognized by the employers for the purposes of collective bargaining. This type of recognition is voluntary. Since the Employment Relations Act 1999 there has been a separate statutory scheme for recognition via a body called the Central Arbitration Committee. The scheme is longwinded and if the union successfully completes the process, the outcome is recognition but only in respect of pay, hours and holidays. The Employment Relations Act 2004 specifically excluded pensions from 'pay'; however, at the time of writing the Government is considering whether or not to include pensions as one of the topics because over time negotiations about pensions have become commonplace in negotiations when recognition has been voluntary.

Redundancy payments—on redundancy (as defined in s. 139 of the Employment Rights Act 1996) the employers are liable to make a redundancy payment to each employee made redundant. The calculation of the amount is the same as that for the basic award (q.v.).

Re-engagement—this is one of the three possible remedies for unfair dismissal. It consists of the employment tribunal ordering the employers to take the employee back into employment but not into the same job she had before dismissal (that is reinstatement (q.v.)). The remedy involves putting the employee into a job of similar status. The tribunal will direct the nature of and remuneration in the new employment, the benefits the employee is to receive, and the date by which re-engagement must take place. If the employers refuse to comply with the order, the remedy is the additional award (q.v.).

Reinstatement—when the employment tribunal finds that the employers have unfairly dismissed the employee, they must consider first whether to reinstate the employee into the same job as he or she had before dismissal. If such an order is made, the tribunal will also order the employers to make up the pay loss between dismissal and reinstatement. If the employers do not comply with the order, the additional award (q.v.) is made.

Statutory discipline and dismissal procedures—by the Employment Act 2002 and the

Employment Act 2002 (Dispute Resolution) Regulations 2004 (SI 2004/752) Parliament has laid down procedures which must be followed before disciplinaries and dismissals. For further details see chap. 6, q. 2. At the time of writing it has been proposed that these procedures should be abolished.

Statutory grievance procedures—by the Employment Act 2002 and the Employment Act 2002 (Dispute Resolution) Regulations 2004 (SI 2004/752) employees must go through the grievance procedure in relation to various claims before the claim may be brought in the Employment Tribunal. This procedure also applies to constructive dismissal (q.v.). For further details see chap. 6, q. 2. At the time of writing it has been proposed that these procedures should be abolished.

Trade dispute—economic torts (q.v.) committed by trade unions are not actionable if committed 'in contemplation or furtherance of a trade dispute', a phrase known as the 'golden formula'. The term 'trade dispute' is defined in s. 244(1) of the Trade Union and Labour Relations (Consolidation) Act 1992 as being:

a dispute between workers and their employer which relates wholly or mainly to one or more of the following:

- terms and conditions of employment, or the physical conditions in which any workers are required to work;
- engagement or non-engagement, or termination or suspension of employment or the duties of employment, of one or more workers;
- allocation of work . . . ;
- matters of discipline;
- a worker's membership or non-membership of a trade union;
- facilities for officials of trade unions;
- machinery for negotiation or consultation, . . . including recognition . . .

Trade union—in law a trade union is one which is an 'organisation, whether temporary or permanent, which consists wholly or mainly of workers of one or more descriptions, and whose principal purposes include the regulation of relations between workers and employers or employers' associations': s.1 (a), Trade Union and Labour Relations (Consolidation) Act 1992.

Transfer of undertakings—under law originally derived from the Acquired Rights Directive 1977 as amended, now the 2001 Directive of the same name, and transposed into English law by the Transfer of Undertakings (Protection of Employment) Regulations ('TUPE') 1981 (SI 1981/1794), now TUPE 2006 (SI 2006/246), employees' terms and conditions are protected on the transfer of an undertaking or part of one as a going concern from the transferor employers to the transferee employers. Continuity of employment (q.v.) is also preserved. Any amendment to the terms is prohibited, even if overall the change is to the employees' benefit: *Daddy's Dance Hall* [1988] ECR 739 (ECJ). A dismissal in connection with the transfer, whether by the transferors or the transferees, is automatically unfair unless the employers have an economic, technical, or organizational reason entailing changes in the work force, in which case TUPE deems the reason to be a dismissal for some other substantial reason (or for redundancy if the reason is one within the definition of redundancy found in s. 139 of the Employment Rights Act 1996); in that event the tribunal must determine whether the dismissal was fair or unfair in the usual way.

Unfair dismissal—this is a claim, first created in the Industrial Relations Act 1971 and now found in the Employment Rights Act 1996, brought by former employees against their former employers. It is based on the ex-employers' dismissal of the employee contrary to the rules laid down by Parliament as expanded on by the courts and tribunals. The remedies that the tribunal may award are reinstatement (q.v.), re-engagement (q.v.), and compensation comprising the basic award (q.v.) and the compensatory award (q.v.). However, only one of these remedies may be awarded and Parliament has instructed the tribunals to consider the remedy in the order stated (e.g. if the tribunal refuses to order reinstatement, it must then consider re-engagement).

Variation—employers may vary, i.e. change, their employees' contracts only with their consent (or that of their union), by having a flexibility clause that covers the variation, or by dismissal and re-engagement on new contracts. The last may be an unfair dismissal (q.v.). Simply notifying the employees of the change is not lawful; also not legal is merely consulting with the employees or their representatives.

Whistleblowing—the Public Interest Disclosure Act 1998 inserts new provisions into the Employment Rights Act 1996 to protect those who blow the whistle on the misdeeds of their employers. Dismissal in breach of these provisions is one of the automatically unfair reasons (q.v.) for unfair dismissal.

Working time—the Working Time Directive 1993 (93/104) was transposed into UK law by the Working Time Regulations 1998 (SI 1998/1833). In brief:

- the maximum hours of work per week are 48 averaged out over a 17-week reference period, but individuals may opt out from this protection;
- each person is entitled to four weeks paid holiday per year;
- special rules apply to young workers and to night workers.

The British Government is one of those that refuse to get rid of the opt out from the maximum hours of work per year; however, at the time of writing, there are proposals from it to extend the number of days of holiday per year to 28.

Written statement—the Employment Rights Act 1996, s. 1 provides that employers must provide their new employees who have at least one month's continuous employment (q.v.) with a written statement of their particulars of employment within eight weeks of their starting employment. This statement is sometimes known as a 's. 1 statement' and 'written particulars'. This is *not* the contract of employment (except when the employee signs the written statement as being the contract of employment), though a written contract of employment may constitute also the written statement. Any change to the particulars must be notified to the employee within four weeks.

Wrongful dismissal—this is a common law action for breach of contract resulting in the dismissal of the employee or the repudiation of the contract by the employers; 'wrongful' in this context means 'in breach of the law on notice' (q.v.); and the employers fail to prove that they had a sufficient 'cause' (justification/reason) to dismiss in breach of contract. Traditionally the sole remedy is damages. Since 1994 actions for wrongful dismissal may be made in the Employment Tribunals provided that the claim is for less than £25,000.

Index